CW00340948

SURVEILLANCE & CRIME

Surveillance & Crime

As Surveillance Studies goes from strength to strength with numerous degree courses, international journals, conferences and symposia dedicated to it each year, the time seems perfect for a book like *Surveillance & Crime* to inspire students and established scholars alike. Written by two of the leading scholars who have had an influential role in shaping the contours of the field over the last decade, *Surveillance & Crime* discusses the subject of surveillance in all its technological and human dimensions.

Like the subject of surveillance itself, this volume is provocative, challenging and continuously fascinating. Drawing on a dazzling array of theoretical ideas from across the social sciences, Roy Coleman and Mike McCahill situate the study of surveillance not only within the familiar contexts of 'security', 'order', 'policing' and 'risk', but also within less well-trodden territories (for a book of this kind, at least), including cultural theory, historical perspectives, globalization and gender politics – all of which make *Surveillance & Crime* a perfect companion to the other volumes in the *Key Approaches to Criminology* series.

Yvonne Jewkes
Series Editor

SURVEILLANCE & CRIME

ROY COLEMAN AND MICHAEL McCAHILL

Los Angeles | London | New Delhi
Singapore | Washington DC

© Roy Coleman and Michael McCahill 2011

First published 2011

Apart from any fair dealing for the purposes of research or
private study, or criticism or review, as permitted under
the Copyright, Designs and Patents Act, 1988, this publication
may be reproduced, stored or transmitted in any form,
or by any means, only with the prior permission in writing
of the publishers, or in the case of reprographic reproduction,
in accordance with the terms of licences issued by
the Copyright Licensing Agency. Inquiries concerning
reproduction outside those terms should be sent to the
publishers.

SAGE Publications Ltd
1 Oliver's Yard
55 City Road
London EC1Y 1SP

SAGE Publications Inc.
2455 Teller Road
Thousand Oaks, California 91320

SAGE Publications India Pvt Ltd
B 1/I 1 Mohan Cooperative Industrial Area
Mathura Road
New Delhi 110 044

SAGE Publications Asia-Pacific Pte Ltd
33 Pekin Street #02-01
Far East Square
Singapore 048763

Library of Congress Control Number: 2010924527

British Library Cataloguing in Publication data

A catalogue record for this book is available from the British Library

ISBN 978-1-84787-352-1
ISBN 978-1-84787-353-8 (pbk)

Typeset by C&M Digitals (P) Ltd, Chennai, India
Printed in Great Britain by CPI Antony Rowe, Chippenham, Wiltshire
Printed on paper from sustainable resources

MIX
Paper from
responsible sources
FSC   FSC® C013604
www.fsc.org

Contents

Acknowledgements and dedication   vi

1   Introduction: Surveillance, Crime and Controversy   1

2   Understanding Surveillance   11

3   The Historical Foundations of Surveillance   39

4   New Policing and New Surveillance   67

5   Globalisation, Surveillance and the 'War' on Terror   91

6   Surveillance, Power and Social Impacts   111

7   'Contesting' and 'Resisting' Surveillance: The Politics of Visibility and Invisibility   143

8   Deconstructing Surveillance, Crime and Power   169

Glossary   187

Bibliography   193

Index   213

Acknowledgements and Dedication

We would like to pass on our thanks to Joe Sim, Dave Whyte and Steve Tombs for reading various chapters in this book, and providing us with useful comments and insights.

We dedicate this book to Denis McCahill and Elizabeth, George and Gary Coleman.

1

Introduction: Surveillance, Crime and Controversy

CHAPTER CONTENTS	
Surveillance, crime and social context	4
A 'surveillance society'?	7
Questioning surveillance and the plan of the book	8

OVERVIEW

Chapter 1 provides:

- An introductory discussion of surveillance as a social issue and the kinds of problems this gives rise to for students of surveillance

KEY TERMS

- Surveillance society
- Tax fraud / social security fraud

- The social construction of crime
- Visibility

> Crime is, above all, a function of the resources available to know it. (Manning, 1972: 234)
>
> Criminality is born [...] by means of ever more closely placed insertions, under ever more insistent surveillance. (Foucault, 1979: 301)

How do we come to recognise crime? Clearly our own experiences are important in forming our perceptions, which in turn rely upon a whole range of activities that 'watch', monitor and report on the crime problem. Official statistics, victim surveys, media narratives and official pronouncements all combine to produce and socially authorise knowledge about crime. All these areas overlap with, and in themselves constitute, forms of surveillance defined in dictionary terms as 'vigilant supervision, superintendence'; as 'a watch kept over someone or something, especially over a criminal (and his or her activities)' (*Chambers Dictionary*, 1993). This watching aspect is aligned fundamentally to a process of categorisation towards the collation of knowledge about crime over time and space. It has technical aspects (the creation of records, databases, tables and maps) as well as normative features (rules, values and standards pertaining to correct behaviour). In this sense, knowledge of the crime problem is accrued and forms the basis from which to intervene, control and correct 'crime'.

Surveillance and crime, then, are intimately connected. By this we mean that knowledge about crime would be impossible without surveillance, along with any attempt to manage crime and criminality. On a common-sense level this relationship may appear straightforward: crime exists as an incontrovertible and self-evident 'fact' requiring little debate because it is outlawed, 'socially harmful', 'bad' and 'immoral'. Surveillance, then, merely responds to crime – it is a key aspect of crime fighting: it prevents, detects, categorises, controls and corrects the criminal and the wayward. We glimpse this view in official pronouncements calling for ever greater vigilance over the 'unruly', the 'anti-social', the 'potential terrorist', the 'hardened criminal' or the mere 'nuisance'. Indeed, knowledge surrounding these categories seems boundless and from this 'crime' is very much seen as a problem of the streets and surveillance as the guardian. Establishing parent and child classes for the 'anti-social', calls for 'respect', child curfews and spy cameras in neighbourhoods and urban spaces, calls for more police powers, more prisons and ways to collate information about the criminal – all attest to the idea that surveillance *responds* to crime and disorder; to both know and control it. In some respects surveillance may serve to make some of us feel better – 'something is being done' – the law abiding are protected and society is kept 'in the know' about criminality. Developments in surveillance are often couched in terms of the 'public interest' along with the common refrain that those 'who have nothing to hide, have nothing to fear' from surveillance.

Moreover, supporters of surveillance point to its 'successes' in identifying and prosecuting criminals (for example, in the use of surveillance evidence in courtrooms or on TV shows such as the BBC's *Crimewatch*). This official perspective tenders the view that extending surveillance (more police stops, community patrols, street cameras, nationality and credit checks and the like) makes for a more secure society and encourages feelings of safety. This view of the intersection between surveillance and crime appears uncontroversial and, for many, even incontrovertible. It is just common sense.

But does surveillance merely respond to crime, trapping wrongdoers and aiding their prosecution, as well as reducing anxiety? Is the knowledge accrued from surveillance an accurate reflection of the spatial and temporal distribution of crime, harm and injury in society? If we were to answer in the affirmative, then any controversies concerning surveillance would be nullified and we could confidently proclaim that surveillance is useful and necessary because it targets society's most harmful activities, which we usually label as 'criminal'. In this book, the assumptions buried in common-sense views will be deconstructed and subject to critical scrutiny. This is because both surveillance and crime are more controversial than first appearances suggest. Indeed, the growth of surveillance has always been accompanied by contentious questions. These include whether surveillance 'works'; to what extent it invades 'privacy'; how surveillance relates to justice (both criminal and social); and how it operates within unequal and divided social landscapes characterised in terms of class, 'race', gender, age and sexuality. There is a need, then, to place surveillance practice within actually existing social relations, political priorities and prevailing cultural practices (McCahill, 2002; Coleman, 2004), which is the main goal of this book.

Surveillance, crime and social context

Surveillance relates to questions of visibility – *what* can be seen, *how* it is seen and what are the consequences of enhanced or decreased visibility? Surveillance does not exist in a social vacuum. Exploring the ways in which surveillance and visibility are practised needs to take into account social, political and cultural factors. Questions concerning what 'surveillance' is, and how it is practised, also engender questions surrounding what 'crime' is and how it is rendered 'visible'. Both categories are rarely straightforward and only become socially meaningful when explored in social relations (and their imbalances of power, hierarchical forms of organisation and contentious debates around what constitutes a 'social problem').

Let us take the example of surveillance and fraud, both in the form of corporate tax fraud and social security benefit fraud. In 2009, corporate tax dodging in the UK was estimated to cost the British state up to £13.7 billion a year in lost tax revenue. This information was garnered through a Freedom of Information request in 2005 and led to a series of debates on the issue in the *Guardian* newspaper from early in 2009. Tax 'evasion' is practised in at least two ways. First, there is *avoidance*, through which companies exploit loopholes or lack of clarity in the law to reduce their tax bill or shift a company's location off-shore as a means of avoidance. In the UK this is not illegal. Secondly, there is tax *evasion*, practised through illegal means to conceal company income (*The Guardian*, 14 February 2009). This vast area of hidden and illegal practices is policed by prosecutors in the Revenue and Customs Prosecutions Office (RCPO). Tax fraud is acknowledged to be a widespread problem but it is difficult to see or accrue knowledge about it because of the legal ambiguities, corporate obfuscation and secrecy surrounding the practice (*The Guardian*, 14 February 2009).

On the other hand, social security benefit fraud in the UK is estimated by the Department of Work and Pensions (DWP). This Department produced figures for 2007–08 to state that 'benefit thieves stole an estimated £800 million from public funds' (http://research.dwp.gov.uk/campaigns/benefit-thieves/index.asp). This problem provides a press and broadcast diet of 'scam' stories, although figures regarding its seriousness and extent are contested (Cook, 2006: 55–56). Typical frauds here are in the hundreds of pounds scale, occasionally going into much higher figures.

These two instances of fraud have quite different social impacts measured in terms of their respective 'costs', the former example of fraud far outweighing the latter in terms of financial costs. In terms of corporate tax evasion and the ability of companies to move to off-shore locations, there is a socially harmful knock-on effect upon public taxation policies reformulated to make up for tax losses and in how states compete with one another to attract businesses with tax exemptions. One may think, then, that surveillance resources, legal controls and cultural censure would accumulate around tax evasion in that this represents a more serious form of social harm, at least as it is measured in financial and human terms. However, making this assumption would be to ignore how surveillance is located in social relations and reflects and reinforces asymmetries of power and social capital within them.

In the mid-1980s the ratio of prosecutions for tax fraud and benefit fraud was 1:30. By 2004 the ratio was up to 1 tax fraud prosecution for 250 relating to benefit fraud (Cook, 2006). The RCPO has just over 300 staff to monitor and investigate tax fraud whereas the DWP has over 3,000 fraud surveillance officers in its team of investigators. Like the RCPO, the DWP favours a selective prosecution policy and uses cautions and benefit withdrawal as penalties. In 2006/07 the DWP's surveillance of benefit fraudsters resulted in sanctions (including prosecutions, cautions and other penalties) that totalled 51,000. In 2009/10, RCPO's surveillance activities resulted in 23 prosecutions for tax fraud (RCPO, 2009). In the UK since the early 1980s, there has been a general trend in the increase of surveillance and targeting of benefit fraud while scrutiny over the tax fraud has declined. Welfare claimants and benefit fraudsters in particular are surrounded by a range of surveillance technologies and programmes that intimately oversee their eligibility for work, leisure patterns and family status (Gilliom, 2006).

These examples show us that 'crime', 'misdemeanour' and 'deviance' are categories which do not speak for themselves. The levels of 'harm' they each generate does not correspond in any simple sense to what one may consider 'appropriate' and proportionate levels of surveillance, control and censure. Here we glimpse controversy in surveillance practice, not only in terms of *what* is targeted, but *how* and *why* it is targeted. The discrepancies in the targeting and pursuing of these types of fraud can only be explained by placing the 'problem of fraud' within its wider social context, out of which 'surveillance' and 'crime' emerge as meaningful social categories. In each of these examples, the decision to enact particular surveillance strategies towards the particular 'problem' highlight how surveillance takes place within, and acts to reinforce, a wider communicative process that encompasses particular values and interests that shape, define and respond to social problems and social groups in specific ways.

There are three aspects to this process. First, as Dee Cook (2006) has shown, there is a wider historical and ideological context at work here. Historically, the idea of the taxpayer has been positively represented as a productive, orderly and useful citizen: taxpayers *give* revenue for state services. On the other hand, the unproductive benefit claimant has been represented as someone who *uses* or *takes* from the state. These two contrasting representations continue to 'serve to shape very different social, political, judicial and public responses to the relatively rich and the poor when they breach citizenship "rules" and/or the law' (Cook, 2006: 47). Secondly, various surveys have shown that only a minority of the population in the UK think that tax evasion is 'wrong' at the same time as reports have appeared stating that a majority of the population believe benefit fraud to be a major problem and deserving of harsh responses (see Cook, 2006: 49). Thirdly, a wider social focus on the problem of benefit fraudsters has been encouraged through negative media portrayals representing them as 'spongers', 'cheats', 'scroungers' and 'criminals': the £800 million in benefits stolen 'from the public' by 'thieves' in 2008, it is argued, could have been spent on public services. Such people are construed as an 'enemy within' (Cook, 2006: 54).

These interlinked contextual factors highlight issues in the politics of surveillance and how the latter cannot simply be understood as a 'natural' outcome or response to the level of harm found in society. Surveillance takes place within, and is the result of, these wider discourses which help frame surveillant responses. Surveillance, then, does not simply respond to 'crime' as such, but responds to socially constructed forms of public anxiety about particular social problems which may come to be defined as 'crime', without any necessary relationship to objective measurements relating to 'harms', 'costs', 'injuries' or 'damages'. Indeed, 'the word "crime" is rarely associated with tax evasion', which is instead understood as compliance with the law (Cook, 2006: 48). So in saturating TV and newspaper space, government campaigns against benefit fraudsters are explicit in this respect. In 2009 the campaign against benefit fraud went under the title: 'We're closing in with every means at our disposal' against 'those who steal benefits [and] are picking the pockets of law-abiding taxpayers'. The campaign trumpeted its '3,000 fraud investigators, carrying out over 2,000 investigations every week, cross-checking the bank accounts of benefit thieves using hidden cameras and mobile surveillance' (http://research.dwp.gov.uk/campaigns/benefit-thieves/index.asp). 'Hotlines' and online reporting services also invite the 'honest' public into this surveillance web by encouraging them to report 'cheaters'. By 2008, 25 housing benefit offices in England and Wales had installed 'voice risk analysis technology' (lie detectors) to test welfare claimants' 'honesty' in providing information about their living and working circumstances (The Guardian, 3 December 2008).

Through these processes, benefit fraud is transformed into a visible 'social problem' and this is reinforced by the surveillance capabilities that have been marshalled to police it. The same cannot be said of tax evasion, where no comparable sustained and negative/deterrent publicity campaigns or public reporting of offenders exists, despite the more costly and prevalent nature of this activity (Cook, 2006: 54).

What impacts do these kinds of surveillance have upon those subject to it? What 'public interest' is being served? Again, the answers challenge one-dimensional views of surveillance. Poverty campaigners and civil liberties groups have argued that the panoply of surveillance and penalties imposed on welfare claimants prosecuted for fraud has a detrimental impact on their lives, in disrupting family relationships and increasing hardships, along with little or no understanding of the causes that underlie benefit fraud. On the other hand, this punitiveness, in making poor families pay back welfare cheques, for example, can be contrasted to the vast tax write-offs that occur in cases of corporate fraud where the recovery of assets is deemed impossible (Cook, 2006: 58). Furthermore, the dearth of surveillance and prosecution of tax fraud leads to significant cash losses that could be accrued through recovery (and these losses need to be placed alongside significant tax increases elsewhere). Investigatory surveillance in the case of benefit fraudsters is uncontrovertibly punitive and justice is seen to be publically done. The process is more permissive in cases of tax fraud, where forms of 'private justice' and negotiated financial settlements with suspects are common (Cook, 2006: 51).

Drawing upon these examples, we highlight a key concern of this book: that is, to raise questions about surveillance and the manner in which it relates to activities and meanings associated with 'crime'. We are concerned to show how surveillance and its relationship to crime are contested and social constructed.

A 'surveillance society'?

Many academics and political commentators have referred to the term 'surveillance society'. Contemporary apprehension over the growth of surveillance has been raised by campaign groups such as Liberty and Privacy International. These concerns relate to the growth of monitoring *without* democratic oversight and debate. In the early twenty-first century, disquiet has been expressed that the citizens in the UK were 'sleepwalking into a surveillance society'. This claim was made by Richard Thomas, the UK's first Information Commissioner, who went on to state that 'more information is [being] collected about people' and is 'accessible to far more people [and] shared across many more boundaries than British society would feel comfortable with' (cited in *The Guardian*, 20 January 2006). The idea of a 'surveillance society' highlights what, for many, are alarming developments in the growth of surveillance – it 'invades' privacy and lacks democratic oversight or constraint, and leaves little or no room for political debate as to the consequences. These are valid concerns that point to key questions about the nature of democracies, the enactment of justice and the management and control of citizens. These concerns have also led to questions about surveillance expansion and intensification into hitherto unobserved areas of social life (including the home, telephonic and web communications, education, health and travel).

However, what we shall develop in this book is a series of critiques that question the notion of a 'surveillance society'. The term 'surveillance society' presents a number of problems as a descriptor for what is going on in practice. The term encourages a view of surveillance as ubiquitous; as something that has unfolded in an even manner and rendered all kinds of people, social situations, organisations and institutions more 'visible'. Given our examples discussed earlier, how accurate is this view when trying to understand the relationship between surveillance and crime? Is, for example, 'privacy' intruded upon in a uniform manner when we consider the surveillance of crime across different groups? As our introductory example illustrates, some forms of privacy may be relatively sheltered while others are dramatically exposed by surveillance practice. Does surveillance categorise what appear to be very similar activities in the same way – supporting and producing even-handed and consistent sanctions? Does surveillance operate in an equal, even-handed manner in judging behaviours found in distinctive aspects of the social world? In short, as the book progresses, we shall critically explore the extent to which surveillance can be characterised as a homogeneous exercise and illustrate the extent to which it is uneven both in its reach into society and in its consequences. And these consequences will be shown not only to have significance for those under surveillance, but also for our understanding of the social meanings and social responses to crime.

We shall provide a focus upon surveillance as a controversial and contested practice and we shall illustrate this practice in relation to a range of criminal justice and social control settings. Indeed, 'crime' itself is a contested concept. It has multiple meanings that were intimated in our earlier discussion relating to 'fraud'. These meanings become energised in a range of contexts – politics, law, media, criminal justice proceedings, 'public' debates and in victim campaigns, and so on. Crime is also an historically evolving category that is never static and is subject to change. Crime 'remains a site of political, legal and moral contestation' (Muncie, 2001: 64) and is surrounded by a variety of competing voices and interests, some of which are more powerful than others.

Questioning surveillance and the plan of the book

This chapter has set the scene for the kinds of questions the rest of the book will raise. These include:

How does surveillance respond to crime?

How does surveillance constitute crime and render it meaningful?

How has surveillance and the 'surveillance society' been understood by scholars from a range of disciplines, including sociology, criminology, political science and cultural studies?

How has surveillance developed historically? How does it intersect with landscapes, institutional priorities and cultural frameworks inherited from the past?

How has surveillance aided the development of policing particular groups?

What are the social impacts of surveillance?

How is surveillance contested and how does this contestation reflect back on surveillance practices?

What are the implications of the surveillance of crime upon broader processes of social ordering?

Chapter 2 provides an overview of the main theoretical perspectives and key concepts that have been deployed in order to understand the 'surveillance society'. What kinds of issues does surveillance raise? Have we arrived at a 'new' surveillance frontier? How does surveillance become implicated in how the few see the many and in how the many see the few – and what are implications for understanding crime? Chapter 2 explores these and other related questions.

As we have indicated in our opening example, surveillance practice takes place within, and develops out of, social relations and these have an historical lineage. In **Chapter 3**, then, we explore the historical development of surveillance and its relationship to crime: how did the intimate relationship between the two develop and what were the consequences of this for understanding the modern surveillance endeavour? Here we pay particular attention to the development of early attempts to reform state practices along more interventionist lines and within this we trace the trajectory of 'policing' within the broader context of capitalist modernity and its attendant power relations.

As a number of writers have argued, the balance between 'public' and 'private' policing provision has shifted in recent years to the extent that a 'pluralized, fragmented and differentiated patchwork has replaced the idea of the police as the monopolistic guardians of public order' (Crawford, 2003: 136). For some writers, this provides a challenge to the state monopoly of 'policing' and is part of a paradigm shift in policing and social control signified by the move away from a 'punishment' mentality towards a 'risk' mentality.

In **Chapter 4** we look critically at the emerging 'risk paradigm' by examining the construction and operation of 'new surveillance' systems by 'public' and 'private' police officers. In line with our focus on *continuity* as well as *change*, we argue, first, that 'risk-based' strategies are mediated by the existing organisational, occupational and individual concerns of front-line operatives; secondly, that there is no easy distinction to be made between 'public' and 'private' actors in moral or ideological terms and that there is often a shared assumption concerning which social groups should be singled out for targeting by 'new surveillance' technologies; and thirdly, that alongside the emergence of the loosely formed 'surveillant assemblage', there are also countervailing trends towards the centralisation of surveillance systems.

Chapter 5 explores the relationship between 'globalisation', the 'war on terror' and 'surveillance' by showing how the rapid increase in the use of 'new surveillance' technologies, post September 11 2001, is in fact being driven by wider global trends which pre-date the 'war on terror'. We argue that this 'technological fix' may not have the desired effects in terms of preventing 'global terrorism', before going on to show how the 'globalisation' of surveillance may have serious unintended consequences which threaten civil liberties and community cohesion.

As indicated in our earlier example, surveillance has impacts and these can vary according to the kind of surveillance enacted and upon whom it is exercised. The social impacts of surveillance have many facets that fall differentially upon the life chances and opportunities of different groups as well as having consequences for how a society comes to understand 'crime' and harm. In **Chapter 6** we critically explore the social impacts of surveillance upon relatively powerless groups as well as more powerful sections of the population.

Chapter 7 continues to unravel the unevenness of surveillance practice by looking at its contested nature. The interface where surveillance meets the surveilled is an important one for shaping the ideological thrust and impact of surveillance. Surveillance shapes but is also shaped by social forces acting within and around it. But again this shaping is by no means an even process. Returning to our example of fraud, tax analysts have, for a long time, argued that 'however good the inspectors [at RCPO] they are no match for the highly paid legions involved in this sophisticated, quite legal, exercise in globalised accounting' (*The Guardian*, 2 February 2009). Millions are spent by individual companies on lawyers and financial experts for the purposes of hiding (sometimes legally, sometimes not) statements of income and potential sources of tax from the inspectors. Such resources aid the negotiation and shaping of the surveillance interface at least, in this example, for rich and powerful business people. What of the benefit fraudster? What resources does he or she have in shaping or negotiating their own surveillance? Along with the ability of all kinds of groups to contest and shape surveillance, Chapter 7 explores the issues, contradictions and discrepancies that groups and individuals bring into surveillance situations.

Chapter 8 concludes the book and revisits the main arguments while considering the implications of what has been discussed in previous chapters. A particular emphasis will be placed upon a reconsideration of what the 'surveillance society' might mean in light of the issues explored. What are the relationships between surveillance, crime and social order, and what forms of 'justice' does this relationship promote? Finally, what are the key processes involved in shaping the 'surveillance society' and is the shape and direction of this society inevitable?

2

Understanding Surveillance

CHAPTER CONTENTS

Issues in surveillance	12
Surveillance, crime and deviance: the limits to visibility	14
The development of panoptic societies	16
The dispersal of disciplinary surveillance	18
The electronic panopticon	19
Risk and the 'new surveillance'	21
The surveillant assemblage	24
Beyond the panopticon? The rise of synoptic surveillance	26
Differential surveillance: women and girls	28
Bringing the material and the ideological back in: surveillance, social ordering and power	31
Summary and conclusion	36
Study questions	37
Further reading	38

OVERVIEW

Chapter 2 provides:

- An overview of the main theoretical perspectives on surveillance and their differing conceptual orientations
- An insight into how power is understood in relation to surveillance practice
- An exploration of the relationship between surveillance technologies and their normative drivers
- The similarities and differences between panoptic and synoptic surveillance

KEY TERMS

- Differential surveillance
- Panopticon
- Power
- Risk / normative technologies

- Social order
- Surveillance
- Synopticon
- Visibility / invisibility

Issues in surveillance

Surveillance practices target and gather information concerning a range of deviations from social norms. These include crime, but also deviations that have a tangential relationship to legal proscriptions. Many writers agree that surveillance is implicated in the process of social ordering or the assignment of groups and individuals into some position or function in a hierarchy of social relations. In this sense, surveillance possesses power – a power that seeks to make many facets of social life 'visible' and 'known' for the purposes of maintaining stability and order in social relations. For Lyon (2007), the power of surveillance can be understood through exploring three interrelated and overlapping types of surveillance relationship, each with the potential of coexisting alongside the other. First, there is *face-to-face* surveillance that takes precedence in local, more confined spatial settings (such as the case of policing on the streets or in being interviewed in a welfare department). Secondly, there is *file-based* surveillance, conjoined with the development of modern bureaucratic systems of classification staffed by professionals and 'experts' whose growth in the field of social control throughout the twentieth century has been 'directed towards creating new categories of deviance and social problems', and 'defining more people as belonging to special populations and then slotting them into one or other category' (Cohen, 1985: 195). Thirdly, there is *interface* surveillance, mediated by digital technologies developed in the later part of the twentieth century and aimed at accruing information from bodies, gestures and traits. Interface surveillance may forgo the need for embodied persons to be present in the surveillance relation as well as speed up the flow of surveillance information across time and space, thus allowing a greater possibility for global surveillance. The interconnectedness of these ideal types of surveillance should be borne in mind as they mediate between a surveillance regime and surveillance subjects. And the latter, of course, react and respond to surveillance in ways not always anticipated by those involved in monitoring (Lyon, 2007).

As we saw in the Introduction, surveillance and its relationship to crime raises controversial questions. Whatever the precise mode of surveillance practice, the heated social debates that surveillance practice throws up are legion and point to questions of what surveillance *is*, *whether and why it is necessary*, and its *impacts* on the power and status of institutions, groups and individuals in the social world. At the risk of over-simplifying, some have argued that surveillance provides a means to deter crime, manage 'risks' and reduce harms and is therefore necessary to the extent that it achieves such aims. Others have argued that surveillance amplifies social risks and social divisions, and infringes on fundamental civil liberties. On this view, its necessity and practice within social situations is therefore in need of careful scrutiny.

What is clear from these kinds of debates is that surveillance is a matter of concern because it is never a neutral exercise. As 'a medium of power' (Giddens, 1985: 341) it works on the assumption that it is necessary to generate categories of suspicion or deviation in the attempt to uphold prescribed social norms. As a result, our common-sense understandings of surveillance may be in need of revision, especially if they proffer a simplistic view that 'it empowers citizens' or 'promotes the public good' or 'deters crime'. Our theoretical understanding can begin by grasping surveillance as a form of power with a number of facets and how this, in turn, raises key questions that take us to the heart of the interrelationship between surveillance and the governing of social relations of which it is a part. This chapter is designed to illustrate different theoretical perspectives, each with its own nuances and questions in approaching the subject. Taken as a whole, these perspectives raise general questions that have come to characterise the study of surveillance. These are:

1 Privacy: Whether and to what extent individual freedoms and civil liberties are reconfigured and even under threat from surveillance.
2 Effectivity: Does it 'work' with respect to its stated aims?
3 Social order: What is the relationship between surveillance and the wider processes of social ordering around class, race, gender, age and sexuality?
4 Equity: What is the relationship between the proliferation of surveillance technologies and 'justice'?
5 Expansiveness: What is the potential of surveillance to become a global phenomenon?

The chapter does not intend to explore all these issues with equal weight and attention, and this is reflected in the different weightings that different perspectives provide in respect of these questions. In outlining the issues, however, it is intended to emphasise some of the key concerns in thinking about surveillance, concerns that will be revisited and alluded to throughout the book.

However, posing these issues forces us to consider how they become constituted in social life. Issues of privacy, power and justice reverberate within many and varied micro and macro spatial settings where surveillance is enacted. This means that we need to be alert to the fact that surveillance that takes place within, as well as helping to constitute, spatial borders – from the realms of the body to the global. In general terms, surveillance aids border maintenance (both formal and informal), effecting groups and individuals as they move between and utilise multiple spaces in the course of time (whether in leisure, at work, through consumption, as national citizens or in the home). Consequently, issues in surveillance arise 'in a wide variety of contexts' and 'often revolve around the appropriateness of crossing, or failing to cross, personal and organizational borders' (Marx, 2005: 29). It follows that surveillance has consequences for the production and reproduction of particular spatial relations. In this sense, and as we saw in the Introduction to the book, surveillance is tied to, and indeed reflects, assumptions and judgements about particular spaces, who inhabits them and how they are used. Surveillance may attempt to create, maintain and legitimate spatial borders – informing our understanding of them and movement between them – in ways that are deeply structured in prevailing relations of power.

Surveillance, crime and deviance: the limits to visibility

As we shall see in Chapter 3, surveillance has a long history in relation to the control of crime. However, its significance stretches beyond this. It is now called upon to perform a range of 'duties' in the monitoring of deviations and transgressions within a given social order. Some theorists have put forward the idea that advanced capitalist societies are in fact 'surveillance societies' (Lyon, 2001). This notion suggests 'the proliferation of social visibility' has been extended by surveillance in that 'more people from more walks of life are now monitored' (Haggerty and Ericson, 2006: 5). As indicated, this extension of surveillance monitoring has been conducted in a manner that extends beyond what we think of as 'crime'. While surveillance may be widespread and endemic to modern societies, it is important to acknowledge that its mode of operation and its purposes display limitations – whether enacted through face-to-face, file-based or interface systems. As Rule has pointed out, surveillance regimes are limited: by their size; the amount of information they can cope with; the degree to which centralisation of surveillance information can occur; and the speed of information flow and intervention that may result from surveillance. These factors impose limitations on 'the agency of surveillance and control' whereby they 'cannot bring ... data to bear on a client quickly enough to act against him [sic]' (Rule, 2007: 27). Accordingly, the *capacity* and *effectiveness* of surveillance systems can be called into question by the structural limitations of the latter alongside the ability of surveillance subjects to avoid or resist control.

These technical limitations, however, do not relay all the issues and problems thrown up by surveillance. Surveillance is a partial exercise, accruing knowledge and information in an uneven and differentiating manner. This may be due to limitations inherent in surveillance technologies, but it is also, more importantly, related to the fact that surveillance takes place within fractured and contested social orders. As already noted, it is a form of power with a number of dimensions and it is these dimensions that are defined through social values and specific interests that, when scrutinised, help us understand how surveillance is used, in what contexts and with what consequences for specific social groups. Consequently, as highlighted in Chapter 1, the idea of a 'surveillance society' is a somewhat assertive and generalised notion and leaves many questions open to debate in theory and practice. The politics of visibility in such a society – what is seen and what is relatively unseen – remains a critical focal point for students of surveillance. What is rendered 'visible' and 'known' through the use of cameras, databases, computing technologies and face-to-face surveillance is in fact premised upon the fact that surveillance 'operates through processes of dissembling and reassembling' based on 'pre-established classificatory criteria' (Haggerty and Ericson, 2006: 4). The tendential nature of surveillance – both in terms of what is monitored, who monitors who and what kind of data are collected – means that it has a role in what Lyon has called a process of 'social sorting'. As he has indicated, surveillance 'obtains personal and group data in order to classify people and populations according to variable criteria, to determine who should be targeted for special treatment, suspicion, eligibility, inclusion, access and so on' (Lyon, 2003c: 20). This general definition of surveillance as social sorting raises further questions in respect of the relationship between surveillance and crime.

1 Which institutions and social groups (both formal and informal) are engaged in monitoring crime, criminality and deviance?
2 What kinds of crime and deviance are most likely to be surveilled or rendered visible – which are not?
3 What kind of social understanding is generated from surveillance with respect to our knowledge about 'the crime problem' or 'the deviance question'?

These questions can also be set alongside other questions concerning the nature of power within surveillance practices. To reiterate, how does surveillance intersect with the power and powerlessness derived in relations of class, 'race', gender, sexuality and age? Furthermore, the extent to which surveillance empowers some social groups and agencies (who and under what circumstances?) and disempowers others (perhaps diminishing their privacy and social status) remain areas of debate within and between surveillance perspectives. It is a matter of theoretical debate, then, as to the precise relationship between surveillance and the structuring of social relationships within the social order. The theoretical perspectives discussed here often compete and contest with each other as to the nature of surveillance, its targeting and social effects. As Lyon has stated, what seems to be emerging is that 'surveillance studies today is marked by an urgent quest for new explanatory concepts and theories' and that 'the most fruitful and insightful ones are emerging from transdisciplinary work' (Lyon, 2003c: 27).

The development of panoptic societies

Lyon has argued that 'the rise of surveillance society may be traced to modernity's impetus to coordinate or control' (Lyon, 2001: 49). As we shall see in the next chapter, surveillance is rooted in nineteenth-century modernity and is characteristic of the rise of the nation state (Giddens, 1985) and the bureaucratic means of institutional organisation (Dandeker, 1990). For Giddens (1985: 321), the development of 'surveillance is fundamental to social organizations of all types, the state being historically the most consequential form of organization, but nevertheless being only one organization among many others'.

As the next chapter will explore in more detail, modern surveillance developed alongside the rise of criminal, moral and legal discourses that consolidated within bureaucratic institutional procedures as the nineteenth century progressed. The work of Michel Foucault has been instructive in excavating this period. He tied the development of modern surveillance within the punishment practices established in modern European prisons between 1760 and 1840. In this period, punishment shifted from the public spectacles of torture and execution (monarchical punishment) to the techniques of 'soul training' mastered in the new prisons and geared towards the production of obedient and 'docile' individuals. Foucault termed this process 'carceral punishment' in that it heralded a constant surveillance of inmates under a new kind of power – disciplinary power. New prisons developed a form of spatial and temporal control via hierarchies of surveillance and classification and sought to instil discipline over a prisoner's body through disciplining the mind. In this way, prisoners were to be the subjects of 'normalising judgements' orchestrated by guards and professional groups who recorded, collated and categorised knowledge of inmate behaviour.

Deviation from the norm was thus identified, recorded and corrected. This surveillance gaze was asymmetrical in that those subject to it were at once the objects of 'knowledge' pertaining to their behaviour but were also unable to verify how, where and when this knowledge through surveillance was being conducted. This kind of surveillance operated through the *panoptic principle* – where the few (guards, doctors and criminologists) could exercise surveillance over the many (the prisoners). Thus, through the panoptic plan, a handful of prison guards could control, monitor and contain hundreds of prisoners, therefore ensuring a new kind of authority that sought a more intense, 'efficient' and automatic functioning of power (Foucault, 1979: 206). The modern prison acted as a laboratory to monitor, train and correct individual behaviour (1979: 203–205) by increasing the numbers over whom surveillance was exercised. Crucially, this was meant to encourage prison inmates to conduct self-surveillance in regulating and disciplining their own behaviour, under conditions of constant, yet unverifiable, watching (Foucault, 1979: 206). In theory, this characteristically modern form of surveillance therefore had a deterrent aspect to it in that the prisoner could never verify when he/she was being watched or not, thus it was hoped instilling self-discipline among its subjects.

For Foucault, panoptic power and the forms of expertise and unverifiable surveillance this gave rise to do not end at the prison walls. This modern form of surveillance gradually became operative outside the prison as a new instrument of social control that would 'insert the power to punish more deeply into the social body' (Foucault, 1979: 82), and bring with it the possibility of 'the utopia of the perfectly governed city' (Foucault, 1979: 198). Here, surveillance as a tool for ensuring obedience proliferated throughout institutions such as schools, hospitals, workplaces, army barracks and asylums, and fostered the birth of a 'disciplinary society'. In such a society, 'the judges of normality are present everywhere'; 'We are in the society of the teacher-judge, the doctor-judge, the educator-judge, the "social worker"-judge'. In this sense, the thrust of modern surveillance is conjoined with the generation of knowledge used to 'normalise' individual bodies, gestures, behaviours, aptitudes and attainments (Foucault, 1979: 304). Accordingly, what once constituted a drive to control illegalities (crime) became applicable to a whole range of behavioural contexts in which 'the norm' reigns supreme and surveillance offers the possibility of countering many forms of non-illegal 'deviation' whether in the workplace, the school, the mental health clinic, the family and in consumer transactions. Panoptic surveillance 'was about whether an individual was behaving as he should, in accordance with the rule or not, whether he was progressing or not' (Foucault, 1994a: 59). Right into the twentieth century and beyond, these expansive surveillance sites aided the maintenance of social well-being and social order. Controversially, Foucault argued that this form of modern surveillance encouraged a 'docile' citizenry – self-inspecting, self-judging and self-correcting in relation to predominant social norms.

For Foucault, surveillance was tied to a process of individualisation which, in turn, was tied to the development of the modern state. Surveillance in this sense encourages a new subjectivity based on an individualising ethos that, for him, was not determined by the state alone, but nevertheless encouraged identification with forms of state power. His work concerned the power of surveillance along with the possibility engendered in its analysis 'to liberate us both from the state and from the type of individualization linked to the state' (Foucault, 1994b: 336). Therefore, Foucault's analysis focused upon the micro aspects of surveillance – how it was enacted – in order to 'undertake a critical investigation of the thematics of power' (1994b: 337) which have a macro reality. Alongside individualisation, Foucault (2004: 253) argued that surveillance operates through a form of 'bio-power'. By this he meant the observation and control of whole populations through the introduction of techniques such as forecasting and statistical estimates that were developed in order to provide regulation over the domains of sexuality, death, birth, production and illness. For Foucault, the surveillance society (or in his words the 'normalizing society') is one 'in which the norm of discipline and the norm of regulation intersect' (Foucault, 2004: 253).

The dispersal of disciplinary surveillance

Stan Cohen took many of Foucault's insights and elaborated upon them in terms of how surveillance generates new visions and practices of social control. Throughout the twentieth century the dispersal of surveillance took on many manifestations – community corrections, intermediate treatment, neighbourhood watch, private security, and latterly the use of public surveillance cameras – all of which Stan Cohen critically traced. For Cohen, the notion of 'dispersal' has a number of important consequences. First, the move to informal, private and communal controls 'widens the net' of the formal system by bringing about 'an increase in the total number of deviants getting into the system in the first place'. Secondly, a 'thinning of the mesh' occurs, increasing 'the overall level of intervention, with old and new deviants being subject to levels of intervention (including traditional institutionalization) which they might not have previously received' (Cohen, 1985: 44). Thirdly, the dispersal of surveillance blurs the 'old' boundaries between formal/informal and public/ private forms of control, resulting in 'more people [getting] involved in the "control problem" [and] more rather than less attention ... [being] ... given to the deviance question' (Cohen, 1985: 231). Accordingly, modern surveillance heralds a more insatiable processing of deviant groups undertaken by 'new' experts in new spatial settings. However, 'the most fundamental fact about what is going on in the new agencies is that it is much the same as what went on and is still going on in the old systems' (1985: 79). Like Foucault, Cohen traced the bedrock of surveillance within an insatiable need to classify – a process that was consolidated in the nineteenth century (see Chapter 3). It is this 'need' that has continued up to the present and is woven into the minutia of social life, bringing with it new forms of expertise without which it is assumed we can no longer function (as parents, travellers, consumers, workers or sexual beings). As the cornerstone of modern social control, surveillance now operates 'right outside the formal punitive system – in consumer culture, welfarism, family, education, systems of private regulation and civic law' (Cohen, 1985: 272).

Cohen's understanding of social control included his predictions for future trends. First, both inclusionary (supervision in the community) and exclusionary forms (the use of prisons for example) of control will merge to reinforce each other and become expanded. Secondly, pre-emptive forms of surveillance (to spot and halt deviance at an early stage) will also expand. An array of evidence for these predictions has been compiled by Blomberg and Hay (2007). We shall return to these issues in throughout the rest of the book.

To recap the lines of theoretical thought discussed so far: surveillance has a tendency to disperse and become operative in a wide range of social settings not merely found *within* the criminal justice state but also *alongside* it; in Cohen's writing, it works towards both visions of inclusion (normalisation, community monitoring) and exclusion (stigma, banishment, separation of deviants, incarceration); and by its complexity, sprawl and spatial decentralisation it tends to become self-sustaining so that surveillance and control leads to more surveillance and control. The notion of panoptic control and its dispersion introduces the idea of the unseen observer (for some the core icon of modern surveillance) and the relentless classification of bodies, thoughts, gestures and actions that modern surveillance produces as a forerunner to intervention and control of targeted populations. The primacy of face-to-face and file-based surveillance is stressed in these earlier formulations as it was these that predominated up until the last quarter of the twentieth century. There is also a stress upon surveillance as developing a capillary-like structure, involving a range of formal and informal agencies. But how and through what means is surveillance spreading, and with what social consequences?

The electronic panopticon

Foucault, and to a lesser extent Cohen, had little to say about the impact of information technology on surveillance. Others following their work did. This reflected changes in technology, with the greater possibility for surveillance becoming mediated through electronic interfaces. Poster (1996), for example, documented how computers and complex databases, have been central in dispersing panoptic principles beyond the prison walls and thus, in Foucault's terms, helping to ensure an efficient and capillary-like operation of power. This is so because databases 'are perfectly transferable in space' and 'indefinitely preservable in time' (Poster, 1996: 182). Poster called this the 'superpanopticon', where 'the subject [of surveillance] has been multiplied and decentred, capable of being acted upon by computers at many social locations without the least awareness by the individual concerned yet just as surely as if the individual were present somehow inside the computer' (1996: 185). In this sense, 'the surveillance gaze has been expanded to a level unimaginable on the basis of co-presence' (Norris, 2003: 253). Thus, the superpanopticon may be overtaking the face-to-face regime of surveillance in that the subject of the database 'has a new form of presence, a new subject position that defines him [sic] for all those agencies and individuals that have access to the database' (Poster, 1997: 189). Furthermore, we all partake in our own database surveillance when, for example, surfing the internet, during bank transactions, making telephone calls or using interactive TV, we leave traces of action which databases can sort into categorical identities. 'Identity' can be constructed remotely and at a distance, simulated by computer tracking and matching. For Poster, the 'superpanopticon' is even less verifiable to the subjects of surveillance than the panopticon – we simply have no way of knowing on this 'global' scale how, where and when data about us is stored, how our identities are fabricated within the 'data image' (Lyon, 1994) or the 'data-double' (Haggerty and Ericson, 2000).

With the advent of networks of computers, 'data mining' has become operational through the extraction of information 'directed towards the generation of rules for the classification of objects' (Gandy, 2007: 149). For example, data mining can be used to classify high and low value customers for corporations, or be used to assess and rank 'high' or 'low' risk groups in relation to criminal behaviour (based on databases of police stops, searches or arrests). Data mining can be used, in theory, in the prediction of future behaviour and for increasing the profits for corporations based on knowledge of consumer behaviour in the name of 'efficiency'. The computerisation of surveillance engendered what Lyon (2001: 16) called the 'disappearance of the body', as social relations (for some) become stretched over time and space – 'disembodied and abstract relationships are maintained not so much in human memory as in data banks and networked computer systems'. Face-to-face contact – though not disappearing altogether – is often displaced by electronic mediation and institutional remoteness. Biometric surveillance appears to consolidate these shifts and refers to the measurement of the body to corroborate identity and thus manage movement and access. Fingerprints, iris scans, hand geometry and facial recognition technology lead the way in this 'informatization of the body' (van der Ploeg, 2003: 58) and appear to 'offer what many believe to be the most reliable ways of perfecting ... tokens of trust' (Lyon, 2007: 125).

As David Lyon states, electronic surveillance creates data-doubles which stand in for real persons. As indicated previously, this produces partiality in knowledge of surveilled subjects: we are 'known' from the abstractions produced and stored by the database. We are thus coded and atomised by surveillance, reduced to bits of information collected about us and deemed relevant to understanding 'the person'. This raises questions about 'how far the data image or the digital persona may be said to correspond to the embodied person who walks the downtown street' (Lyon, 2001: 147). However, 'dataveillance' of this kind constructs virtual bodies to be investigated, disseminated and in some cases stolen in cases of identity theft, raising questions relating to the impacts of these technologies on 'the integrity of the person' (van der Ploeg, 2003: 71). In this sense, surveillance – whether linked to digitised information storage or more direct forms of watching – can posses an alienated quality by its sheer remoteness, institutional distance and procedural invisibility.

Risk and the 'new surveillance'

The issues discussed so far illustrate what for many writers is a shift in contemporary surveillance patterns in relation to the use of computer technology that has redrawn, in quantitative and qualitative terms, modes of surveillance different from 'older' surveillance practice. This is reflected in 'new' concerns with the identification and anticipation of 'risk' and concurs with the notion of the emergence in late twentieth century of a 'new penology' or *politics of prevention* which attempts to predict dangers upon which proactive interventions can occur. Here, surveillance in general, and crime control policy in particular, is guided by 'techniques for identifying, classifying and managing groups assorted by levels of dangerousness' (Feeley and Simon, 1994: 180). Castel (1991) argued that modern social orders are moving towards a 'post-disciplinary' form of rule, less concerned with changing people (as in Foucault's concern with normalisation) and more concerned with surveillance policies which aim to 'anticipate all the possible forms of irruption of danger' and promote 'suspicion to the dignified rank of a calculus of probabilities' (Castel, 1991: 288). 'To be suspected' one only has to 'display whatever characteristics the specialists responsible for the definition of preventive policy have constituted as risk factors' (Castel, 1991: 288).

Shearing and Stenning (2003) argued that surveillance techniques could also assume various forms without necessarily being moral or normalising in orientation. The growth of private policing and mass private property in the late twentieth century was thought to be signalling a 'reconstruction in the social world' towards 'instrumental' ordering practices. Shearing and Stenning argued that the shift to preventative strategies hinged around the 'language of profit and loss', thereby replacing moral questions of right and wrong (2003: 338). Consequently, some have argued that a reorganisation of institutions for the maintenance of order and a significant erosion by the private sector of the state's assumed domination over policing and justice has occurred (Shearing and Stenning, 2003). For these authors, it has been the rise of large commercial complexes, such as Disneyland, that has undermined the unitary order of the sovereign state. The spread of disciplinary surveillance power into a range of spatial settings driven by a new instrumentalism has not only sought the maximisation of profit but brought with it 'not one conception of order but many' (Shearing and Stenning, 2003: 428).

Such theoretical observations reflect some of the ideas found in the work of Gary T. Marx (2007) and his argument that we are in the midst of a 'new surveillance'. He contends that the 'new surveillance' gathered momentum in the last quarter of the twentieth century: it is routine, relatively hidden, yet ubiquitous. It renders advanced societies such as those in Europe and North America, *surveillance societies.* Examples of 'new surveillance' practice are found in everyday situations and include smart surveillance camera monitoring found in streets and shops that scan faces in the crowd to match against a database of known or potential troublemakers; mandatory provision of DNA samples; parental monitoring of children using cameras; phone tracking or smart clothing equipped with locator chips; computer programes that track and collect keyword-related information regarding to subjects discussed or searched for on the internet; monitoring workers in time and space using smart cards, chips or covert camera surveillance. We could continue this list, but the point about what is 'new' in such practices is found in relation to a number of generic tendencies contained within them. For Marx, the new surveillance is less visible to those subject to it; it is relatively inexpensive; more likely to involve low levels of consent; can be operated remotely; appears less coercive – 'soft surveillance', as he calls it; it involves surveillant experts but is also conducted through self-monitoring. What appears to be new is the enhanced power of information collation and the speed of intervention that takes place if deviation or suspicion is aroused. Furthermore, 'low visibility and the involuntary and remote nature of much contemporary surveillance may mean more secrecy and less accountability' and, as a result of diminishing costs in respect of surveillance technologies, an even greater widening of the surveillance net than that which Cohen predicted is possible because 'the sacred value placed on interior life would be eroded' (Marx, 2007: 89).

Bogard (2007: 97) has extended these points in arguing that many features of the new surveillance exist as 'simulated surveillance' because, for him, they involve 'observation before the fact' and have the goal of pre-ordering and pre-emption. The proliferation of profiling exemplifies this as it exists across a range of social sites, including policing, insurance, banking, teaching and advertisement. Profiling is an attempt at pre-emption in that it diagnoses and targets, *in advance*, problematic behaviour, individuals or groups. As Bogard puts it in relation to policing, 'if your skin colour, sex, age, type of car ... matches the computer profile each officer carries while on duty, you're a target, whether you have actually done anything wrong or not' (2007: 97). In terms of policing, profiling prescribes 'typical' offender behaviour or patterns of suspicious conduct. The offender or deviant is simulated from patterns of appearance, spatial movement or behaviour. This triggers a form of action – not necessarily to an offence or deviation that has *actually* occurred – but to the appearance of a risk that an offence or deviation *might* occur. Thus the 'new surveillance', it is argued, is concerned with the identification of risk where all problems are foreseen and 'all contingencies planned for in advance' (2007: 101). Bogard stretches the Foucauldian idea to its limit in inviting us to view surveillance as simulated into complex networks. It is all encompassing in its ability to design out danger and conflict. In this scenario, power itself is so amorphous in its targeting and so decentralised in its non-location, that it is seemingly impossible to resist and to identify any particular power interests served by 'simulation'. As he puts it, 'there are too many virtual connections, too many observers of observers, too many points of recording: all products ... of the networks themselves' (Bogard, 2006: 118).

Lianos and Douglas (2000) develop these arguments in tracing what they see as a move away from face-to-face surveillance and its replacement with the rise of 'automated socio-technical environments' (tracking devices, machine-based access control, automated CCTV, and so on). In their view, automated surveillance has little or no need for human input and even less room for subjects to negotiate with a surveillance regime. It is argued that these technical environments render deviance 'impossible' because 'the norm becomes a technical rule of action' – a kind of 'neutral parameter independent of decisions and values' (Lianos and Douglas, 2000: 108). These 'new surveillance' technologies have been conceptualised as 'profoundly reductive; they utilize no other logic than whatever is programmed into their software' whereby 'access is accepted or denied; identity is either confirmed or rejected; behaviour is either legitimate or illegitimate' (Norris, 2003: 276). The idea of the 'new surveillance' depicts a situation in which discretion *and* moral judgement are peripheral in the sense that that the former is almost non-existent and the latter has become a technical issue.

More broadly, what are the implications of these arguments for thinking about contemporary surveillance? First, it has been argued by some that the kinds of order that surveillance intersects with can have instrumental as well as moral foundations. Secondly, it is argued that advanced forms of governing are exercised through forms of 'power beyond the state' characteristic of political action being practised 'at a distance' (Miller and Rose, 1990). New forms of surveillance are thought to reflect 'advanced liberal' developments in government by audit, privatisation, quangoisation and the devolution of responsibility for the management of various risks – 'for health, wealth and happiness' – to non-state institutions and private individuals (Rose, 1996: 54–57). Surveillance technologies are understood as operating through plural systems of rule aimed at regulating the movement of goods, persons and the control of criminality. Under neo-liberal conditions, therefore, 'centres of government are multiple' (Rose and Miller, 1992: 185). Thirdly, multiple centres of government 'seek to employ forms of expertise in order to govern society at a distance, without recourse to any forms of direct repression or intervention' (Barry et al., 1996: 14).

Indeed, these developments may not be as simple as they first appear. Simon and Feeley (2003) have argued that the 'new penology' is not entirely dominant in advanced capitalist societies and may be limited to some but not all groups of professionals in and around the criminal justice system. Neither has it displaced 'older' forms of control upon which contemporary 'public discussion [about] crime remains rooted in the moralism' and a politics of vengeance that has developed over the last two centuries (Simon and Feeley, 2003: 101; see also Chapter 3). In this sense, many have argued that 'new' developments exist alongside 'older' ones in societies that are characterised as being increasingly 'governed through crime'. This governing is thought to be underpinned as much by technical discourses of risk as by a 'culture of control' in which punitiveness and surveillance play a large part (2003: 108; Garland, 2001). We shall return to these issues later in the chapter.

The surveillant assemblage

As already indicated, Haggerty and Ericson (2006) have argued that surveillance in the late twentieth and early twenty-first centuries has proliferated and generated greater social visibility. Contemporary surveillance transforms social hierarchies, rendering them less rigid 'as people from all social backgrounds are now under surveillance' (2006: 6). This is because of the rise of the 'surveillant assemblage' (Haggerty and Ericson, 2000), which encompasses the advances and extensions in information and data gathering we have noted so far. For these writers, such an assemblage is 'rhizomatic' and the result of infinitesimal offshoots, interconnections, dispersed flows of data across borders and between institutions. Such information and knowledge, and its speedy crossing of institutional borders, has had consequences whereby 'it is increasingly difficult for individuals to maintain their anonymity' (Haggerty and Ericson, 2000: 622) under the surveillance gaze. This obliteration of anonymity, or 'the disappearance of disappearance', in Haggerty and Ericson's terms, is manifest in a 'fractured rhizomatic criss-crossing of the gaze such that no major population groups stand irrefutably above or outside of the surveillant assemblage' (2000: 618). For example, while police can and do videotape demonstrators, so too do demonstrators (with cheaper and more accessible technologies) videotape police in order to monitor their (mis)conduct.

The idea of the 'surveillant assemblage' runs against views of surveillance as necessarily top-down or as a tool of the powerful which is evident in the institutionally fixed conceptions of panoptic surveillance. This 'new' surveillance situation 'allows for the scrutiny of the powerful by both institutions and the general population' (Haggesty and Ericson, 2000: 617). There are a number of related consequences of this view of surveillance. First, privacy may not only be eroding for more and more social groups, but that privacy (or its loss) is being traded in by surveillance subjects for benefits, services and rewards offered by surveillance bodies (such as in the case when some of us allow supermarkets to gather information about us in return for targeted better deals and offers relating to consumables). This allegedly highlights a shift in the rationality for surveillance increasingly being organised around, and operated through (at least for some), seduction. In other words, the 'acceptance' of surveillance is greater not because of any oppressive and coercive characteristics connected with earlier views of institutional power associated with the prison, but because it is contemporaneous with processes whereby we are 'seduced to conform by the pleasures of consuming the goods that corporate power has to offer' – as is the case with leisure patterns associated with entry into shopping malls and theme parks like Disneyworld (Shearing and Stenning, 2003: 432). Secondly, the assemblage of surveillance allows for greater expandable mutability (Norris and Armstrong, 1999) as surveillance regimes intended for one purpose find themselves being applied for another. This is evident in how policing agencies can access non-police databases for the purposes of fighting 'crime' and 'terrorism' (see Chapter 5) and could include those databases relating to media, educational, financial or insurance organisations. Thirdly, it is supposed that the rhizomatic nature of surveillance is underpinning an (as yet) unfinished 'democratisation' of surveillance. This is because the panopticon (where the few see the many) has in many senses been supplanted by, or at least joined with, another equally pervasive surveillance medium – synopticism. In a world in which surveillance now enables the scrutiny of 'the demeanour, idiosyncrasies and foibles of powerful individuals' (Haggerty, 2006: 30), it is no longer merely the case that the few see the many (panoptic power), but in fact it is just as likely that the 'many come to see the few' (synoptic power).

Beyond the panopticon? The rise of synoptic surveillance

The observations above have provided analysts of surveillance with new questions and points of debate, not least of which is: are we all subject to the *same degree* of surveillance and with *the same social consequences*? Is the 'disappearance of disappearance' an omnipresent and convincing notion? Is surveillance, as now practised, breaking down socio-spatial hierarchies? The idea of the 'new surveillance' tends to homogenise the reach of surveillance power – assuming rather than demonstrating its powers of penetration across the social world. We can no doubt follow Haggerty and Ericson's view of surveillance that takes account of technological advances and in grasping its multifaceted character – but does this amount to a democratisation of the gaze? Elsewhere, Haggerty and Gazso (2005: 174) acknowledge that it is 'not possible to adequately understand how surveillance operates if we do not attend to how surveillance capacity is related to, and derives from, efforts to align and integrate a host of different visualizing systems'. Thus, integration of surveillance networks is possible by states and governments who have the resources and political will to marshal such integration (as was the case after the attacks in the USA in September 2001 and in the UK in July 2005). However, attempts at coordinating surveillance systems by powerful bodies with the means to do so have been in evidence since the birth of modern surveillance in the nineteenth century (see Chapter 3). Indeed, as others have argued, 'rhizomatic' surveillance has existed from this time and has been the result of continuous technological innovations that have persistently accompanied it (Hier, 2007). In this sense, authors like Bogard unintentionally emphasise the determinate qualities of technologies and lose sight of how they are embedded in social-spatial relations and wider structures of power and have been for a much longer historical time period (McCahill 2002; Coleman, 2004; Monahan, 2006a). This is a critical point worth holding on to as we progress through the chapter and indeed the rest of the book.

Moreover, many theorists now recognise a 'new surveillance' has indeed been accompanied by the rise of synopticism – where the many see the few. Some of the effects of this were first elaborated by Thomas Mathiesen (1997) when he observed that panoptic models of surveillance had 'overlooked an opposite process of great significance which has occurred simultaneously and at an equally accelerated rate' (1997: 215). The growth of the mass media and digital and internet-based forms of communication have transformed the surveillance landscape and indeed created what Mathiesen terms a 'viewer society'. In such a society, 'literally hundreds of millions of people at the same time' are encouraged 'with great force to see and admire the few' (1997: 215).

The expansions in database technology, the internet and the mass media in the late twentieth century have at the same time led to a situation where surveillance has become enacted and spread across different social groupings. This, it is thought, has had at least two effects. First, extending Mathiesen's insights, Lyon argued that scopophilia (the love of looking) had become a cultural condition evidenced in the growth of surveillance-based reality media that conferred a greater visibility upon celebrities, politicians and criminals. Thus, 'the question of why people permit themselves to be watched [and "accept" the surveillance society] may be paralleled by the question of why people want to watch' at least in the realms of what passes for 'entertainment' (Lyon, 2006a: 48). Secondly, as mentioned above, synoptic surveillance, enables greater scrutiny of groups previously 'unseen'. In many respects, surveillance has 'become a more public and collective phenomenon' and in the case of broadcast TV has helped 'create a new type of watching public', underpinning 'a shared experience' that arouses 'collective sentiments' (Doyle, 2006: 218). Thus, in Mathiesen's terms, synoptic surveillance power – generated through our viewing and utilisation of media technologies – allow for a situation where great numbers of people are invited to focus on the 'commonality' of certain social problems and 'problem' people. For Foucault, it was the disciplinary power of panoptic surveillance that provided the main route to control an individual's soul and consciousness. However, others have argued that synoptic surveillance brings greater weight to this process of normalisation. For example, the media provides an arena for synoptic surveillance where viewers, readers and listeners (the mass audience) are encouraged to watch the few: celebrities, politicians, VIPs, the notorious and the banal criminal. The media inculcates a process of surveillance aimed at presenting 'a general understanding of the world' in which the 'personal and the individual, the deviant, the shuddering, the titillating' is emphasised (Mathiesen, 1997: 230).

However, 'the love of looking' is not without its problems as it raises new areas of concern within surveillance studies. First, what are the social messages contained in this mass looking exercise? Exactly what is being looked at and with what social consequences? Are the subjects of synoptic surveillance, be they street criminals, celebrities or political leaders, scrutinised and rendered 'visible' in the same way? Secondly, the cultural condition that forms the backdrop to a love of looking may in fact – at least for Mathiesen – lead us to a situation 'where the answers to the [most] basic questions are taken for granted' (1997: 230). Thus, the knowledge reproduced in synoptic surveillance remains highly partial in relation to the basic questions as to what is 'crime', who commits it and where (Coleman, 2009a). More broadly, it has been argued that synopticism reinforces a system of social stratification. Media imagery has attached great value to 'success' in work and leisure as well as through material gain with a particular valorisation of celebrity 'lifestyle'. At the same time, the media spotlights those failing to live up to this vision of success (aka the 'underclass'). This kind of media spotlighting veils social inequality (Young, 2007: 64–65). Consequently, the partiality of surveillance practice and the kinds of knowledge it produces – whether panoptic or synoptic – promotes a specific kind of social 'understanding' and exposure to events in the world that at the same time creates 'a spiral of silence' in relation to what is not seen and not foretold (Mathiesen, 2004: 103). Thus, as well as producing 'knowledge' and 'understanding' (which is always partial), surveillance is also imbued with a process of silencing in relation to social debate and understanding.

There is a third and related aspect pertaining to the rise of synoptic surveillance. This concerns how synopticism reinforces developments in real-world panoptic expansion. This aspect has two related components. One is the manner in which synoptic surveillance is limited in its apparent quest for enhanced social visibility. For Mathiesen, there remain relatively secret spaces, closed off from synoptic scrutiny. This relates to social visibility of panoptic processes themselves, as in the case of criminal justice practices that include police decision-making, state punishment, political policing concerning 'the war on terror' and other aspects of surveillance found in, and enacted by, powerful corporations. For Mathiesen, such arenas 'try to keep synopticism at arms length' (1997: 231). On the other hand, other aspects of the panoptic process become the staple diet of synoptic media – what are often referred to as 'human interest' stories – whereby social understanding or knowledge 'is purged of everything except the purely criminal' and 'hurled back into the open society as stereotypes' that operate in a 'panic-like' fashion in the form of 'terrifying stories about individual cases' (1997: 231). In this way, Mathiesen urges us to focus on the complex processes that are at work through which synoptic surveillance – particularly in its negative portrayal of threats, deviations, rising crime and the perceived insufficient protection from these phenomena – reinforces panoptic surveillance. Fear-inducing tales of criminality and 'terror' are often the basis for establishing expansions in real-world panoptic surveillance, thus endorsing calls for more street cameras, more prisons, more data checks and greater police powers.

Differential surveillance: women and girls

Surveillance technologies only make sense when understood within the social relations in which they operate. The power of surveillance is therefore the power of the social forces acting in and through surveillance practice. In this way, surveillance systems 'are both socially shaped and have social consequences, some of which go beyond the intentions inscribed in their shaping' (Lyon, 2001: 25). Without seeking to over-generalise, writers in the area of the 'new surveillance' have tended to explore it as driven by cold and seemingly disinterested technical factors at the expense of a focus on the moral, emotional and punitive underpinning of contemporary surveillance (Coleman, 2004). Although it is possible to depict how 'the general tide of surveillance washes over us all' (Haggerty and Ericson, 2000: 609), we may also wish to explore, in theoretical and practical terms, how what we might call *surveillance reach* is uneven and inconsistent in this watching process. In the new surveillance literature, the question of exactly *who* and *what* comes to be monitored, and who and what does not, and *why*, is left largely unexplored. The previous discussion around the 'new surveillance' leads us on therefore to consider the *differential and differentiating* nature of surveillance. For if surveillance can be defined as the 'collection and analysis of information about populations in order to govern their activities' (Haggerty and Ericson, 2006: 3), this governing aspect will be subject to a process of boundary maintenance through which surveillance produces lines of demarcation between 'normal'/'law abiding' and 'abnormal'/'criminal' behaviour. Consequently, '"deviance" is not a set of activities or attitudes separate from ... surveillance operations ..., but is formed in and through them' (Giddens, 1985: 309). This crucial insight restates a point we made in Chapter 1 concerning how surveillance both responds to *and* constructs crime and deviance. As noted above, this can be further exemplified in the proliferation of synoptic surveillance and the growth of reality-crime-TV in which partial understandings of crime and punishment are constructed (see Chapter 6).

Further points relating to the differential and differentiating nature of surveillance can be made here in relation to surveillance and the social divisions constructed around gender. As we have seen, Foucault's carceral model of surveillance directed us to how surveillance increasingly proliferates into more and more formal *and* informal spaces which in turn propels monitored subjects towards self-surveillance. Again, we can specify this process of dispersal and think about how self-surveillance may also operate in relation to 'female deviance' inscribed within everyday beauty and feminisation practices. In this realm, it has been argued that female self-surveillance is differentiated through gendered norms and values which arise as part of a cultural disciplinary continuum that proscribes female body 'management' and subjectivity (Bordo, 1993). In the realm of popular culture, it is argued, we are encouraged to see female 'deviance' in relation to prescribed images of 'beauty', 'worth' and 'attractiveness'.

Surveillance plays a role in objectifying bodies not least in terms of biometrics. However, the body-objectifying aspect of surveillance takes on a differential character when applied to women and girls in both formal and informal settings. A number of feminist theorists have explored this in terms of the kinds of technologies used and the gendered nature of the spaces within which they operate. Surveillance, it is argued, will have different effects and outcomes if we explore it alongside patriarchy as a key social construct and social division. In terms of popular women's magazines, for example, forms of self-surveillance (what Foucault called 'disciplinary technologies of the self') directed at the body may, for women, denote 'disgust', self-denial or 'shame' in the perceived failure to live up to prevalent feminine codes of appropriate body size, shape or demeanour – and this can have the effect of inducing self-directed panoptic control that includes self-harm (Bartky, 1988; Bordo, 1988). This self-surveillance may be encouraged by articles in women's magazines that delineate 'appropriate' behaviour in relation to domestic roles, bodily cleanliness, dietary habits, dress sense and sexual performance. Delineating 'conventional feminine behaviour' encourages surveillance directed towards 'the discipline of perfecting the body as an object' which can have harmful results, found in cases of anorexia nervosa and bulimia (Bordo, 1993: 179). For Bordo, the fact that women's magazines are underpinned by a discourse of 'liberation' and 'empowerment' renders the forms of surveillance they promote insidious: 'to *feel* autonomous and free while harnessing body and soul to an obsessive body-practice is to serve, not transform, a social order that limits female possibilities' (Bordo, 1993: 179). Bartky emphasises how self-surveillance operates 'as a form of obedience to patriarchy' underpinned 'with a pervasive feeling of bodily deficiency' (1988: 81–82). This reinforces some of the points already made concerning how particular social (embodied) stereotypes, relayed synoptically for public consumption, both reflect and discipline 'popular anxieties' as well as attempting to frame popular ways of seeing (for example, in relation to celebrity, criminality or one's body). While some have argued that women's magazines encourage surveillance as selfloathing, other feminist writers have countered that the genre is more complicated. Instead of promoting 'docile' female bodies in Foucault's sense, magazines allow space for debate (however limited) about women's issues outside stereotypical concerns (Wolf, 1993).

As a consequence of such issues that have been thrown up by feminist theorising, Howe (1994: 40) has argued that the literature on disciplinary control is a 'more penile-than-penal discourse' and has failed to account for the differential forms of control directed towards women within the formal justice setting and beyond. Disciplinary practices developed in women's prisons, for example, are quite distinct from those found in men's prisons in respect of gendered norms underpinning surveillance regimes geared to 'training' for domesticity, motherhood and dependency (Carlen, 1983). Moreover, outside the space of the women's prison, control is enacted through discourses of femininity in a range of situations: the home, in public, at work and through social policy (Heidensohn, 1996). Within the public realm, for example, women have been subject to the regulation and supervision of their 'femininity' through the threat and implementation of male violence, the labelling of women's behaviour (via the importation of negative sexual stereotypes), and the continual reinforcement of the dominant discourse that a 'women's place' is in the private sphere where violence will also be utilised to control 'deviant' behaviour. The surveillance of women has therefore been socially constructed through the lens of gender that has differentiated between the 'proper' roles of men and women, along with a prevalent ideology that has posited these differences as 'natural'. Feminists have drawn attention to the differential treatment of women within the criminal justice system and how regimes of control found here are gendered, resulting in differential forms of intervention aimed at women that are as much about penalisation for stepping outside ascribed 'feminine' boundaries as they are about the control of 'crime'.

Some feminist writers have noted that surveillance theorists have downplayed the control of women within civil society but they have also ignored how state control, far from being always negative, can – when exercised – have progressive consequences for women through interventions concerning protection from domestic and sexual violence (Howe, 1994: 115). Others have further complicated our understanding of 'privacy' in relation to the surveillance of women, particularly in western societies. Defences of privacy have often cloaked violence against women, making it difficult to render it visible either through surveillance or through the voices of women themselves. Furthermore, it has been argued that 'the power to invade the privacy of women's bodies is not easily curtailed by scrutiny and surveillance or by policies and legislation' but is more likely to be rendered knowable and potentially curtailed through the campaigns of women's groups themselves (Jones, 2005: 593).

Bringing the material and the ideological back in: surveillance, social ordering and power

From the discussion above we can see that theorists of surveillance have begun to open up questions as to how both panoptic and synoptic surveillance differentially scrutinises the foibles and machinations of differently situated social actors which can reinforce already existing ideas and practices. Indeed, many within surveillance studies are beginning to deploy the hermeneutic devices we have looked at so far to 'find that what is being secured [by surveillance practice] are social relations, institutional structures, and cultural dispositions' (Monahan, 2006a: xi). This reinforces the need to *contextualise* surveillance in spatial relations and practices along with the recognition that these relations are structured asymmetrically through key social divisions, including those based around class, 'race', gender, age and sexuality. Ultimately, surveillance cannot be divorced from social, political, economic and cultural struggles. It is these struggles that both shape surveillance and are shaped by it.

An exploratory task for theoreticians, as well as researchers in the field of surveillance will penetrate what Monahan (2006a: 2) has argued are the 'deeper motivations and logics behind surveillance and security'. Indeed, Foucault was at pains to stress not only 'the question of "how"' surveillance practice is exercised but also 'the questions of "what" and "why"' in relation to understanding developments in surveillance (Foucault, 1994b: 336). As Haggerty and Ericson (2006: 4) have argued, 'no single factor has caused this expansion of surveillance'. Furthermore, surveillance has not 'proliferated because it renders the state, capital, or power more effective' (2006: 4). Is this the same as arguing that surveillance (however intended or unintended in its consequences) *does not* render major institutional agents and agencies (such as states or corporate bodies) and their interests more powerful and effective? Is it the case that surveillance is so 'ubiquitous' and 'diverse' that 'it is almost impossible to speak ... coherently about "surveillance" more generally'? (2006: 22) These questions take us to the sociological heart of surveillance debates: *what kinds of power relations, if any, does surveillance reflect and reinforce?*

As we saw earlier, ideas about the 'new surveillance' have a tendency to stress technical automation that may be leading to the decline in discretion and moral judgements in surveillance practices. Clive Norris has questioned some of the assumptions found here in that these perspectives have been based on 'the premise that everyone is equally subject to the same surveillance regime' (Norris, 2003: 277). In the field of crime control, electronic and technically 'automated' surveillance cannot, in all instances, be entirely divorced from 'previous discretionary decisions that are already the result of selective law enforcement which prioritise some kinds of crime as opposed to others' (2003: 277). Similarly, McCahill has argued that the 'social shaping' of surveillance processes has not entirely disappeared. How surveillance technology is used depends on 'how the introduction of this technology fits in with existing social practices' (McCahill, 2002: 200). In contrast to the view that we are in the midst of a 'new surveillance' network, research has suggested that the use of technologies such as CCTV are driven by CCTV operators 'who bring with them taken-for-granted assumptions about the distribution of criminality within a given population' (Norris and Armstrong, 1999: 118). In other words, the recourse to 'risk'-based assessments and classifications are not divorced from moral categories (Coleman, 2004). Furthermore, many people may 'experience the facts of risk assessment', and the surveillance that underpins them, 'as normative obligations' (Haggerty and Ericson, 1997: 451). Rigakos (1999: 145) reinforced this point when he stated that there has been 'a tendency among risk theorists to overstate the importance of cold, actuarial calculus'. He cautioned theorists 'not to misread risk systems as operating on a separate or detached logic from "unscientific" impulses such as racism, heterosexism, classicism' (1999: 146). Thus, even the most technologically advanced, predictive and dataveillance-based systems incorporate previous assumptions and stereotypes into their models of what constitutes 'normal' behaviour and these can be relatively fixed in not allowing for ambiguity in the real-life flux of bodily expression and practice. Predictive surveillance is thus part of a wider set of social relations and assumptions embedded in material relations. However, 'to disentangle information from its material instantiation is inevitably to do some violence both to the data and the material' that will have a greater detrimental impact upon 'non-normative physical bodies' (Conrad, 2009: 386) defined in prevailing class, 'racial', gender and sexual terms.

Others have also sought to retain an analysis which focuses on 'centres of power'. As Garland (2003) has argued, while a whole range of technologies, institutional sites, activities and rationalisations around 'risk management' appear to be in play in contemporary surveillance societies, this does not fore-close analysing centres of power and continuities in the field of surveillance and crime. In an earlier article, Garland illuminated this point in relation to the state and its engagement in 'responsibilization strategies'. Here, states experiment 'with ways ... of activating the governmental power of "private" agencies, of co-ordinating interests and setting up chains of co-operative action' (Garland, 1996: 454). Thus, while surveillance and crime control may well disperse beyond the state:

> The state does not diminish or become merely a nightwatchman. On the con-trary, it retains all its traditional functions – the state agencies have actually increased their size and output ... and, in addition, take on a new set of co-ordinating and activating roles, which in time develop into new structures of support, funding, information exchange or co-operation. *Where it works ... the responsibilization strategy leaves the centralized state machine more powerful than before, with an expanded capacity for action and influence.* (Garland, 1996: 454, emphasis added)

Developing these points, others have raised questions around what is 'new' about the new surveillance. Coleman and Sim (1998: 40) argued for a 'dialectical analysis which emphasizes continuity, discontinuity and intensification rather than ideal-typical shifts'. It has been argued that while an array of institutional, technological and political 'innovations' continue to shape surveillance practices, so too do 'older' discourses surrounding what constitutes 'the proper object of surveillance power' (Coleman and Sim, 2000: 632). Despite the seem-ing diversity and 'rhizomatic' nature of agencies involved in the surveillance of particular crime problems, some have argued that it is important for surveillance studies to explore the normative dimensions of 'diverse' surveillance activity and analyse the discursive and ideological correspondences *between* networks and not merely their technical aspects (Coleman and Sim, 2000). Thus, both 'the capacity and ideological fervour' of seemingly unconnected surveillance agents and agencies 'to govern through *particular forms of crime* has been neglected in risk orientated analysis' (Coleman and Sim, 2005: 104, emphasis in original). Neglected too has been the coercive impacts of surveillance upon particular groups whose mere presence in specified spaces, or non-compliance, is deemed problematic and subject to processes of banishment (Beckett and Herbert, 2010) and fear-inducing responses among its subjects (Gilliom, 2006).

Borrowing Nicola Lacey's argument in relation to thinking about criminal justice practice as a whole, surveillance can be understood as a 'related but not entirely coordinated set of practices geared to the construction and maintenance of social order' (Lacey, 1994: 28). This argument would apply irrespective of whether the consequences of surveillance were intended or unintended. The classificatory impulse of surveillance has always been related to the ability to socially sort and order activities, people and events based on normative criteria. These criteria place differential value and meaning on classifications such as 'young' and 'old', 'foreign' and 'national', 'black' and 'white', 'poor' and 'affluent', and 'feminine', and 'unfeminine'. Therefore, someone or some agency makes a decision about what it is necessary to know and for what purpose and in doing so initiates surveillance that reinforces and reflects predominant institutional or social values and power networks. Consequently, the power of surveillance lies not just in its classificatory schema but in how this schema reflects back on material relations of power and control, enabling some circuits of power while disabling others (Coleman, 2004).

According to David Lyon, it is important that surveillance studies keeps 'a place for realist investigations of the [differential] experiences of subjects of surveillance *and* of specific analyses that show which groups are able to use surveillance power to their ends' (Lyon, 2007: 63, emphasis added). In developing this position, our understanding of surveillance will involve attending to what we call the 'surveillance discourses' that surround the development, maintenance and targeting of surveillance practice. Not all groups and populations stand on an equal footing in relation to a surveillance regime, and therefore cannot all engage in the same terms of a prevailing surveillance discourse. As many of the writers in this section have argued, surveillance is not merely technical in nature but is constituted by a value-laden communicative process between the agencies and agents involved in networks driving and maintaining surveillance systems (see McCahill, 2002; Coleman, 2004). The discursive tactics that form the communications between all those involved (from the watchers to the watched) in the surveillance process are an important aspect of setting the agenda for surveillance practices. Surveillance discourses entail formal and informal rules about what can be said, how it can be said, and who can speak what to whom. The outcomes arising from such discourses impinge upon the regulation of action and the preferred mode of intervention of a surveillance regime. In this sense, surveillance discourses are 'regulatory' and exist as 'vehicles through which attempts may be made to build meaning and to change existing ... behaviour' (Black, 2002: 179). Surveillance discourses are constructed upon asymmetrical terrains of power exhibited within differing levels of social, political and cultural capital that underpin the capacity to successfully engage the terms of a surveillance discourse.

Understanding the regulation of discourse is thus central to understanding the monitoring of populations and how normative evaluations, that are often unwritten, underpin this monitoring. How the terms of surveillance discourse are framed (and opposed), along with who is involved and who is not, help us understand how surveillance works in practice. Exploring such discursive formations will also shed further light on the relationship between surveillance and the 'public interest' and how this relationship – far from being obvious or unmediated – is socially shaped. This shaping is evident within the parameters of a surveillance discourse which will ask what and who is to be surveilled, to what extent and for what purpose (to enforce criminal law or gain compliance with rules?). It may be the case, for example, that surveillance measures such as CCTV in urban centres in the United Kingdom were introduced with little or no public discussion (Coleman, 2009a). However, the discursive frameworks that emerged during the 1990s were, and remain, structured within a network of power relationships which in turn were limited to those between government agencies, business consortia and public and private police who, not without conflict, produced shared meanings around the purpose of surveillance and the kinds of crime and disorder to be targeted (Coleman, 2004a). Thus, surveillance discourses involve networks of primary definers whose power and influence over the parameters of debate can work towards a form of linguistic closure whereby some voices and issues are kept marginal to the 'surveillance debate'. For example, surveillance discourses surrounding CCTV in the urban core have left the extent of CCTV, and its terms of use, relatively unproblematised (Coleman, 2009a). At the same time, it could also be argued that while the space for democratic debate and dialogue has been increasingly restricted, public 'opposition' has been either muted or rendered inconsequential (Davies, 1996a).

As we saw in the previous chapter in relation to 'fraud' committed by powerful groups and less powerful groups, there are different incarnations of surveillance discourses, ranging from those that are combative to those that are more conversational and relaxed in their tone, and these need specifying in particular contexts. In exploring particular surveillance discourses we can ask: is it an adjunct to criminalisation (for example, in relation to young black men on the streets) or less punitive techniques of persuasion (as applied to the powerful)? Or is the process taking into account rights to privacy – if so, whose? How does the communicative process either promote or sanction risk taking? As we saw in relation to benefit fraudsters in Chapter 1, a combative and punishing tone has no necessary relationship to levels of harm, but is more a reflection of longstanding and already existing discourses that negatively represent, sanction and demonise particular 'outsider' groups. These issues will be explored more fully in Chapters 6 and 7 in relation to the constitution of surveillance discourses *vis-à-vis* the powerful and the relatively powerless. How surveillance discourses develop is crucial to whether or not populations are subject to intensive and wide-ranging punishment-based surveillance or in being subject to forms of enabling surveillance. Therefore, questions relating to how 'crime', 'deviance', 'threat' and 'fear' are understood in communicative actions are central to understanding the surveillance of particular groups, activities and spaces. Later in the book we shall see how some groups targeted by surveillance are in a position to shape the surveillance discourse and influence the level of intensity and boundaries assigned to surveillance regimes. Indeed, in some instances, surveillance discourses can and are shaped through the medium of a 'conversation' (and its connotations of negotiation, cooperation and dialogue among 'equals') between surveillance agents and more powerful social actors. The latter, unlike those groups on the margins of political and economic life, may constitute inside players with influence in relation to the formation of a surveillance discourse and a surveillance regime as a result of their cultural credibility, status and enhanced bargaining power (see Chapters 6 and 7 in particular).

We end this section with the observation that surveillance produces knowledge about crime and deviance. This knowledge is always partial, uneven and incomplete. But surveillance is also developed and constituted through surveillance discourses and these themselves constitute forms of knowledge that are drawn upon in developing and targeting surveillance practice. Once again, however, this will not be just any knowledge found free-floating in society, but knowledge that is constructed and positioned by specific historical agents and endorsed by a strategic set of political alliances. Thus, as we have indicated here, the knowledge base that surveillance developments draw upon will also subjugate other forms of knowledge (for example, from the experience of 'criminals', workers, 'suspects' and specific targeted groups) and disqualify them as inadequate, naïve and unqualified to the task of surveillance (Foucault, 1984: 202). In this view, then, surveillance is tendential in both its development and affects.

Summary and conclusion

In theoretical terms, there may be broad agreement about the continuing expansion of surveillance but less on the impacts of this expansion upon different social groups and prevailing understandings relating to the 'problem of crime'. In relation to the surveillance of crime, some have stressed the diversity of technologies and practices, while others have stressed a by no means entirely coherent ideological unity across the field of surveillance and crime control. Various theoretical perspectives have probed the extent to which surveillance (in both its panoptic and synoptic forms) is integral to the process of *constructing* social understandings of 'crime', 'security', 'order', 'disorder', 'risk' and 'threat'.

A number of conceptual debates have been gained from this discussion and underpin the exploration of surveillance practices to follow. These can be listed as follows:

- Surveillance technologies exist within social frameworks, shaped by 'risk' discourses, alongside normative judgements containing emotive and punitive components. More often than not, surveillance does not merely seek to monitor, but is also ensconced in attempts to change or shape social behaviour. It 'legislate[s] norms for acceptable and unacceptable behaviours and actions' (Monahan, 2006a: 12).
- What may be 'new' in twenty-first-century surveillance practice is a matter of debate with respect to the novelty and increasing use of the technologies deployed (CCTV, searchable databases, and so on) rather than with respect to *how* surveillance is deployed, over *whom* and upon what types of crime it focuses as well as its impact on social divisions.
- Surveillance possesses a classificatory impulse related to the ability to socially sort and order activities, people and events. This renders it a medium of power which goes beyond its technical functioning, whereby someone or some agency makes a decision about what it is necessary to know and for what purpose and in doing so initiates surveillance that reinforces and reflects predominant institutional, common-sensical or social values.
- The classificatory impulse of surveillance means that it is entwined with social relations and social divisions – in work, migration, popular culture and consumption – as it is in fighting crime and political violence. Whatever the spatial context, surveillance will have intended and unintended impacts upon the social order and the structuring of class, 'race', gender, sexuality and age relations.
- Surveillance does not take place outside or apart from techniques of coercion and violence as processes of social ordering. What kind of spaces and for which groups does surveillance take on a more coercive and repressive character?
- As we have intimated here, surveillance is partial in both the kind of information it abstracts about individuals and groups. At the same time, these individuals and groups maintain an ability to negotiate, evade or neutralise surveillance (see Chapter 7). As a partial and uneven exercise, surveillance reduces individuals and collectivities of individuals to coded fragments of data used to decide entitlement in respect of receiving social 'goods' or in assigning social worth. Accordingly, surveillance possesses an inclusionary *and* an exclusionary logic.

STUDY QUESTIONS

1 In general terms, what are the main goals of surveillance?

2 What is panoptic surveillance and in what kinds of sites does it operate?

3   In what ways does surveillance create 'docile bodies'? What are some of the
    drawbacks with this understanding of surveillance?

4   'Surveillance increases social visibility.' What are the strengths and limitations
    that can be gleamed from this statement?

FURTHER READING

Cohen, S. (1985) *Visions of Social Control*, Cambridge: Polity Press.

Coleman, R. (2004) *Reclaiming the Streets: Surveillance, Social Control and the City*, Cullompton: Willan.

Lyon, D. (2007) *Surveillance Studies: An Overview*, Cambridge: Polity Press.

McCahill, M. (2002) *The Surveillance Web: The Rise of Visual Surveillance in an English City*, Cullompton: Willan.

Marx, G.T. (2007) 'What's new about the new surveillance? Classifying for change and continuity', in Hier, S.P. and Greenberg, J. (eds), *The Surveillance Studies Reader*, Maidenhead: Open University Press.

Mathiesen, T. (1997) 'The viewer society: Michael Foucault's "Panopticon" revisited', *Theoretical Criminology*, Vol. 1, No. 2, pp. 215–234.

3

The Historical Foundations of Surveillance

CHAPTER CONTENTS	

Excavating the roots of a 'surveillance society'	40
Representations: how the many saw the few in popular print	42
Practices: early-modern surveillance and disorder	45
The new theoreticians of surveillance	47
The policeman-state and urban order: unevenness in surveillance reach	52
The 'problem' of the poor and the Poor Law	53
The 'problem' of youth	53
Controlling the factory system and financial crime	54
Classifying 'deviant' women and girls: from the streets to penal institutions	56
The 'new police' and urban order	58
Contesting police surveillance	61
Consolidating police and surveillance power	62
Summary and conclusion	65
Study questions	66
Further reading	66

OVERVIEW

Chapter 3 provides:

- An overview of the historical foundations and processes that have shaped both the practices of surveillance and the meanings attributed to 'crime'
- An exploration of the key social forces and the kinds of power relations involved in the development of surveillance and crime
- An emphasis on the continuities and discontinuities in the discourses and practices of surveillance
- A consideration of the differential nature of the targets of surveillance

KEY TERMS

- Classificatory power
- Continuity and discontinuity
- Policeman-state
- Public order
- Workplace

Excavating the roots of a 'surveillance society'

In this chapter we explore the roots of the 'surveillance society' and frame these roots not so much in terms of 'advances' in technological innovation but in terms of the interests and values that shaped surveillance. In doing this, the chapter begins to trace the unevenness of surveillance targeting as an historically inherited feature of current surveillance practice.

There has been broad agreement among scholars that the roots of contemporary surveillance are evident within the growth of 'capitalist modernity', the early shoots of which appeared in the seventeenth century and greatly accelerated from the late eighteenth and into the nineteenth century amidst the tumultuous changes affecting all aspects of modernising social orders (Dandeker, 1990; Lyon 1994; McMullan, 1998a). Significant transformations relating to population growth, working practices and the expansion of urban living accompanied debates that laid the seedlings for the expansion of surveillance as it enmeshed with conflicts surrounding the prescribed 'causes', maintenance and governance of social (dis)order.

A number of writers have characterised developments from the early nineteenth century to its close as one of 'great transformation' (Dandeker, 1990) in which 'master patterns and strategies for controlling deviance in Western societies' were laid down (Cohen, 1985: 13). In brief, these patterns – upon which 'all subsequent deviancy control systems' were rooted (Cohen, 1985: 13) – developed a particular trajectory of surveillance along with the nature of power that underpinned it. The patterns of change discussed separately by Dandeker (1990: 111) and Cohen (1985: 13–14) overlap with each other and shall provide a useful backdrop to this chapter. They can be summarised as follows:

1   An increase in state participation in the practice of monitoring deviancy and crime control leading to centralised and bureaucratic sites for the control and punishment of crime.
2   An increased resort to forms of surveillance with the aim of differentiating and classifying 'criminal' and 'deviant' groups fuelled by new domains of 'expertise' and knowledge brokers.
3   An increased emphasis on surveillance as a tool for the segregation and containment of the 'undesirable' within both civil society and closed institutions. The prison provides an example of a site both of segregation *and* intensified inspection and classification of deviants (see Chapter 2).
4   A decline of forms of surveillance-come-punishment aimed at the body (for example, public executions) replaced with a less visible though no less intense surveillance aimed at monitoring the mind, individual consciousness and behaviour of offenders.

By the latter half of the nineteenth century, surveillance had reconstituted itself from a relatively disorganised, *ad hoc* and socially variegated exercise characteristic of the eighteenth century and earlier, to one of a modern, codified, systematised, formal and centralised process of state control (Cohen, 1985; Foucault, 1994a). This gradual development encompassed a more routine and professionally administered practice of incarceration (for criminals and the insane) and of state-authorised policing, particularly in urban public space (Brogden, 1982). However, this broadly painted picture of change should not be taken as evidence for cataclysmic ruptures in surveillance practices. Instead, we should be alert to connections between discourses and practices over time. As Gatrell (1990: 246) has argued, 'watersheds in history are always debatable [and] continuities have to be acknowledged'.

In this chapter, we can begin to unravel the continuities and discontinuities in the development of a 'surveillance society'. What interests and whose voices – supportive and resistant – surrounded and shaped surveillance discourses and practices in the period under discussion? What kinds of problems and problem populations did surveillance seek to monitor and manage, and why? As an increasingly important aspect of governing modern social orders, what kind of order did surveillance come to both reflect and reinforce? To begin with we shall explore how crime came to be represented to an increasingly widening audience.

Representations: how the many
saw the few in popular print

This section considers, in synoptic terms, how 'the many' were encouraged to
see deviants, 'criminals' and policing agents between 1700 and the late nineteenth century. Surveillance developed during this period as a form of intervention in and over what were perceived to be disorderly people and spaces,
bringing with it new ways of talking about and identifying deviance, and in
particular 'a new definition of the criminal' as 'the social enemy' (Foucault,
1994a: 54). These ways of perceiving crime traversed many institutional sites,
including the development of popular communication through which 'the
problem of crime' became socially meaningful and responded to. Changes in
the perception of the criminal and the deviant during this period took place
within broader shifts *away* from a form of surveillance rooted locally, based on
local custom and collective responsibility for the 'potential for social inclusion'
of outsiders, to one characterised by more complex, formal and bureaucratic
societies in which *exclusion* of criminals and deviants became more marked
(McMullan, 1998a: 96).

From the beginning of the seventeenth century, a steady growth in literacy
reached beyond elites and, fuelled by developments in printing, cultivated a
steadily expanding market for stories, images and news in which crime and
criminality figured prominently. The proliferation of pamphlets, ballads and,
in the late eighteenth century, newssheets and newspapers gradually circulated news of crime beyond provincial settings. These can be seen as early-
modern precursors to the arrival of mass communications in the twentieth
century. Ballad storytelling and pamphlet reportage focused upon formulaic
accounts (part fiction, part fact) of the life circumstances leading to crime and
the mindset of the condemned or the offender. Often romanticising the criminal, such portrayals evoked sympathy for the dismal life histories that led to a
life of crime, or stressed the heroic aspects of highway robbery and the 'jolly
capers' in outlaw confrontations with the forces of law and order. Such early
narratives of synoptic representation had contradictory effects on the wider
society. First, they carried the message that criminality must and will be
suppressed – 'good must triumph, and the irrational and disorderly world of
the delinquent be overturned by the order and rationality of the law' (Sharpe,
1999: 228). Secondly, such narratives also served as entertainment through
stirring emotions such as fear, anxiety and excitement. Throughout the eighteenth and nineteenth centuries periodic fears were expressed around these
narratives themselves in that they were thought to entice some into a life of
crime. However, their key role 'was to act as a caution or warning to their
readers' and this was most graphically illustrated in relation narratives around
the execution of the criminal (Sharpe, 1999: 228). In particular, depicting the

criminal's remorse 'left in little doubt as to the consequences of sin' to those attending executions or reading about them (Sharpe, 1999: 232).

The growth in availability of prints in this period had great purchase on the visual representation of a body of new 'outcasts' in the context of increasing urbanisation, changing working practices and population growth. In these formats, depictions of 'peddlers, vagabonds, tricksters, sojourners, masterless men and sturdy beggars', and their association with sin and criminality, figured prominently (Shesgreen, 2002: 7). Prints visualised scenes pertaining to the behaviour and correctness of attitude of the lower orders and were often collected by elites in part to 'aestheticize, regulate and order on paper the collective lives of city streets with their burgeoning commerce and carnivalesque turmoil' (Shesgreen, 2002: 1). Prints representing the life worlds of a range of mobile street folk – the banished, traders and hawkers, beggars, drunks and prostitutes – were 'active instruments in moulding values and reinforcing beliefs' as to one's 'natural' place in the emerging hierarchy of social order (2002: 15). In relation to crime, portraits, often modelled around the consequences of hard work and idleness, reinforced 'a set of stereotyped ideas about crime and its origins' (Sharpe, 1999: 234). Popular representations focusing upon 'crime' and its 'threat' from particular populations also mirrored official concerns and pronouncements as to 'solutions'. Crime was rendered 'comprehensible' and remedies were suggested through a medium that 'allowed contemporaries the luxury of reacting to crime with a stock response rather than thinking too deeply about the issues involved' (Sharpe, 1999: 236).

In the nineteenth century the thirst for 'information' about crime and marginal people dovetailed with a shift towards a scientific classification of outsider groups. This was underpinned by new statistical measurements purporting to show a rise in crime along with moral panics aimed particularly at working-class youth in the early nineteenth century and again in the 1870s (Pearson, 1983). Although the evidence presented for this rise may have been spurious, prosecution rates did begin to grow alongside statistical alarm bells that were 'used to inflame unreal fears and to give shape to unreal problems' (Gatrell, 1990: 251). Again, it was the idea of the 'criminal classes' that took centre stage as a group to be made 'known' to an initially middle-class audience. The tools of popular knowing were becoming fused with the professional knowledge of social scientists driven by statistical and moral calculus emanating from governmental bodies 'anxious about the unwieldy masses confronting the authorities' (Shesgreen, 2002: 269). In the anonymity and density of continuing urban growth, this 'criminal class' was continually the source of anxiety in terms of its identity and whether or not it would contaminate the 'honest worker'. In popular narratives, this 'class' was increasingly delineated by their deficiencies in moral, psychological and social habits, and the 'professional or hardened offender' emerges in the narrative to express the 'hopeless intransigence of these people' (McGowen, 1990: 37). These later, and seemingly more sophisticated, renderings of criminality circulated the idea that crime resulted from individual failings and that anti-social tendencies were written on the bodily appearance and demeanour of the criminal. Moreover, sympathy was aroused for those in danger of falling into the criminal group, whereas those already in it were subject to outrage (McGowen, 1990: 40).

Popular narratives of this time were concerned with exposing the criminal as an 'enemy within' – someone who could feign 'respectability' for dishonest ends. In exposing the 'criminal class', newspapers and periodicals had a role in interpreting the secret 'signs and signals' of the latter in order to put 'the public on its guard' (McGowen, 1990: 43) and produce a sense of 'caution' from the perspective of the powerful which 'neutralized the power of the criminal' (1990: 44). Within these narratives the formation of the new police in 1829, as the embodiments of law and order, played a significant role. Knowledge from their surveillance of criminals featured significantly – a reassuring presentation of police applauded 'their ability to see and know', thus depriving 'criminals of their cloak of secrecy' (1990: 45). As McGowen has noted, there is little controversy found in these media surrounding the inception of the police role, nor is there recognition of the 'fact that most of their activities involved the regulation of public spaces' (1990: 45). Rather like today's 'reality' TV shows and associated narratives on crime (such as *CrimeWatch UK*, *World's Stupidest Criminals*, etc.), the authors (journalists and experts) worked closely with police in producing these narratives pertaining to criminal activities and places (1990: 49).

These early developments in synoptic surveillance carved out 'knowledge' of the 'crime problem' and limited this to the lower orders. In enabling the many (law-abiding, responsible citizens) to see the few (criminals), contradictory attributes ensued over what was seen and how what was seen was understood. In the stirrings of a modern mass media the 'criminal class' was exposed as a problem located at the lower margins of society and constructed as 'hidden' yet observable; 'powerful, threatening and skilled', yet 'degenerate and ignorant'; and 'recognizable yet strange' (McGowen, 1990: 48). McGowen reminds us that in producing a 'reality effect', popular media narratives on crime did not reveal 'the "reality" of the criminal class', but *shaped a belief* that was 'real' (McGowen, 1990: 35). Such beliefs had the effect of entertaining, comforting and outraging public attitudes. After 1850, media storytelling began to overlap with the concerns of expertise (in the form of police, legal specialists, criminologists and social reformers) that, taken together, took to the task of classifying, labelling and stereotyping urban marginal groups generally and criminal groups in particular.

The steady growth of popular media forms in this period, and in particular 'reality' genres that focused on crime and criminality, were not neutral narratives. They reflected and reinforced elite and popular anxieties relating to social order through which '*a* problem of crime' was constructed. We will return briefly to the present day context regarding these issues in Chapter 6.

Practices: early-modern surveillance and disorder

In their earliest form, ideas of 'police' referred to a range of overseeing activities relating to trade, commerce, health and public morals (including public dress and behaviour). In seventeenth-century European societies a range of social bodies beyond the state took part in surveillance of this kind and included religious societies, paramilitary bodies and powerful economic coalitions (Foucault, 1994a). The conditions of surveillance, police and government changed significantly during the seventeenth century and intensified throughout the eighteenth century. In England, for example, expansions in capitalist global trade, increases in population and the growth of London as the first economic, consumer and leisure market highlighted problems for methods of surveillance and control designed for localised and familiar territorial-based control 'whereby all members of a community had an obligation for the appropriate surveillance and conduct of each other' as a form of communal duty (McMullan, 1998a: 95). Throughout the seventeenth century, and indicative of an intensification in the debates that would come to predominate over the next two centuries, shifts in economic and social relationships drew consequences for how these new kinds of bewilderingly complex social orders and the problems they threw up were to be maintained. A new category of 'outsiders' emerged, who were feared for their growth in numbers and their unshackling from the emerging social ties of property and urbanity. These were the 'masterless' men and women in search of work and food along with homeless rovers – 'highly visible but in constant motion', who allegedly created problems of prostitution, begging and theft (McMullan, 1998a: 97). Along with the growing illegal underworld of organised criminals, these threats to the emergent order 'exposed the obsolete nature of traditional mutual surveillance and security' and brought 'upon themselves the anger and moral opprobrium born of a new anxiety' (1998a: 97).

Early attempts to deal with these problems of disorder were chaotic and fragmented, involving Justices of the Peace, militias and the army. Taken together, their attempts to surveil and coerce unsettled migrants were discretionary and parochial, and ultimately were eroded by the mid-nineteenth century when their legitimacy was questioned for lack of coordination, underfunding and corruption. As well as failing to decrease crime, the 'old' system was subverted by the masterless who learnt how to avoid monitored space (McMullan, 1998a). One achievement of this variegated activity was to focus more clearly on a definition of 'the problem', rendering its visibility more marked. The uses and additions to the English Vagrancy Act of 1572 continuously conflated hawkers, beggars and peddlers with vagabonds, tricksters and masterless men, thus collapsing 'distinctions among people living on the edges of society, mandating that all the mobile, insubordinate and frugal be punished as the "devil's poor"' (Shesgreen, 2002: 7). Here surveillance, visibility and physical coercion went hand in hand. For example, branding was introduced in 1547 and the vagabond could be sold into slavery. From 1572 they were to be flogged and have their ears bored and by 1604 they would be branded on their shoulder with the letter 'R' for rogue.

By the eighteenth century the visibility of the lower orders as the proper object of surveillance increased as 'a problem to be managed, something to be designed for, organised, supervised and consciously invented' (McMullan, 1998a: 100). For Foucault, these developments were pushed along in this period by a series of 'obscure' mechanisms of control that lay outside the state. Yet these mechanisms based themselves around the surveillance, governance and policing of social norms that where later 'superimposed on penal practice' in the next century (Foucault, 1994a: 60). Religious groups dominated these early societies for surveillance, as in the case of The Society for the Reform of Manners established in England in 1692 (later to become The Proclamation Society in the late eighteenth century). Surveillance activities here were numerous and attempted to prevent gambling, prostitution, cursing, drunken-ness and 'everything that might show contempt for God' (Foucault, 1994a: 61). At the beginning of the nineteenth century, the Society for the Suppression of Vice (SSV) was formed by members of middle-class religious groups dismayed and angry by what they saw as state failure to enforce law and set a moral example. As one SSV representative stated at the time: 'The laws are good, but they are eluded by the Lower Classes, and set at nought by the Higher. The Laws are good: but they have fallen into contempt, and require the Zeal, the Activity, the Discretion as such a Society as this to renovate their vigour' (cited in Wilson, 2007: 122). The SSV worked with a wide definition of 'immorality' and included idling in public houses, swearing, blasphemy, lewdness, dances, non-attendance at church, lack of obedience to parents and employers – all of which were perceived to undermine respect for authority. Such infringements of social norms were seen as forms of anti-social behaviour leading to more serious forms of crime (Wilson, 2007). The Society sought to 'remind consta-bles and watchmen of legal statutes and their duty to police the morals of the lower classes' (2007: 123). Although the SSV identified immorality in the higher classes – as perceived in female fashions, gambling and adultery that set a bad example for standards lower down the social hierarchy – these were not to be policed. Instead, surveillance of elites was directed at *advising* them to self-regulate and at least 'give the appearance of virtue' at a time when ill-repute towards the aristocracy could tarnish their right to rule and fuel revo-lutionary attitudes in the years following the French Revolution (2007: 145). This voluntarist 'policing' took place alongside sterner interventions for the lower classes – for example, the Society for the Suppression of Mendicity (1818) scrutinised and tested 'the beggar' as either worthy of help or an imposter to be punished.

Such moralising calls for surveillance of the lower orders were not without critics, who saw meddling in 'English liberties' and social affairs, and hypocrisy in the actions of reformers. At the same time, the work of the SSV and similar bodies demonstrated 'the often close relationship between private vigilance and public authorities' throughout the nineteenth century that, for example, successfully persuaded the state to push through the Obscene Publications Act of 1857 (Weeks, 1989: 84). Such voluntary surveillance flowed from religious commitments and were often sponsored by businesses keen to curtail popular pastimes and see a more disciplined labour force as the factory system advanced (Fitzgerald et al., 1986). Indeed, these relatively autonomous surveillance experiments over the habits, behaviours and spaces of the poor gradually 'disseminated into a state appropriated penal system' (Foucault, 1994a: 64) spurred by a wider 'long-term "civilising" process' and underpinned by a 'growing demand for security in daily life and a rising standard of personal self-discipline' (Bailey, 1993: 224). Such a process symbolised and represented particular interests and fed into calls for more bureaucratic and rationalised policing and surveillance concomitant with today's ideas of policing. These rationalist and 'enlightened' arguments around the surveillance and control of lower-class criminality implied new thinking about the role of 'responsible authorities' and the state in maintaining order.

The new theoreticians of surveillance

The notion of 'civilisation' became a powerful driving force in the 150 years after 1750, not only to suppress and restrain the more 'vulgar' public emotions, behaviours and displays of vice, but also to target and control them in a more rational way using recognisably modern surveillance techniques. A bourgeoisie that was growing in confidence 'produced new forms of regulation and prohibition governing their own bodies' as well as deriding 'ever more loquaciously ... the body of the Other – of the city's "scum"' (Stallybrass and White, 1986: 126). The tendency to differentiate within civilising sensibilities in the late eighteenth and early nineteenth centuries combined with calls for more regular surveillance – a civilising eye – as a means to classify, control and manage what were seen as the uncivilised lower orders: a 'populous that was expanding, increasingly insubordinate, unshackled from rural controls, and politically opinionated' (Gatrell, 1990: 254). In short, the presence of 'the unshackled' placed established hierarchal orders under threat. In the minds of the powerful, the ideas of poverty, crime and social unrest clashed with what they believed to be inviolable civilising sentiments that found practical expression in calls to protect and stabilise urban property relations, the process of wealth creation and trade.

New theoreticians of surveillance emerged in this period to articulate a more rational surveillance project as part of a new legal order instilled with disciplinary controls, moral instruction and regular supervision 'justified in the name of progress and enlightenment' (McMullan, 1998a: 103). Writers and reformers such as John Fielding, Patrick Colquhoun and Jeremy Bentham 'shared a common frame of mind in their thought' geared towards developing civilising 'cultural controls over the poor that combined benevolence with coercion, relief with restraint, and supervision with punishment' (McMullan, 1998b: 100). Fielding expressed many ideas ahead of his time. He laid out what he saw as policing and surveillance deficits in London in the 1760s and 1770s which were failing to deal with wealth creation ('the vast torrent of luxury') and the excesses in 'immoral entertainments' that 'changed the Manners, Customs, and Habits of the People, more especially the lower sort' (Fielding, cited in Dodsworth, 2007: 445). Money itself, particularly if in the hands of the lower orders, undermined social deference and law, encouraging greed and licentiousness leading to threats and crimes against property. In Fielding's view, while the 'responsible' management of wealth might be a problem across society, the rich were able to check their own vice through displaying self-restraint through gentlemanly codes of honour, whereas the poor had no such restraining force and, consequently, contributed most to a growing threat of crime and violence (Dodsworth, 2007: 446). This latter group therefore were to be subjected to a 'general preventative machine' with its 'civilising effects' of moderation and surveillance, along with 'swift and solemn punishment' (Fielding, cited in McMullan, 1998b: 102). This would require a policing of popular culture with respect to the vices of gambling and drinking, which not only undermined the principle of hard work, but were also central in shaping popular culture and how the many saw the deviant. Ballads and newspapers were envisaged as key synoptical tools towards cultivating virtuous messages to the citizenry in general and the poor in particular, as to the immorality of crime and the decency of hard work. For Fielding, the growth in media could be harnessed to the preventative cause – advertising crime, naming and shaming, and enlisting the help of the citizenry in tracking the criminal (McMullan, 1998b: 102–103). Fielding, like those to come after him, was also interested in developing classificatory and cataloguing methods to store information on criminal locations and habits, creating a criminal register to be drawn upon for investigating and detecting particular crimes. Fielding's is an early formulation in how to mark off the criminal from respectable society – spatially, physically and morally – using surveillance as a classificatory tool of policing the streets. In London by the 1790s, Fielding had managed to assimilate some of these ideas into his Bow Street Police, but his was a broader set of ideas that articulated more than a manned presence on the streets and envisioned a more comprehensive regime to regulate the poor than was developed by others.

Colquhoun carried forward and developed many of these ideas in arguing for a centralised police force replete with records of known offenders and their haunts, alongside a Police Gazette as a means to educate the citizenry on the errors and consequences of crime. Writing in the 1790s and into the first decade of the nineteenth century, he too saw that 'offences of every description' as having 'their origin in the vicious and immoral habits of the people' whose 'vulgar life' led to the temptations of drink and gambling (Colquhoun, cited in Dodsworth, 2007: 450). The target of policing and surveillance in the early nineteenth-century city was partly founded upon elite fears that any 'wealth, power and luxury' that filtered down to the lower orders 'would lead to contempt of authority and ultimately anarchy' (Dodsworth, 2007: 441). Mechanisms aimed at 'policing' the cultural and material advancement of working-class people were also evident in rendering them and their popular culture as subjects of ridicule in the nineteenth century (Maidment, 2000). Even today, a strand of this kind of surveillance is evidenced in the punitive identification of the 'chav' or 'scally', who although conforming to patterns of consumption do so in ways 'deemed vulgar and hence lacking in "distinction" by superordinate classes' (Hayward and Yar, 2006: 14).

For Colquhoun, the poor were uncivilised, unruly, noxious, and idle. Their poverty may have been necessary to wealth creation ('it is the source of wealth'), but their indigence was the source of violence and crime (cited in Linebaugh, 2006: 428). As Linebaugh noted, it was it perceived that indigence nurtured idleness among the poor. Idleness was a moral and economic category and a statement of 'the refusal to accept exploitation' in the workplace (2006: 428). For Colquhoun, this aspect of poverty became fused with the wider problem of police and surveillance – the latter being necessary 'to prevent the class of poverty from falling into indigence' (Neocleous, 2000: 715). Not being in work through idleness contributed 'in no small degree to the general phalanx of delinquents' (Colquhoun, cited in McMullan, 1998b: 109) for which the 'cure' was a restraining morality which would 'preserve this poverty in a discrete state by preventing its collapse into indigence and idleness whence came the temptation to commit crime' (McMullan, 1998b: 110).

The morality, decadence and behaviour of particular segments of the working class became the proper objects of surveillance. Public houses, drinking and gambling were a particular source of concern, leading to calls for a police force to keep an eye on, and regulate (through licensing), working-class entertainments. Moreover, like other voices at the time, there was a concern to assert property rights over customary rights. The custom of labouring and agricultural workers taking 'extras' in the form of goods from work or hunting on private land became subject to attacks from landowners and businesses keen to outlaw these practices as a means of establishing wage relations and the protection of private property (Linebaugh, 2006). As an agent in the sugar trade himself, Colquhoun was supportive of the establishment of the Marine

Police on the London Thames in 1789 to deal with the customary illegalities of working-class dock labour. Supported by businesses and with the sanction of government, policing here had a role in restraining the act of pillage, searching dock workers, enforcing dress codes, and setting wage rates. This first 'preventative police system' was thus an attempt to regulate labouring people to the discipline of the wage and the sanctity of private property (Neocleous, 2000: 719–720) as well as playing a role in the process of redefining 'crime by reclassifying traditional relations of custom and conduct in the production of private property' (McMullan, 1998b: 112–113) – a process that continued throughout the nineteenth century.

More broadly, Colquhoun's notion of police was expansive and insisted upon all respectable individuals and agencies (teachers, charities, and clergy and law officials) to morally instruct the poor along with his idea of specialised criminal policing. In their efforts to secure a systematic surveillance of the poor, albeit with largely private sponsorship, writers such as Fielding and Colquhoun redefined the meaning of 'liberty' – from one that entailed a defence of elite property interests from the state to one of a defence of the same property interests in the name of extended police powers of surveillance (Gatrell, 1990: 255). This shift to state-orchestrated intervention was more clearly stated in the work of Edwin Chadwick in the first half of the nineteenth century. His call for a centralised police force to oversee the poor stressed the control of vagrancy and crime, but also the hygiene of the poor as the source of immorality (Mort, 1987). His vision sought to pull together 'poor relief and control, prison administration, factory inspection, child support and police surveillance' into an integrated inspection machine (McMullan, 1998b: 120–121).

These 'rationalist' theoreticians of a surveillance society reflected and reinforced elite thinking of the time. However, while interests originating in property, commerce and the market played a key role in arguing for the 'improvement', reorganisation and restructuring of responses to crime, it was not always agreed as to what was the best way forward. While agreement that the old ways of social control were no longer tenable, and that the challenges of a new economic order required new methods of control were evident, a range of overlapping discourses were becoming increasingly drawn upon to meet these challenges (Hall and McLennan, 1986). First, as we have seen with our theoreticians above, there was an increasing emphasis on classification and codification within the legal realm and an attempt to ensure clarification and greater predictability in detecting and punishing crime. Secondly, there was the argument that a more humane legal system (one which would train the mind of the criminal as opposed to seek retribution upon his or her body) would be more effective in regulating and correcting crime. Writing in the late eighteenth century, the prison reformer John Howard epitomised contradictions in humanitarian ideas. He criticised the old prison system as inhumane and brutal while at the same time pushing for greater disciplinary surveillance of inmates in the new prisons, where cleanliness, prayer and work would inform the prisoner experience as a socially excluded subject to be treated impersonally (Hall and McLennan, 1986: 52). Thirdly, matters of crime and punishment became subject to utilitarian ideas pertaining to 'rational men' whose motivations and actions were understood as rationally calculated. Thus, 'men' would be deterred from crime if punishment (pain) outweighed the pleasure or rewards gained from crime. Jeremy Bentham's ideas influenced Colquhoun and both saw prevention and deterrence as the keys to surveillance and inspection of the 'pleasure-seeking poor' as derivative of their views of punishment and policing. For both of these utilitarian thinkers, their belief in minimal state intervention and free economic competition was set alongside an increasing perception of the need to quell the disorder that undermined this 'freedom'. They articulated the desire to police and punish (on the streets and in the prisons) as a means 'to civilise, to transform and shape' the criminal and morally wayward (McMullan, 1998a: 107). Fourthly, repression was also a motive informing change, exemplified in Fielding's work in which curtailment of the rights of the accused figured prominently. Lastly, moral reform remained a key imperative for many commentators and surveillance societies and organisations keen to instil codes of civility, decorum and repentance among the lower orders (Hall and McLennan, 1986).

These arguments, couched in humanitarian, rational, and efficiency and social defence terms, all played a part in the birth of modern surveillance and the desire to subject the criminal to a greater degree of order, inspection and classification. Not all the ideas of the reformers were put into practice in the ways they envisaged, but the work of such thinkers 'paved the way for that persistent surveillance which characterises modern policed society', signifying 'an important starting point for unravelling the beginnings of carceral and surveillance-based societies' (McMullan, 1998b: 123). This is exemplified by Bentham's panoptic inspection model, formulated as a moral architecture for prisons. The idea of creating a comprehensive gaze inside prisons (anonymous, unrelenting and encouraging prisoner self-surveillance – and all run by commerce) failed to gain parliamentary approval in 1810. However, principles of panoptic inspection and classification survived and morphed into a range of institutional sites up to the late twentieth century and beyond (Lyon, 1991). For Foucault, the aim of institutionalising panoptic techniques of control, beginning in the prison system (see Chapter 2), was *not* to punish less, but to establish a more 'formidable right to punish the offender' as the 'common enemy' (Foucault, 1979: 90).

This period also left traces of the modern view of crime as not only emanating almost exclusively from lower down the social hierarchy, but as something that lay extrinsic to what was assumed to be a healthy and morally upright social body (Mort, 1987: 36). As the nineteenth century developed, the criminal became the deposit of a social type, spoken of through a language of individual decrepitude, disease and contamination. Tensions between the experts and other political forces were evident concerning 'what should be done' about the health, sanitation and immorality of the poor, but proposals and resolutions rarely if ever challenged the civilising potency thought to be located in 'the commercial system as a force whose movement was inexorable' (Mort, 1987: 36). How, then, did the actual practice of surveillance take off from this period?

The policeman-state and urban order: unevenness in surveillance reach

What Gatrell (1990) called the shift to a 'policeman-state', beginning in the nineteenth century, also signified shifts in surveillance practice within which the 'new police' became one, albeit important, dimension. Moreover, as explored later, the surveillance activities of the 'new police' from 1829 and after, were not only directed to the prevention and detection of crime (in lower-class areas), but at a range of 'practices antithetical to the development of the new relations of production' (Neocleous, 2000: 723). This class-based strategy occurred alongside broader developments in the policeman-state which had an impact on social divisions more broadly. Drawing upon classificatory and disciplinary tools, state intervention expanded in the nineteenth century towards a wider notion of 'social policing' (Donajgrodzki, 1977; Neocleous, 2000), alongside the development of concerns around lower-class political organisation as well as habits regarding leisure and family life. At the same time, the extension in surveillance reach over these areas remained uneven in its development and targeting.

Surveillance classification systems underpinned urban reform programmes throughout the nineteenth-century city and constructed class- and gender-related polarities around virtue/vice, cleanliness/filth, morality/depravity, civilisation/animality (Mort, 1987: 41). Throughout the nineteenth century concern was expressed about the proximity between 'respectable' middle-class groups and what became known as the 'great unwashed' (the poor). This turbulent mass of people were deemed problematic *both* because of their 'offensive' visibility (too many, too rowdy, too dirty, and threatening) and because of their 'unknowability' (they were seen as 'secretive', 'alien' or a 'race apart'). Both of these issues conjoined in the overall problem of the governability of this seemingly ungovernable group. State interventions were stamped with a medical and scientific legitimacy in order to identify 'all the practices of working-class life leading to ungovernable and disruptive behaviour: lack of individual self-reliance, ignorance, criminality, the threat of political sedition and ... sexual impropriety' (Mort, 1987: 37). Regimes of compulsory inspection, detention and education formed the bedrock of surveillance 'solutions' to these problems and became preferred techniques of regulation which were manifest (although not uniformly) in a range of penal and semi-penal institutions – prisons, factories, schools, workhouses and asylums. The key practice here was that of classification around the 'norm'; a targeted practice increasingly resorted to in the assessment of what constituted 'socially acceptable' behaviour. As noted below, this classificatory impulse was not applied evenly.

The 'problem' of the poor and the Poor Law

The Poor Law Amendment Act of 1834 sought to suppress idleness, which it was thought led directly to crime. This legislation set in train a utilitarian rationale that stated that any relief offered to the poor must be set below the rate of that received by working for a living. This was to deter 'pauperism', understood not merely as poverty but as 'moral degradation'. The basis of Poor Law relief dovetailed with earlier concerns that money (or luxuries) gained by the poor would inevitably lead to their own moral corruption and lead to idleness and a belief on their behalf that something (relief) could be gained for little effort (industry). Paupers, then, were to be identified and segregated into workhouses where rations would be reduced to the bare minimum, overseen by disciplinary codes concerned with instilling regimented and compulsory work. The main objectives here were to 'affect the conditions of subsistence of the working class in such a way as to hasten their acceptance of disciplined factory work within a capitalist political economy' (Squires, 1990: 82). The austere regimes of the workhouse were to deter 'incorrigibles', 'rogues' and 'idlers', and encourage industriousness among the poor. The institution of the workhouse remained until the early twentieth century and their classificatory schemas carved out the basis for future welfare interventions, through which those seeking state benefits would be subject to stringent testing and surveillance over attitudes to work, their 'lifestyles' and consumption patterns. As we saw in Chapter 1, the construction of categories of 'appropriateness' assigned to those who may be in need of state relief remain central to surveillance practices in a penal welfare complex in which 'genuine claimants' and those deemed to be 'actively seeking work' are marked out from the 'fraudster' and 'scrounger' (or as the Victorians called them, 'the undeserving poor').

The 'problem' of youth

Many reformers fixated upon 'dangerous' youth and the Society for the Improvement of Prison Discipline and the Reformation of Juvenile Offenders

(1817) pushed forward debates on the issue of juvenile delinquency as well as the development of specialist institutions for the reform and reclamation of the 'depraved' and 'corrupted' children of the labouring poor. The moral magnitude of the problem was stressed by reformers, and the establishment of Reformatory Schools in 1854 consolidated surveillance and training in the habits of work for those youngsters convicted of an indictable or summary offence. Industrial Schools were established in the same period for children found begging or with no obvious means of survival. They could be sent here indefinitely and by the 1890s both types of school housed over 30,000 inmates (see Muncie, 2009: 54–62). As well as classifying, segregating and training children (and girls were separated from boys to be given specific instruction on domestic duties expected later in life), these surveillance institutions developed alongside growing interventions into 'the failings of parents – the apparent absence of supervision and control [and] the failure to imbue their children with proper moral habits' (Muncie, 2009: 58). Here we begin to see recognisably modern conceptions social disorder being tied to the deficiencies purported to be intrinsic to the family units of the poor, where surveillance and instruction have most often gone hand in hand.

Controlling the factory system and financial crime

The 1833 Factory Act was an attempt to establish a 'regular working day' in the textile industry and included the provision to stop children (aged 14 to 18) working more than 12 hours a day and children (aged 9 to 13) not working more than 8 hours (with an hour lunch break). Such measures, and their oversight, were resisted by employers and their representatives in Parliament. As was noted at the time:

> Such a measure would be tyranny of the grossest kind to the operatives and perfect destruction as regard our manufacturers. Capital and industry would then find their way into other countries and England ... would be undersold. (Thomson, 1836/1973: 203)

Such opposition points to the contradictions and unevenness integral to the surveillance momentum in the nineteenth century, and with particular regard to the variety of 'protective' factory legislation attempted from 1802 onwards. Legislation variously provided – at least on paper – 'protections' for women and children in the workplace (for example, through restrictions on age and working hours) as well as attempting to define standards in clean and safe working conditions. The earlier factory legislation was meagrely policed and challenged in political debates by factory owners who resisted the law regularly in practice (Carson, 1981). In the 1830s just four Inspectors and several

Superintendants were commissioned to enforce factory laws. They developed and relied upon allegedly persuasive communication channels with employers to confer the benefits of regulation. This kind of surveillance relationship with, and over, factory owners often meant Inspectors were 'loathe to prosecute' and 'even joined with some of the more influential manufacturers' in calling upon government to repeal some aspects of legislation (Carson, 1981: 137). Early attempts at policing the factory system were bound up with questions of legitimacy for the emerging industrial order and the attempt to control some of its most brutalising features without sacrificing economic competitiveness. The ability of manufacturers to influence legal surveillance (and even evade it) in this early period can be contrasted with the lack of communicative input the working classes had on matters of their own surveillance, where the law appeared more certain and coercive in its consequences. Moreover, as Carson demonstrates, the uncertainty of law, and particularly of surveillant enforcement, relating to factory sites allowed space for powerful industrialists to displace responsibility for illegal acts often on to workers themselves. Inspections relied on factory record-keeping to determine breaches in the regulation of working hours, sanitary conditions and use of child labour, but these were often resisted on the grounds of 'unfamiliarity' – as an 'inconvenience' and unnecessarily expensive to business (1981: 144–145).

As a consequence of this ambiguity regarding surveillance over the powerful, little can be discerned about the extent of illegalities within the productive process – even though some Inspectors at the time reasoned that illegality was widespread. Two-thirds of convictions between 1836 and 1842 resulted in a £1 fine (Whyte, 2009), heralding the long-running unwillingness of courts and legislators to attach the criminal label to 'captains of industry' and consolidating a form of surveillance in which prosecution would be the last resort. Legal 'protection' and the modes of regulatory surveillance applied to enforce them point to the contradictory and perhaps unintended effects of monitoring practice. For example, working conditions for adult male workers in particular was intensified as a result of protective measures in terms of their increased work rate, dictated by the installation of speedier machines to maintain the rate of profit (K. Marx, 2009).

On the one hand, business activity in general and financial crime in particular was becoming subject to parliamentary and legal scrutiny after 1850, and pointed to a process that began to 'cast suspicion on respectability' on the respectable class (Wiener, 1990: 244). On the other hand, and at the same time, surveillance and judicial oversight over areas such as business fraud and embezzlement often, but not always, fell short of a full criminalising discourse and sanctioning process. From the outset, establishing full criminal liability in trials of businessmen relied (because of insufficient specialist understanding of the commercial world) upon the expertise of business actors themselves. Businessmen, as recognised 'expert' witnesses and advisers in legal proceedings, constituted a means by which 'City interests' gained 'a substantial hand in determining what amounted to "acceptable" ... business conduct' in determinations of criminal liability (Wilson, 2006: 1085). For Wilson, this pointed to the emergence of 'self-regulation' regarding business crimes, in which the 'cooperation' of business in identifying its own crimes and misdemeanours was induced alongside the construction of 'legal rules (e.g. company law)' as an 'enabling rather than prescriptive' form of oversight (Wilson, 2006: 1086).

It was in these kind of spaces, made 'known' by *particular* discursive and practical surveillance routines, that 'criminality' became 'more rather than less' obscure and 'mysterious' (Wiener, 1990: 245). In particular, these developments articulated the 'problem of crime' and its negotiated character, particularly between legally constituted surveillance agents and the powerful, reflecting the interrelated issues of visibility, invisibility, regulation and non-regulation regarding the crimes of the powerful that remains with us to this today. This will be discussed more fully in Chapters 6 and 7.

Classifying 'deviant' women and girls: from the streets to penal institutions

One of the concerns within the factory legislations was the position and status of women in the public realm. This concern can be discerned across a range of reformatory sites in which normative constructions of 'femininity', as part of a 'civilised' society, were forged. Here reformers depicted female sexuality, often conjoining it with notions of 'depravity'. Mort (1987) shows how factory Inspectors, far from displaying concern with female working conditions, produced in their reports sexualised images of the 'filth' in which working women toiled that was apparently reflected in their 'depraved' sexual character. This was in opposition to idealised images of restrained middle-class female sexuality. In the manufacturing areas, female work too was being perceived through the eyes of reformers as a hindrance to performing 'proper' domestic habits associated with family duties and motherhood (Mort, 1987: 48–61). The Contagious Diseases Acts of the 1860s were provoked by concerns for the decline of the British Empire – particularly thought to be located in the decline in virile fighting men who contracted venereal diseases from prostitutes – and the role women as mothers and domestic caretakers were thought to play in this decline (Davin, 1978). These Acts targeted working-class street prostitutes as 'women who were identified as the human agents of infection, threatening national health and security and challenging the social order by their active and autonomous sexuality' (Mort, 1987: 74–76). Many actual and suspected prostitutes were put in Lock Hospitals and subjected to moral and physical discipline, including medical examinations, lessons on personal hygiene, domestic duties and class deference as means to re-educate 'fallen women' for their place in the conjugal household. Many at the time thought these practices unfair and reflective of double standards in the coercive surveillance of women's sexuality while leaving male sexuality and its use of women as 'whores' unchecked. Although prostitutes were seen as immoral and diseased, the economic subordination of women as the impetus for entering 'the trade' was ignored.

Although the Acts were repealed by the 1880s (partly as a result of feminist campaigns), their legacy for the surveillance of female sexuality remained. One of the principal functions of police registration and surveillance of prostitutes was to name and shame and mark out 'women of disrepute' from the 'respectable'. Police officers had difficulties in determining the prostitute from the 'respectable' women, particularly in surveilling and assessing a woman's presence in public space. Surveillance of women's sexuality seemed to be doing more harm than good by ostracising prostitutes from community support and forcing many of them into ever more dangerous habitats. Moreover, the Acts also possessed an element of function creep and were used by the police to reinforce the trend of containing the occupational and geographical mobility of the poor as a whole (Weeks, 1989: 89). The social purity movements that emerged after this period and into the early twentieth century – some elements of which did attack male sexual violence relating to women – became overwhelmingly concerned with building 'responsible' motherhood and directed forms of surveillance-as-instruction for working-class 'girls and women in cooking, hygiene, and child care' (Davin, 1978: 27).

Regimes of discipline aimed at criminal women in the new prison system from the early nineteenth century differed significantly from that of male criminals. Layers of expertise – shaped particularly by a medical discourse – constructed a form of training for confined women around prevailing notions of domesticity, sexuality and pathology, in which moulding the personal and moral life of women was central (Sim, 1990). Domestification through surveillance extended to the 'care' of women once outside prison, where a number of agencies aimed to provide 'suitable' living conditions and work for women upon release (Sim, 1990: 144). Barton (2005) has demonstrated that a range of semi-penal institutions have developed from the late eighteenth century to surveil and control categories of 'immoral', 'wayward', 'drunk' and 'mad' women. Both formal and informal regimes of control have developed to construct and 'police' the boundaries of 'normal' femininity. Official forms of surveillance over confined women (in prisons and asylums) that developed in the nineteenth century underpinned a process of muting and silencing women's voices under regimes of strict monitorial power (Showalter, 1987; Worrall, 1990).

As we have noted in the previous chapter, the developments discussed here provided Foucault with the ground upon which his ideas of the development of panoptic surveillance were constructed. Hierarchical supervision, incessant categorisation and grading of individuals united with segregation techniques to isolate the 'dangerous' from the 'normal' and to categorise and coerce the 'deserving' and 'undeserving'. As with many surveillance practices since, education and welfare were entwined with control and coercion. However, from this brief excursion it can be noted that surveillance reach was uneven and impacted upon different social groups depending on their abilities to contest surveillance. While many of the reformers' actions were important in 'reforming some of the most brutalizing aspects of working-class life (for example sanitary reform) this has to be considered against what this intervention, and others, meant in terms of social order' (Fitzgerald et al., 1986: 132).

The 'new police' and urban order

This section explores the development of the 'new police' that broadened surveillance networks in and around a more interventionist state. The establishment of local police forces in England from the 1830s did not straightforwardly reflect the views of the new theoreticians of surveillance discussed earlier. In arguing ideologically for a developing 'policeman-state', such views were instructive and influential but never fulfilled in all their 'authoritarian and centralizing rigour' (Gatrell, 1990: 257). On the other hand, the establishment of the 'new police' was not entirely 'new' and may be best understood as revealing longer-term trends in consolidating past ideologies, tactics and legal codes in dealing with 'crime' (Gatrell, 1990: 260).

From the late eighteenth century many of the new theoreticians of surveillance constructed statistically based arguments purporting to show rises in crime and associated idleness. This buttressed the view that the urban landscape afforded refuge to 'depraved habits and loose conduct' of the lower classes within 'the unexampled growth of the Metropolis' (Colquhoun, cited in Gatrell, 1990: 249). In contributing to alarmist campaigns for reform, such ways of perceiving the problem served as a model for later moral entrepreneurs and their ideas about the 'dangerous' and 'criminal' classes (Bailey, 1993). Not only apparent rises in crime, but food riots in 1795–96 and again in 1799–1801, along with major industrial disturbances in 1811–12 and other sporadic protests (around a free press and trade union rights), alarmed elite opinion and led many to question local solutions (discretionary procedures of law, the use of parish constables, who were sometimes perceived as corrupt and illiterate, Justices of the Peace, thief takers, etc.) to what appeared to be national problems. Many commented upon the fusion of criminality with political agitation, encompassed within the phrase the 'dangerous classes', along with that other emerging category, the 'criminal classes', who were deficient in moral restraint. Such views consolidated an emerging 'respectability' as the 'often unspoken premise of social policy': that respect and admiration of authority underpinned a harmonious social order and were in need of resurrection (Gatrell, 1990: 258).

The concern of lower-order crimes was reflected within parliamentary government committees from 1815 onwards that set out to determine the effectiveness of policing the lower class in the metropolis. These governmental inquiries were important in bringing together actors in the surveillance discourses and in balancing the calls for disciplinary surveillance with notions of liberty. In line with what went before, the voice of the poor themselves was missing from such discursive frameworks. As the objects of surveillance, their life experiences were inferred from statistics and expert conjecture. The committees focused upon the behaviour, 'brutal' popular pastimes, decorum and even the costume of the lower orders, with a particular emphasis on how these were influenced by rises in alcohol consumption. Committees heard evidence *for* policing public houses out of existence. Others argued that the 'boisterousness' and minor disorders of the poor should be allowed as a means of averting more serious forms of disorder. The committees up until 1822 took the view that a coordinated police force over and above existing local practices was an unnecessary encroachment into 'English freedoms' that was not commensurate with making spies of citizens (Fitzgerald et al., 1986). This dovetailed with strong opposition to such a force from the captains of finance based in the City of London.

By the 1820s, however, the discourse around 'crime' began to change. By the early nineteenth century, and bound up with the developing complexity of penal, police and law reform, problems of 'crime' and 'disorder' became heightened. In this context, 'crime' was rapidly assuming importance as 'a vehicle for articulating mounting anxieties about issues which really had nothing to do with crime at all'. Fears for the stability of social hierarchy 'invested crime with new meanings' and 'justified vastly accelerated action against it' (Gatrell, 1990: 249).

This shift helped transform the political landscape within which surveillance interventions in general, and the formation of the 'new police' in particular, were undertaken. Many reformers argued that 'rising crime' provided the rationale for increasing police surveillance. However, attempting to discern rises in crime in this period is less important than recognising *the contemporary belief that it was increasing* along with 'the growing demands that a new threshold of order and decorum be established' (Emsley, 1996: 16–17, emphasis added). This is an important point that highlights how care must be taken when interpreting the introduction and extension of surveillance practice.

Official references to 'objective' rises in crime as drivers for surveillance cannot be accepted at face value.

A Bill [as amended by the committee] for Improving the Police in and near the Metropolis empowered the police to prosecute all those 'loose, idle and disorderly persons' found 'disturbing the public peace' and who cannot give 'a satisfactory account of themselves' (Parliamentary Papers, 1829: 450). The establishment of the Metropolitan Police in 1829 was followed by the Rural Constabulary Act of 1839, which aided the organisation of the first uniformed police in and outside London, mainly under local authority control. Although elite anxiety continued to be found around the potential for centralisation of this new force, there were 'few quibbles' about the police mission. These developments were fuelled by a new consensus in elite opinion that popular disorder, whether political in content or not, and including recreational activities such a dog fighting, drinking and horse racing, constituted a threat to social order. Robert Storch argued that the new police 'received an omnibus mandate: to maintain a constant, unceasing pressure of surveillance upon all facets of life in working-class communities' reporting on political activities, drinking habits and recreational life (Storch, 1981: 88). While the broad remit of the police seems fairly well established in the literature, the study of different locations provide nuance in the debates as well as highlighting the continuities between localities.

The city of Liverpool provides an example of how the direction, meaning and eventual targets of police work became routinised. In 1811, the Town Council reorganised the police in appointing 21 constables and seven head constables to patrol the seven boroughs of the city. The wealthy residents financed their own force to patrol the line between their estates and the city centre. By the 1830s, the poor in Liverpool consisted of a shifting mass of migrants, both under- and unemployed, who formed a casual residuum segregated from the 'respectable' working class. Writers on this period refer to the alarm of 'respectable' citizens in viewing the streets of Liverpool as filled with pathological pursuits and immoral activities, the scale of which threatened to overwhelm the growing social construction of the city as a centre of mercantile trade, and civic and commercial propriety (Coleman, 2004). In the light of these concerns, the Liverpool City Police force was established in 1836. For Brogden (1982), the formation of the new police straddled the volatile economy with its casualised labour force and a huge 'illegal' secondary economy serving the casual poor in the streets. This economy included street traders, gaming houses, pubs and brothels, creating a problem of control for the local merchant class. Thus, what spurred the formation of the Liverpool City Police in 1836 was the desire 'to suppress the manifestations of direct economic conflict' (Brogden, 1982: 52). The emergence of the new police extended and reformulated older practices established by the Corporation, Town and Dock Watches. The new police gained a substantive legal remit and acted from Watch Committee directives. During these formative years the police gained considerable autonomy in enacting social control on the streets in the city. In particular, the new police directly demarcated 'the territories of the dominant classes in the city – the merchants, the shopkeepers, and the new professional and white-collar strata – from the territories of the poor' (Brogden, 1982: 62). As with Storch's findings, the control on the streets and the activities within them figured prominently in police surveillance and control. Indeed, between 1836 and 1910 the policing mandate in Liverpool aimed to 'to divide off, to map out, the lower class areas' (Brogden, 1982: 52). The subjects of police work penalised the sources of mercantile discomfort – 'disorderly boys', 'children trundling hoops', 'rough characters', 'prostitutes', 'hawkers', 'Arab children', and adults playing 'pitch and toss' (1982: 63).

Communications from merchants, shopkeepers and other businesses to the Watch Committee in Liverpool between 1836 and 1872 show that demands for police deployment were targeted overwhelmingly at 'disorderly street behaviour', followed by 'sabbatical disorder', 'traffic obstructions', 'street traders', 'thieving', 'brothels and prostitutes', 'gambling and street games', and 'public houses' (1982: 65). Such police practices became routinised and amounted to a form of street cleansing in which officers operated 'as a kind of uniformed garbage-men' where 'arrests, other than for minor misdemeanours were rare' (Brogden, 1991: 1).

Contesting police surveillance

One of the continuous problems for those orchestrating surveillance practices has been that of gaining consent for their operation. As with the development of the 'new police', consent was subject to negotiation and compromise. Here the differential ability to contest, change or modify surveillance becomes a significant feature. We discuss this more fully in Chapter 7. For now, we wish to look at the early manifestations of these issues in relation to the 'new police', where there has been much debate as to the reception of the police across the population.

As already indicated, initial opposition to the new police was articulated around the idea of threats to liberty and also the costs of that policing from taxation. Rural elites felt that policing may have been relevant to big towns but not to the countryside (Storch, 1981). This opposition was largely short-lived and managed by recourse to indicators of rising crime and the proliferation of moral panics around social disorder that underpinned a perception that something 'new' must be done. After 1850, middle-class people came to see new legal forces as 'dependable' – as a resource that proved little in the way of a hindrance to their lives (Gatrell, 1990).

Indeed, there is evidence to suggest that throughout the nineteenth century a growing upwardly mobile and skilled working class came to 'side condition-ally' with new legal processes as an expression of their investment in social status as well as distinguishing themselves from the 'roughs'. After the 1870s, many have argued that the new legal order and the police in particular had gained broad legitimacy, but this would ignore a longer history of working-class opposition to surveillance. Increases in the battery of police legal powers, along with the development of new technologies and crowd control tactics, had some success in quelling lower-class disorder (Gatrell, 1990). But as Storch has argued, anti-police violence was a feature of working-class life, with policeman being 'beaten all through the nineteenth century' for snooping into family or neighbourhood relationships, interfering with recreational events, in being shepherds for strike breakers and in moving people off the streets, par-ticularly when unemployment was high (Storch, 1981). In many working-class communities, the police were seen less as a civilising force and more in terms of 'a plague of locusts'.

The force of working-class contestation was most strongly felt in relation to policing these practices up until 1850, after which more sporadic battles ensued in the context of industrial disputes. Although the presence of police surveillance in working-class communities continued and became consoli-dated, the 'domestic missionary' role of the new police and the attempt to instil 'respectable' and 'civilised' values in poorer communities ultimately failed. The moral assent of law into such communities continued to be with-held into the twentieth century (Storch, 1981: 108) where the 'alacrity' of the policing endeavour continued in the task of patrolling aliens, black people and street youth (Gatrell, 1990: 271). Phil Cohen (1979: 131) notes the changes and continuities into the nineteenth century here, in how policing of public order reflected geographical changes in urban segregation patterns between central and peripheral areas and the poorer class's movement between the two. In policing 'public propriety', the police operated 'new norms' that 'imposed a system of unofficial curfew' – an 'informal out-of-bounds, to define what were the wrong people, wrong age, wrong sex, in the wrong place at the wrong time'. Working-class assent to this was not easily forthcoming and resulted in real and symbolic battles between police and lower-class subjects (usually male) over the control of urban space (Cohen, 1979: 131).

Consolidating police and surveillance power

The discussion of early policing practices in Liverpool mirrors practices in other urban localities, where police surveillance became increasingly tied to expand-ing national and local state forms. As Gatrell (1990) has noted, the disciplinary and coercive aspects of police surveillance have always been most acutely felt

by lower-class subjects in the urban realm, where the construction and maintenance of ideas of 'public order' underpinned a variety of legal powers.

The development of the police relationship to 'crime' is a curious one. The
growing manpower, financial leverage and legal power of the policeman-state
through the twentieth century may lead to thinking that this growth was in
response to rises in crime or the increasing difficulties faced by police in controlling it. A number of scholars have demonstrated that this is not the case. For
example, the costs incurred from conventional crimes such as theft have,
throughout the twentieth century, been small in comparison to the 'disproportionate' expenditure on law enforcement (Gatrell, 1990: 264–265). Moreover,
studies have shown that the vast majority of police patrol work has little or
nothing to do with incidents that might be labelled 'criminal', and instead can
be construed as patrolling 'the petty' and 'disorderly'. Thus, expenditure on
police – and the official announcements that justify this as 'crime prevention' –
misconstrue the role of the police patrol, which is better understood as engaged
in the reproduction of order (Ericson, 1992). This involves the regulation of
industrial and political dissent, surveillance and intelligence collation and 'the
symbolic enunciation of social, economic and sexual norms' (Gatrell, 1990: 265).
Patrolling the 'offensive' is as much, if not more, derivative of the police role as
patrolling offences.

From the outset, organised surveillance, legally mandated through the police
institution, has always been subject to controversy, as evidenced in the differential policing of white-collar and corporate crime. Into the twentieth century,
police forces did develop some expertise in this area. However, surveillance and
arrests for corporate illegalities such as fraud have always remained small in
number (with prosecutions of lowly clerks as opposed to company directors
featuring prominently) compared to the pursuit and penalisation of 'ordinary
crime'. Moreover, 'the law's attention was as ever fixed on offenders who had
breached the trust of their employees, not on the employing class itself'
(Gatrell, 1990: 271).

Thus police surveillance practices have, over time, reinforced ideas about
the social and spatial location of crime. This was because policemen were
legally mandated to police streets where poorer people tended to congregate.
There discretionary powers under the Vagrancy Act (1824) and the
Metropolitan Police Act (1839), for example, led to intensified surveillance of
marginal street people that reflected and reinforced stereotypes of both
'criminal types' and 'criminal areas'. Under the Penal Servitude Act (1864)
and the Prevention of Crimes Act (1871) people convicted twice of a crime
and sent to prison could be placed under police supervision for up to seven
years (Bailey, 1993). These, and other legislative changes, extended discretionary powers of arrest, giving police flexibility in defining terms like 'reasonable suspicion' and 'loitering with intent'. Such legislative inducements to the
police role, and attempts to categorise 'habitual criminals' (using fingerprints and

photographs – see Norris and Armstrong, 1999) from this time, consolidated public perceptions that a hardened (lower) criminal class existed (Bailey, 1993: 250). Modern policing consolidated the notion of *criminal areas*, with the power to define and impose sanctions upon symbolic locations signifying 'disorder'. In this sense, surveillance has developed a territorial impetus, developing police technologies that allow 'greater intrusions into the lives of the more "publicly" visible' while ignoring other commercial and industrial spaces and respecting the 'privacy' of actors within them (McCormick and Visano, 1992: 239).

As part of this process, policemen on street patrol developed – within and alongside legal discretion – their own standards of moral purpose and procedural etiquette in dealing with the objects of their surveillance (Gatrell, 1990; Brogden, 1991). Such a police 'culture', relatively impervious to scrutiny, remains a feature of policing to this day and renders a situation in which it is difficult to 'see' police malpractice, illegality and violence. The difficulties in making incidents of wrongdoing visible, then as now, have been placed alongside maintaining public trust and legitimacy in police organisations – at least to those 'respectable' publics that matter (Gatrell, 1990). The history of watching the watchers, and the exposure of wrongdoing, has taken official forms of inquiry that have often denied and discredited claims of widespread police abuses and protected the idea and practice of discretion. Tactics of evading the nature of police malpractice (in drawing attention to individual 'corrupt' officers, for example) consolidated an 'ideological solidarity in the trade of law enforcement'. This left relatively immune from scrutiny the presumed discretionary necessities of street policing (Gatrell, 1990: 275) against 'which poorer people had little defence' (1990: 278) and from which they often withheld their consent.

Finally, the nature of police power and thus the power to surveil has been drawn within the complex of constraining and enabling relations forged between the police command structure, the rank and file and governing authorities. Resistance to outside 'interference' (including from its own management) has been a feature of rank-and-file police culture since its inception (Gatrell, 1990). More recently, policing has come under 'new' forms of managerial control and scrutiny (fiscal controls, performance indicators and auditing), which have redrawn the balance of power between management and the rank and file and framed police accountability around a 'value for money' ethos. However, such measures have taken place alongside a shift away from proposals for direct democratic forms of control (McLaughlin, 2007), leaving 'operational matters' (who gets policed, by what methods, when and where) firmly in the power of the police organisation. The potential areas for action concerning local democratic accountability of the police are still to be realised (McLaughlin, 2007: 196).

Summary and conclusion: continuities and discontinuities

This chapter has sought to provide an historical perspective in order to better situate contemporary relations between surveillance practices and crime control that the rest of the book will explore. The focus has been on what Cohen termed 'the master patterns' laid down in the nineteenth century and the changes and continuities that have accompanied their development. These developments fall under what Garland (2003) called 'penal modernism'. This modernist undertaking succeeded in establishing the forms of investigation, record-keeping, classification and predictive procedures discussed here and applied unevenly to powerless and powerful groups. The 'master patterns' included discursive renditions of the 'crime problem', constructed predominantly around concerns about lower-class space and activities.

The trajectory of surveillance practices derived within the key surveillance institutions and technologies of the nineteenth century, along with their differential impacts on sections of the population, continue to be a source of debate. There is nothing inevitable about differentiation in surveillance reach and, as the chapter has shown, this has been the result of struggles and debates in and around the surveillance endeavour. These debates continue as to how *much* surveillance is necessary? *Where* should it be applied? *What* kind of sanctions (criminal or otherwise) should accompany it? *Whose* voices are to be heard concerning its development and operation? *Whose* are not? The struggles and debates surrounding such questions are situated within an uneven and asymmetrical terrain of power relations that equip some groups to shape the surveillance agenda and the nature of the 'dialogue' that surrounds it. Moreover, as we have seen, it was powerful groups who were able to engage in and shape (through propagating particular ideas and with greater access to material resources) surveillance targeting and mitigate its impacts upon themselves while other groups felt its full force. These are concerns we return to in Chapters 6 and 7.

This historical exploration of the relationship between surveillance crime points to the development of the 'surveillance society' as something akin to a *process* and not a discrete episode. Importantly, the history of the developing relationship between surveillance and crime should be not read as a straightforwardly progressive one in which surveillance growth is characterised as one of greater 'accuracy' and 'precision', and that these refinements will eventually come to 'know' triumph over the 'crime problem'. As we have seen from this historical survey, the practice of 'surveillance' and the meaning of 'crime' raise questions that have only been prematurely 'settled'. Put simply, moral discourses, new legal statutes and practices of surveillance occur in historical processes and have the effect of generating categories of 'crime' in a manner that has stimulated their further reproduction.

STUDY QUESTIONS

1 What were the main impacts derived from the development of synoptic representations of disorder upon the social construction of crime, its location and in terms of its meaning in modernising societies?

2 What were the main motivations for reformers, particularly in the nineteenth century?

3 How would you characterise the role of the 'new police' in the nineteenth century? Were they successful in this role?

4 What would you consider to be the main continuities in the development of surveillance across the period discussed in this chapter?

FURTHER READING

Cohen, S. (1985) *Visions of Social Control*, Cambridge: Polity Press.

Coleman, R. (2004) *Reclaiming the Streets: Surveillance, Social Control and the City*, Cullompton: Willan (see Chapter 5).

Gatrell, V.A.C. (1990) 'Crime, authority and the policeman-state', in Thompson, F.M.L. (ed.), *The Cambridge Social History of Britain 1750–1950, Volume 5: Social Agencies and Institutions*, Cambridge: Cambridge University Press.

McMullan, J.L. (1998b) 'The arresting eye: discourse, surveillance and disciplinary administration in early English police thinking', *Social and Legal Studies*, Vol. 7, No. 1, pp. 97–128.

Storch, R.D. (1981) 'The plague of blue locusts: police, reform and popular resistance in Northern England 1840–57', in Fitzgerald, M., McLennan, G. and Pawson, J. (eds), *Crime and Society: Readings in History and Theory*, London: Routledge and Kegan Paul in association with the Open University.

4

New Policing and New Surveillance*

CHAPTER CONTENTS	
Surveillance and criminal justice – reigning in the 'assemblage'	69
'Prevention' versus 'bandit catching' – police 'culture' and the mediation of 'risk'	75
Police co-option of 'non-state' surveillance systems	78
Plural police property and entrepreneurial cityscapes	83
Summary and conclusion	87
Study questions	89
Further reading	89

*An earlier version of this chapter appeared in McCahill, M. (2008) 'Plural Policing and Surveillance', in M. Deflem (ed.) *Surveillance and Governance: Crime Control and Beyond*. Bingley: Emerald Group Publishing Ltd, pp. 199–219.

OVERVIEW

Chapter 4 provides:

- A critical examination of the emerging 'risk paradigm' in the 'plural policing' literature
- A look at how 'new surveillance' technologies are mediated by the existing organisational, occupational and individual concerns of 'plural police' actors
- An emphasis on continuity by showing how 'plural police' surveillance practices continue to fall disproportionately on the 'usual suspects'
- An examination of how the emergence of 'new surveillance' technologies and 'plural policing' networks is bound up with wider urban transformations, entrepreneurial landscapes and the politics of exclusion

KEY TERMS

- Co-option
- Plural policing
- Police property

- Risk mentality
- Surveillant assemblage

In this chapter we look critically at the emerging 'risk paradigm' by drawing upon recent research conducted on the use of 'new surveillance' technologies in relation to contemporary policing. First, you will recall that we discussed in Chapter 2 how a number of theorists have drawn attention to the emergence of decentred and fragmented networks of surveillance and policing under the notion of the 'surveillant assemblage'. This chapter begins to map out a critical engagement with some of the ideas found in this literature and its relevance for thinking about the contemporary surveillance of crime. We suggest that in the context of surveillance, policing and criminal justice there are also countervailing trends towards the centralisation of surveillance systems. Secondly, in line with our focus on *continuity* as well as *change*, we show how 'new surveillance' technologies are shaped by existing and inherited institutional formations, social relations and political practices. In relation to the 'public' police, for example, we draw upon the findings of empirical studies to show how 'risk' is mediated by the normative, organisational, occupational and individual concerns of 'system managers' and 'street-level bureaucrats'. We argue that when 'new surveillance' technologies are used 'proactively' by the 'public' police, it is often in support of traditional 'law enforcement' rather than 'problem-solving' or 'prevention'.[1]

---

[1]Many writers, including Les Johnston (2000: 79), have recognised that 'many police practices remain reactive rather than proactive and are, to that extent, incompatible with risk-based thinking'.

Thirdly, we also look critically at the idea that the strategies pursued by the 'private' police are driven solely by 'instrumental' factors, gutted of notions concerning moral wrongdoing and based purely on notions of 'actuarial justice'. We suggest that there is no easy distinction to be made between 'public' and 'private' actors in moral or ideological terms and that there is often a shared assumption among 'public' and 'private' actors about which social groups should be singled out for targeting by 'new surveillance' technologies. We show, for example, how the construction of 'public–private' surveillance networks has created a situation in which 'private' security officers have adopted aspects of the 'punishment' mentality and the concern with 'bandit catching' and 'law enforcement' that, from the beginning of the nineteenth century and throughout the twentieth has preoccupied state-centred forms of policing and surveillance. We also draw attention to how a number of writers have placed these public–private initiatives within the broader material and ideological shifts in urban governance to have occurred since the 1980s. It is argued that these wider developments, under the tutelage of entrepreneurial city building, have drawn upon surveillance and control strategies that reinforce spatial divisions and raised questions concerning who has 'the right to the city' (Coleman, 2009b).

Surveillance and criminal justice – reigning in the 'assemblage'

As we saw in Chapter 2, some writers have argued for the idea that we are witnessing a 'paradigm shift' towards 'risk-based' strategies of social control. This is a recurring theme in the sociological and criminological literature and has been echoed in the context of 'criminal justice' policy, where Feeley and Simon (1994: 173) described a shift from the 'Old Penology' to the 'New Penology'. The Old Penology was characterised by 'punishment' or 'treatment' programmes directed at individual offenders. On the other hand, as we saw in Chapter 2, the New Penology is based not on individualised suspicion, but on the probability that an individual may be an offender. These developments, it is argued, have given rise to 'actuarial justice', whereby criminal justice interventions have become increasingly based on risk assessment, rather than on the identification of specific criminal behaviour. This has led to 'an increase in, and legal sanction of, such actuarial practices as preventative detention, offender profiling and mass surveillance' (Norris and Armstrong, 1999: 25).

In the context of 'policing', Johnston and Shearing (2003) have described a move away from a 'punishment' mentality towards a 'risk' mentality. In the former paradigm, the central state exercises its security responsibilities through the employment of specialised professionals, such as police officers, whose main concern is the apprehension and punishment of suspected wrongdoers (Johnston and Shearing, 2003: 14). Under the 'risk' paradigm, on the other hand, security is exercised under plural auspices beyond the central state and is characterised by a 'corporate' mentality that emphasises 'proactive prevention' rather than 'reactive punishment', and 'actuarial calculation' rather than conventional 'moral prescription'. This future-oriented approach to policing and security, it is argued, is no longer the exclusive preserve of corporate security, because the state police have also become more and more preoccupied with risk-based policies and practices (Ericson and Haggerty, 1997).

The debate concerning the emergence of a fragmented and pluralised network of policing has parallels with Haggerty and Ericson's (2000) notion of a 'surveillant assemblage', which we discussed in Chapter 2. As noted in that chapter, the 'assemblage' refers to a set of loosely linked systems, to be distinguished from the operation of the central state or government. This has been variously conceptualised in terms of the emergence of a 'new lateral surveillance' (Chan, 2008), which takes place 'below' the state in the community; the emergence of 'global' surveillance networks operated by 'transnational' actors operating 'above' the state (Mathiesen, 2006); the emergence of corporate-driven 'dataveillance' (Whitaker, 2006), which takes place 'beyond the state' in the marketplace; and the rapid growth of 'private security' officers, who conduct surveillance in 'mass private property' (Shearing and Stenning, 1983). The emergence of a 'risk mentality' in policing is also said to provide further impetus for the use of 'new surveillance' technologies. As Johnston (2000) points out, the concern with 'actuarial calculation' and 'pre-emptive' policing requires 'the systematic generation of information for analysis' and 'in order to produce such information it is necessary to undertake systematic surveillance of those individuals, groups and locations which might be a source of risk' (2000: 74). In this respect, surveillance technologies, such as CCTV cameras, are 'an exemplar of "actuarial" technology which encourages the targeting of aggregate populations rather than individual suspects' (Johnston and Shearing, 2003: 69). As indicated in Chapter 2, these arguments are supported by Gary T. Marx (2002), who has spoken of the emergence of a 'new surveillance' that monitors geographical places, time periods and categories of person rather than individual suspects (Marx, 2002: 10; also Lyon, 2002). When exploring practices on the ground, however, such 'paradigm shifts' are more difficult to discern and maintain at a conceptual level.

In some respects, it could be argued that the emergence of a pluralised and differentiated patchwork of policing has been exemplified most acutely by the introduction of open-street CCTV surveillance networks. The rise to ubiquity of visual surveillance systems in the UK began in the early 1990s when government-initiated 'responsibilisation strategies' (Garland, 1996) mobilised a whole range of 'action groups' and 'public–private' partnerships, including 'the media, the police, local authorities, retailers, insurance companies, surveillance industries and property interests' (Graham et al. 1996; cited in

McCahill, 1998: 56). 'Blurring' across the 'public–private' divide was particularly evident in relation to the 'purchaser–provider' split (Jones and Newburn,
1998). For example, in the UK the 'CCTV Challenge Competitions' in the
1990s stated that bids had to be in the form of a partnership, with the Home
Office providing 50% of the capital costs while the remaining 50% was to be
found from within other sources, such as the business sector, the local authority, the police or other government agencies. These trends became reflected in
the day-to-day management and operation of CCTV control rooms, where a
diverse range of surveillance personnel could be found. These included 'police
officers', 'police civilian staff', 'special constables', 'private security', and
'local authority personnel' (Norris and Armstrong, 1999: 57).

The growth of 'public–private' partnerships in town centres has meant that
the private sector has been closely involved in both the construction and
operation of public space CCTV surveillance systems (McCahill, 2002;
Coleman, 2004). This is clearly evident in the use of Retail Radio Networks,
which have allowed 'private' actors to initiate the targeting practices of 'public' CCTV systems. The UK produced the first national evaluation of public
area CCTV, where it was reported that several CCTV control rooms had retail
or pub radio schemes 'which accounted for the reporting and observation of
significant numbers of incidents' (Gill and Spriggs, 2005: xiii). Also, five out of
six of the CCTV control rooms in Goold's (2004) study of open-street CCTV
had 'established radio links between all of the major retailers and shopping
centres' (2004: 145). In Lincoln, a Business Improvement Group provided
'two-way radios to nearly 200 pubs, clubs and shops' in the town centre, with
'incidents initiated by radio contact accounting for 70% of the control room
staff's activities' (*CCTV Image*, 2006b: 16). Similarly, the CCTV system in
Liverpool was established and monitored by a private security company
which liaised with the 'state' police and in-house store security via a retail
radio link that made possible 'the monitoring of persons through both open
public space and private shop space' (Coleman, 2004: 159). Meanwhile, Norris
and Armstrong (1999) found that one of the CCTV control rooms in their study
became 'almost entirely co-opted by and subservient to the demands of the
private security nexus of the town centre store detectives' (1999: 160).

Thus, while many contemporary urban policing developments have been
understood with reference to the 'plurality' of actors involved in surveillance,
there are strong countervailing trends towards the centralisation of surveillance as the state attempts to reign in the dispersed 'surveillant assemblage'
(Haggerty and Ericson, 2000). For example, from the 1990s to the present the
police have orchestrated a number of organisational changes that could, in
principle, facilitate a more centralised coordination of operational procedures.
In London there are plans to link each local authority CCTV control room to
one of the three new purpose-built police communications centres at Hendon,
Bow and Lambeth. This will facilitate greater cooperation between CCTV

control rooms and the police Borough Operational Command Units (BOCUs), with 24-hour operations, including 'radio communications and CCTV feeds' (*CCTV Image*, 2006a: 26). The CCTV control rooms will also utilise the new 'Airwave' radio system (the secure police cellular radio system), which means that CCTV operators will 'be able to provide responding officers with advance information about what's going on at a particular incident – perhaps warning them of potential risks before they arrive' (2006a: 26). A more recent initiative includes the plan to develop a Facial Images National Database (FIND) 'which will allow the police to contribute to, and access, a library of photographic and video images' which the police will be able to cross-reference with 'all the associated data held on the PNC' (Norris, 2007: 146).

The move towards a more centralised and coordinated approach towards police use of visual surveillance networks is also evident on the UK roads where the 'public' police are beginning to utilise Automatic Number Plate Recognition (ANPR) schemes as a mainstream policing tool (Kelly, 2006: 34). ANPR technology works as follows: when a vehicle passes and is observed by an ANPR camera, a digital image is recorded and then processed to identify the Vehicle Registration Mark (VRM). The VRM is then checked with relevant databases (e.g. DVLA and PNC) and, if a vehicle is flagged up for attention, the police can be deployed to stop the vehicle and investigate (ACPO ANPR Steering Group, 2005). ANPR cameras can be used as part of a dedicated mobile unit, as part of an in-car unit, or integrated with existing Local Authority town centre CCTV surveillance networks (Kelly, 2006: 36). In 2005 the Association of Chief Police Officers (ACPO) stated that the 'the intention is to create a comprehensive ANPR Camera and Reader infrastructure across the country' (ACPO ANPR Steering Group, 2005: 17). This will include the establishment of a 'National ANPR Media Strategy', a 'National ANPR Programme Board', and a 'National ANPR Data Centre' (NADC). This will eventually facilitate the creation of a nation-wide 'reader infrastructure' which will integrate the NADC with Local Authority ANPR-enabled CCTV systems, highway agencies cameras, police cameras, commercial and retail sites such as garage forecourts, and other agency cameras such as the DVLA (ACPO ANPR Steering Group, 2005: 17). The ANPR has also been used to spot vehicles belonging to public protesters and resulted in peaceful demonstrators being repeatedly stopped and searched by police (Lewis and Evans, 2009) – an issue we shall explore in more detail below.

The centralisation of 'state' surveillance is also evident in relation to other surveillance technologies, including the National DNA Database and the Police National Computer (PNC). As McCahill and Norris (2003b) point out, the National DNA Database was set up on 10 April 1995 by the Forensic Science Service (FSS) on behalf of ACPO. The database was originally established as a forensic source for helping to identify those involved in serious crimes (i.e. murder and rape). However, as McCahill and Norris (2003b) point out, an amendment to the Criminal Justice and Public Order Act (1994) allows samples to be taken without consent from any person convicted or suspected of a recordable offence (McCahill and Norris, 2003b: 127). As McCartney (2006) has reported, in April 2000, a DNA Expansion Programme was announced which 'aimed to increase the NDNAD until all of the "known active offending population" (estimated at the time at 3 million individuals) were on the database' (2006: 176). By March 2005, the government had invested £240.8 million facilitating further expansion, including the recruitment of an additional 650 Crime Scene Examiners to devote resources towards 'the collection and analysis of more DNA material at crime scenes' (2006: 176). By 2005, 237,500 profiles had been collected from crime scenes (McCartney, 2006: 176). In 2009 it was announced that there were 10.8 million profiles on the National Database, including 'one in three of all young black males' (Travis, 2009: 12).

Plans for a Police National Computer (PNC) in the UK were first announced in 1969 when the then Labour government announced that they were going 'to set up a Police National Computer Unit at Hendon in North London' (Mainwaring-White, 1983: 55). The PNC was then launched in 1974, at which time each of the 47 police forces in England and Wales had one terminal providing access to the central computer (Mainwaring-White, 1983: 55). As Norris (2007: 144) points out, today the PNC is 'linked to more than 30,000 terminals across the country' and is integrated with a whole range of databases, including the DVLA, the National Automated Fingerprint Identification System (NAFIS) and the Violent Offender and Sex Offender Register (ViSOR). As Norris has stated:

> The surveillant solution enacted as part of the British criminal justice policy is not rhizomatic, but profoundly arboreal. The last decade has witnessed the development of a centralized IT strategy placing the infrastructure under direct central control ... [including] the creation of nationally coordinated software platforms for the exchange and integration of information across the criminal justice system. (Norris, 2007: 152–153)

Moreover, much of this technological know-how has also been used to police and monitor public protest, which is not necessary criminal in law. Indeed, the longer historical development of policing has ensured that 'those who have dissented from prevailing norms have always been penalized' (Gatrell, 1990: 266). Since their inception in the first quarter of the nineteenth century, the police have developed public order maintenance techniques, covert surveillance and specialist departments for the tackling of political dissent, most notably in the form of trade union and anti-war activities. This policing of politics has involved longstanding, though usually secretive, 'partnerships' and informal links between public and private police, businesses and government departments, which have passed intelligence information between each other regarding protests and protest groups (Bunyan, 1977). It was reported in the UK in 2009, for example, that government officials in the Department of

Business, Enterprise and Regulatory Reform handed confidential police intelligence about environmental activists to the private energy corporation E.ON in the run-up to a demonstration against a coal-fired power plant (Taylor and Lewis, 2009). This came at the same time that police admitted to paying hundreds of informants for covert surveillance and intelligence duties within a range of protest organisations in order to pre-empt and disrupt protest activity (Lewis, 2009a). In the UK, the National Extremism Tactical Co-ordination Unit (Netcu) was developed by ACPO in response to pressure from big business concerning their anxieties over public protests against their activities. Large corporations concerned about protests targeted at them regularly engage in surveillance discourses that take the form of conversations between government ministers, civil servants and police, where threats to 'public order' are identified and information can be shared (Evans et al., 2009). According to a senior police officer, Netcu has provided security advice and information to banks, retailers and pharmaceutical industries in order to 'minimize disruption' to their activities (cited in Evans et al., 2009: 6). This group works alongside the National Public Order Intelligence Unit (NPOIU) which maintains overlapping databases on what the police call 'domestic extremists' in England and Wales. The databases are supplied with information from Forward Intelligence Teams (FIT), which record footage and take photographs of campaigners (including environmental activists, animal rights groups, far right groups and left-wing groups) in order to make a record of political activities and movement around the country. Although the term 'domestic extremism' is not defined in law, the police define it as 'people and activities' that 'seek to prevent something from happening or to change legislation or domestic policy, but attempt to do so outside of the normal democratic process' (cited in Evans et al., 2009: 6). The police acknowledged that being on the database did not signify criminal wrongdoing and that 'just because you have no criminal record does not mean that you are not of interest to the police' (2009: 6). The secretive nature of these databases and the close working relations between police, government departments and big business has raised many questions around the policing of legitimate protest and organised dissent in a modern democracy. While for some, in theory, public dissent exists as a democratic freedom and basis of democratic debate, for others, who take a longer historical view, 'the history of public order in the United Kingdom is essentially a history of restrictions' (Supperstone, cited in Gatrell, 1990: 268) targeting the innocent as well as guilty under the broad umbrella of 'enemies within'.

What these examples point to is the continuing importance of state–police agencies in orchestrating large-scale surveillance practices. However, the issue of whether 'new' technologies and centralised surveillance databases are incorporated into 'existing' police intelligence systems and investigative techniques remains an empirical question that we now turn to by reviewing some of the literature on policing and information technology.

'Prevention' versus 'bandit catching' – police 'culture' and the mediation of 'risk'

The shift towards a 'pre-emptive' or 'proactive' approach to policing can hardly be described as a recent development. This was demonstrated in Chapter 3 in relation to developments in policing and surveillance in the eighteenth and nineteenth centuries. During that period policing experts such as Fielding, Colquhoun and Chadwick 'regarded prevention as more important than retrospective functions of arrest, detention and prosecution that later came to characterise modern policing' (Zedner, 2006: 85). Writing in the late eighteenth century, Henry Fielding argued that it was 'better to prevent even one man from being a rogue than apprehending and bringing forty to justice' (quoted in McMullan, 1998b: 102). However, while we may question the novelty of 'risk-based' strategies, many writers have argued that a number of developments in 'late modern' society have given a renewed impetus towards the adoption of a 'risk mentality' in contemporary policing. As Johnston (2000: 69) points out, 'the transfer of private business practices to the public sector by means of New Public Management (NPM) reforms ... required police organizations to behave, more and more, like commercial enterprises'. For Johnston, this has led to a 'melding of mentalities' whereby the 'public' police have become more preoccupied with 'risk management' defined as 'the anticipation, recognition and appraisal of a risk and the initiation of some action to remove the risk or reduce the potential loss from it to an acceptable level' (Broder, 1999, cited in Johnston, 2000: 74).

For many, the introduction of 'new surveillance' technologies fits neatly with the 'risk mentality' by allowing interventions to be made by the police before any deviant act has taken place (Graham, 1998). However, as a number of writers have argued, the way 'new technologies' are applied in practice depends upon how they fit in with existing social relations, political practices and cultural traditions. Writers working with the Social Construction of Technology (SCOT) approach, for example, have argued that 'individuals, social groups and institutions ... have some degree of choice in shaping the design, development and application of technologies in specific cases' (Graham and Marvin, 1996: 105). In relation to the impact of 'information technology' on policing in the United States, Peter Manning (2008: 262) suggests that the idea that 'the police are now an information-based organization, focusing on managing risk and enhancing security, is both premature and flawed'. For Manning, the police remain an institution that 'react[s] to something that might get worse' (2008: 250). Similarly, observational research conducted in the UK on the police use of 'new surveillance' technologies, such as CCTV cameras, has concluded that the way these systems are used in practice depends upon how they fit in with existing organisational, occupational and individual concerns of front-line operatives (Norris and Armstrong, 1999; McCahill, 2002; Goold, 2004). Let us take a more detailed look at these arguments by reviewing some of the empirical literature conducted in the USA, Canada and the UK.

In the USA, Peter Manning (2008) looked at the introduction of Crime Mapping (CM) and Crime Analysis (CA) in three US police forces. Crime Mapping and Crime Analysis, he explains, includes a range of techniques 'designed to gather information on the temporal, spatial, and social aspects of crime' (2008: 4) so that this information can be disseminated throughout the organisation to pre-emptively reduce crime levels. However, as Manning shows, these new technologies and practices are mediated by the organisational and occupational concerns of front-line officers. In the Western Police Department, for example, the CM/CA system was operated by a 'retired clerk' and by 'one person with a master's degree in criminal justice and some flair for computer work, who spent his time checking his investments on MSN, checking his e-mail, and looking forward to retirement' (Manning, 2008: 126–127). In Washington, the computer databases 'represented a sort of archaeology of systems, lying on top of each other yet not linked' and were 'used to track current decisions rather than to plan, anticipate, prevent, or control the "external environment" of crime and disorder' (2008: 150). Finally, in the Boston Police Department the introduction of CM/CA simply led to an 'increase [in] the number of *ad hoc* queries to databases' which 'were incident based, not problem based' and 'had little to do with altering the social conditions or access to criminal opportunities or "crime prevention"' (2008: 189).

Police decisions in relation to the adoption of information technology for 'proactive' policing continues to be shaped by the different and often competing organisational and occupational concerns of those involved in the operation of surveillance systems. In her study of an Australian police force, for example, Chan (2003: 663) reports that 'the perception among operational police ... was that central administration, civilians, management and information technology staff did not understand operational policing needs'. Even in those organisations that did adopt 'a more analytical and problem-oriented approach to crime', there was often a 'clash of cultures between police and analysts' with some officers expressing 'a cultural aversion to depersonalised and decontextualised data generated by crime analysts' (Chan, 2003: 667). Similar findings were reported by Sheptycki (2003) in his study of detectives who had 'a tendency to "co-opt crime analysis for the purposes of crime investigation", thus reducing "the intelligence process to evidence gathering and evaluation", instead of broader analysis of trends and patterns from crime prevention' (Sheptycki, 2003, cited in Chan, 2003: 667).

The literature from the USA has been supported by empirical research in the UK that has focused on the construction and operation of open-street

CCTV surveillance systems. As Goold (2004) has shown, in the early years of construction this new technology was not readily incorporated into police information gathering and intelligence systems (see also Gill and Spriggs, 2005; Fussey, 2007). In his study of six open-street CCTV surveillance systems, Goold (2004) found that while many senior police officers publicly welcomed the efforts of local authorities to bring CCTV to their towns, many adopted a 'wait and see' approach. This meant that they had little say over the design of the systems, camera placement or operational procedures. The first major national evaluation of public-space CCTV also found that the police were often reluctant to become involved in the construction of CCTV systems. Police reluctance was due to a number of factors, including 'a concern that the new CCTV system would increase workload or place a strain on already stretched financial resources' (Gill and Spriggs, 2005: 68). These findings were supported in a study carried out by the Metropolitan Police in 2001 which found that many police officers regarded CCTV as 'a demand on their time or as a tool to be used reactively during investigations to crimes' (*CCTV Image*, 2006a: 25). Meanwhile, another study found that the 'state' police were entirely unaware of the existence of a public CCTV scheme in an inner-city area of Metropolitan City (Fussey, 2007).

The operation of open-street CCTV surveillance networks is also shaped by the competing organisational and occupational concerns of front-line operators. For instance, as we saw earlier, many public-space CCTV systems are monitored not by the police but by local authority employees or private security officers. In his study of six open-street CCTV systems in the Southern Region Police area, Goold (2004) found that police officers were less than enthusiastic about their working relationships with some of the CCTV operators, particularly those in local authority-led schemes who lacked the police officers' 'sixth sense' and often passed on jobs perceived by the police as 'rubbish'. As one police constable explained, 'at the end of the day, however hard civilians try ... they still don't have the gut feeling and never will have the gut feeling that a police officer is so often trained to have' (Goold, 2004: 134). Thus, in three local authority-controlled CCTV control rooms, the author found that out of a total of 243 'targeted surveillances', a police officer was deployed to the scene on just one occasion (2004: 164).

As Chan (2003: 674) has pointed out, when information and communications technologies *are* incorporated into police intelligence gathering systems, it is usually those 'technologies that support a traditional law-enforcement style of policing' that are the most successful. Chan et al. (2001), for example, found that mobile data terminals (MDTs) in police cars to check for outstanding traffic offences were enthusiastically embraced by the police officers in their case study. Similarly, in a case study of a small US police force, Meehan (1998) found that police officers were enthusiastic about the use of MDT for 'running plates' and offenders with 'outstanding warrants' (cited in Chan, 2003: 666). The officers in this study used MDT for 'proactive checking and stopping of motorists' and 'to engage in "investigative work" through "running plates" in parking lots of restaurants known to be frequented by drug dealers or other criminals, often leading to arrests' (cited in Chan, 2003: 659). These findings were supported by Ericson and Haggerty's (1997: 390) research in Canada, where police officers reported that Computer-Aided Dispatch (CAD) systems in police vehicles 'were used frequently during routine patrols to run checks on licence plates'.

In the UK, the introduction ANPR cameras have been readily incorporated into police intelligence and targeting for the purposes of 'bandit catching'. In 2003, the Home Office announced a national pilot of the ANPR scheme which involved 23 police forces setting up 50 ANPR-enabled intercept teams consisting of officers operating from cars and motorcycles. As Norris has pointed out, during the

> first nine months of operation over twenty million vehicle registrations marks were read and 900,000 of these were flagged on police databases as being of interest to them. As a result over 130,000 vehicles were stopped and over 10,000 people arrested. (Norris, 2007: 3)

The findings reviewed above would seem to support Chan's (2003: 668) argument that the introduction of information and communication technologies into 'public' police organisations often leaves 'more continuities than changes in the habitus of policing'. The technologies may be 'new', involving remote, electronically-mediated monitoring, but the police remain a 'rational-legal organisation' whose main concern is the policing of 'class-based street crimes' (Manning, 2008: 23). This is an important point and something we shall return to later in this chapter and in Chapter 6, which explores the social impacts of surveillance techniques.

Police co-option of 'non-state' surveillance systems

As Shearing and Stenning (1983) have argued, the policing strategies adopted by 'private security' focus not so much on the apprehension and punishment of known offenders, but on the goals of 'private justice' and 'loss prevention'. Rather than 'draw on the slow and costly criminal justice process in pursuit of sanctions' (Wakefield, 2005: 532), private actors will choose the most cost-effective option by trying to prevent problems before they occur. Moreover, when deviations from the rules of the organisation do take place, these are likely to 'be dealt with administratively by warnings rather than by criminal prosecution' (Ericson and Haggerty, 1997: 269; see also Henry, 1987). The use of CCTV surveillance and private security patrols in the industrial workplace, for example, are used to monitor compliance with health and safety regulations, time keeping, access restriction, unauthorised breaks, and so on (McCahill, 2002: 161). In shopping malls meanwhile, CCTV surveillance systems are used to deal with issues that relate to 'health and safety', 'lift breakdowns', and 'accidents' which might involve 'comeback' in the shape of 'insurance claims' (McCahill, 2002). However, in this section we want to suggest that the introduction of 'new surveillance' technologies in a range of 'non-state' settings, such as the 'workplace', 'retail sector', 'community' and 'mass private property', can be easily and routinely co-opted for 'traditional' policing and surveillance.

As Ericson and Haggerty (1997: 439) have argued, over the last decade or so the 'public' police have become 'knowledge brokers' for a whole range of organisations to the extent that policing is now 'shaped by the knowledge requirements of external institutions that operate within a compliance-based mode of regulation'. Equally though, as Crawford (2003: 78) has pointed out, information exchange between 'plural policing' bodies 'is not a one-way process from police to private security'. As Crawford (2003) has shown, 'the local intelligence gathered and collected by private security in shopping and commercial centres such as Liverpool Gold Zones and the MetroCentre can be highly sophisticated' (2003: 78). Private security officers at the MetroCentre, for example, have a photographic database to which the 'public' police have access. Recent years have also seen the introduction of new legislation which allows shopping mall managers and town centre managers to use the courts and criminal justice agencies for exclusions, through the use of Anti-Social Behaviour Orders (ASBOs) or exclusions attached to bail conditions. In their study of 'plural policing' in Liverpool, Crawford et al. (2005) found that local business leaders worked closely with the local ASBO Unit and Youth Offending Service to encourage 'the use of exclusion from certain stores in the city centre as an aspect of such contracts' (2005: 51).

Research on the use of CCTV surveillance systems in 'mass private property' has also shown that the information flow between 'public' and 'private' police is not a one-way process. The localised knowledge of 'private security' officers in suburban shopping malls, for example, can be extremely useful for 'state' police officers. In one case study, it was reported how the CCTV control room situated in a shopping mall (Housing Estate Mall) in an extremely deprived area of a northern city came to act as an intelligence base for the state police (McCahill, 2002). On this site, the majority of the security officers were local people with extensive knowledge of the area and its inhabitants. The security officers and those who frequented the mall had gone to the same schools, drank in the same pubs and played for the same darts teams and Sunday league football teams. This localised knowledge was very useful for the police who, with the help of the security officers, used the control room as an intelligence base to monitor suspected drug dealers. Some uses of the system included CID officers sitting in the control room and using the cameras to zoom in on a local public phone booth to watch the telephone numbers dialled by suspected drug dealers or clients; the local beat officer sitting in the control room and watching the screens to put names to faces and faces to names; policing officers asking the CCTV operators to film the registration number of cars driven by suspected drug dealers; and CCTV operators ringing the local beat officer on his mobile telephone to let him know when any 'wanted' persons enter the shopping centre (McCahill, 2007).

CCTV surveillance cameras are also widely deployed in the commercial and industrial workplace and these can also prove useful for criminal investigations instigated by the state police (McCahill, 2002). The Security Manager of a newspaper publishing plant, for example, explained how the police brought a tape to the control room and asked him if he would use one of the site's external cameras to record people visiting a second-hand electrical shop suspected of receiving stolen goods. Meanwhile, a CCTV operator employed by a frozen foods factory explained how the police had used external cameras on the site to monitor a person living in a nearby residential area who was suspected of drug dealing. When asked if the police came to the control room to watch the monitors, the CCTV operator replied:

> No, they gave us a tape and we were taping it 24 hours a day on one channel. They were watching this house here (the security officer zooms in on a house across the road). The guy used to go out on Friday night and come back on Monday morning and apparently what it was he was drug dealing so we caught him on camera. We were recording what time of the day and night people came in, the registration numbers of cars, what people looked like, and as I say it was all on tape. (McCahill, 2002: 83)

As Johnston (2000) points out, 'neo-liberal' projects of 'responsibilisation' referred not only to the 'privatisation' of state institutions such as 'public' policing, but also to 'attempts to disperse governmental responsibilities to communities through "community policing", "community education", "community justice", "punishment in the community"', and so on (2000: 70). Against this background there have been many public pronouncements from politicians in the UK designed to encourage the 'active citizen' or 'communities' themselves to take responsibility for the prevention of crime. As Johnston and Shearing (2003: 74) point out, some of these strategies simply reinforce the old 'punishment mentality' by 'mobilising citizens as informers so as to facilitate better bandit-catching'. Recent years have also witnessed the growth of Community Safety Officers (CSOs) who also provide 'extra eyes' and 'extra ears' for state actors. As Crawford (2003) points out, the deployment of CSOs in Bradford, 'combined with the introduction of the NIM (National Intelligence Model developed by the NCIS) required the police to recruit two extra crime analysts to input on to the police database the extra intelligence generated'. Crawford points out that 'the CSOs alone produced approximately 120 intelligence forms per week' (2003: 77).

As Rodger (2008) has shown, government-initiated 'responsibilisation' strategies have also mobilised the 'policing' and 'surveillance' activities of other organisations and individuals in the community. Rodger points to the recent growth of 'social housing', which has created new surveillance and policing roles for 'housing managers' and 'tenancy enforcement officers'. Rodger argues that in some respects these actors could be interpreted as 'usurping the authority of the police in the investigation and decision-making about anti-social tenants and anti-social families', a role that 'has been formalised by the passing of the anti-social behaviour legislation' (2008: 8). As Brown (2004: 206) has pointed out, 'landlords attempt to reform dysfunctional families' by offering 'a support worker to help develop positive discipline and regular routine in the home' (quoted in Rodger, 2008: 8). Flint and Pawson (2009), in their empirical account of the role of social landlords, have shown that it is not only the 'household dynamics' of those living in social housing that come under greater scrutiny. Rather, the home itself

> becomes the site for facilitating the surveillance and regulation of others ... through the use of covert surveillance (such as installing cameras in front doors to monitor a neighbour's property) or providing tenants with real-time monitoring images beamed into their domestic television screens from CCTV cameras in their neighbourhood. (2009: 423–424)

However, while 'housing managers' may be 'usurping' the role of the police in some neighbourhoods, the introduction of CCTV surveillance systems in housing estates can also be co-opted by central state actors as the CCTV control rooms come to serve as an 'intelligence base' for traditional policing. Many local authority housing departments in the UK have installed concierge-operated CCTV systems that monitor the communal areas of high-rise flats (McGrail, 1998; McCahill, 2002). In one study, informal liaison took place between the police and local authority employees responsible for monitoring the images displayed by a network of 222 CCTV cameras that had been installed in the city's 16 high-rise flats (McCahill, 2002). As the local authority employees responsible for monitoring the system explained:

> 'We can watch the "drug flats" and count how many visits there are to those flats. We've got a list there where we jot down the number of visits which we can then show to the police.' (Concierge Worker)

> 'Well, we gather information for the police. They'll say, "where does so and so live?" or "we think this flats dealing keep an eye on it". I'll keep a record then of who visits the flat and pass it on to the intelligence field officer.' (Senior Concierge) (McCahill, 2002: 176)

There is some evidence that CCTV surveillance systems in urban and sub-urban housing estates are also being used to provide evidence for the enforce-ment of ASBOs.[2] These practices have been reported in several areas, including Portsmouth, where the digitally recorded images displayed by the CCTV cam-eras operating in 45 council housing blocks have been used in the enforcement of ASBOs (Cohen, 2005). The CCTV operators in the control room operated by Newark and Sherwood District Council also work closely with a council-employed ASBO officer who provides the control room staff with details of any ASBOs issued to local residents. As the control room manager stated, 'CCTV can provide us with irrefutable evidence that an ASBO has been bro-ken' (*CCTV Image*, 2005b: 21). In this context, 'below-the-state' surveillance networks in the community are being used to enforce ASBOs, the breach of which can result in 'the ultimate sovereign sanction – the prison' (Crawford, 2006: 455). These developments reinforce the 'formalization of secondary social controls' (Jones and Newburn, 1998: 142, 2002), whereby problems that would have once been dealt with informally by caretakers or housing officers are now dealt with by 'security-oriented personnel' equipped with sophisti-cated surveillance systems and working alongside state police officers.

However, the incorporation of 'non-state', 'local state' or 'commercial' secu-rity into state policing networks is by no means straightforward. Competing organisational goals and different cultural traditions can create conflict among the actors involved in 'plural policing' and surveillance networks (Coleman, 2004). Tensions between 'public' police and 'private security', for example, have been reported by Norris and McCahill (2006) in a South London shopping mall. In theory, everything on this site was in place for 'proactive' or 'pre-emptive' policing conducted in close cooperation with the police. The CCTV operators in the control room had the facility to pull down images from the councils' network of 250 CCTV cameras on to a TV monitor. There was a retail radio link that allowed the CCTV operators to communicate with the police and other security officers working in the town centre. Also, 'public' police officers based in the local Crime Prevention Shop (located in the mall) had been given a radio handset that allowed them to communicate with security officers during unfolding incidents. However, many of the 'private security' officers at the mall reported a range of 'out-of-work' and 'on-the-job' problems with the police. These problems came to a head when one security officer was arrested for assaulting a police officer on the mall during an altercation with a customer. Following the security officer's arrest, the surveillance infrastruc-ture, which had formerly facilitated cooperation between the two organisa-tions, was dismantled. The security team removed the radio handset (which allowed the police to listen to the security officers on the shopping mall radio

---

[2]It is estimated that 'between April 1999 and June 2005, some 6,500 ASBOs were issued in England and Wales' (Crawford, 2006: 465).

link) from the Crime Prevention Shop to stop the police from 'interfering' during incidents that take place on the mall. Meanwhile, the police and the local authority responsible for managing the open-street public CCTV system in the borough responded by removing the microwave link that had allowed the security officers to access images from the borough's public CCTV system (Norris and McCahill, 2006).

Plural police property and entrepreneurial cityscapes

While the construction of CCTV surveillance networks has led to a diversification of the number of 'policing' bodies involved in the operation of 'policing-at-a-distance', this has *not* led to any radical transformation of surveillance processes in terms of *who* and *what* is seen as problematic. Such problem groups have been coined by critical social scientists as 'police property'. Categories or groups become the property of the police when 'the dominant powers of society (in the economy, polity, etc.) leave the problems of social control of that category to the police' (Lee, 1981: 53–54). As we saw in historical terms in Chapter 3, the poor, powerless and politically marginal groups formed the bulk of 'police property' whose 'disorder' was to be policed using a range of resources, including law. There is evidence to suggest this has continued in the era of partnership policing and surveillance. Empirical research conducted on CCTV operator targeting practices, for example, has shown that the gaze of both police-operated and local authority-operated CCTV control rooms continues to fall disproportionately on young, working-class males (Norris and Armstrong, 1999; Goold, 2004; see Chapter 6 of this book). Similar findings have been reported in relation to the use of CCTV surveillance systems in 'mass private property' and city centres, which also focus narrowly on the 'usual suspects'. At one shopping mall in the North of England, for example, the CCTV operators targeted 'known criminals', 'suspected drug addicts', and those 'wanted' for the breach of bail conditions (McCahill, 2002). Similarly, in her study of the use of CCTV in three different leisure centres, Wakefield (2003) reported how private security officers often aided the police in imposing bail conditions on offenders and how this reflected 'a shared sense of those who were deemed "outsiders" or "troublemakers" ... so that the movements of many individuals were tracked by the police outside the centres and the security staff within' (Wakefield, 2003: 218–219).

   Nor are the strategies pursued by commercial actors completely 'instrumental' and gutted of morally toned or punitive language (Ericson and Haggerty, 1997). The employment of 'tough-looking', ex-military personnel, trained in the use of force means that '*de facto*, many private security personnel now occupy important positions of trust and authority' (Morgan and Newburn, 1997: 139; Wakefield, 2003). Empirical research has also shown that the language used by private security officers in mass private property to describe 'out-groups' is often the same as the police officers' description of 'police property'. CCTV operators in two shopping malls in a northern city, for example, targeted young, working-class males who were described as 'scrotes', 'scumbags', 'shit', 'druggies', 'G heads' (i.e. 'glue sniffers'), and 'scag heads' (McCahill, 2002). Meanwhile, in Goold's (2004) study, CCTV operators in police-controlled systems adopted police terminology referring to suspects as 'scrotes', 'scumbags', and 'tealeafs'. Most of the operators also appeared comfortable using the police 'IC' categories, a system used by the police to classify individuals according to their apparent ethnic background (Goold, 2004: 139). In practice, therefore, the gaze of CCTV cameras in both 'public' and 'private' space is mediated by the selective concerns of the operators, who tend to disproportionately target young, working-class males (see McCahill, 2002; McCahill and Norris, 2002; Lomell, 2004; Smith, 2004; Urbaneye, 2004). Thus, while the construction of 'public–private' CCTV surveillance networks may have diversified the network of personnel involved in 'policing-at-distance', there is a shared assumption and correspondence of interests among these policing bodies about who constitutes 'police property' and should therefore be singled out for targeting and intervention.

Chapter 2 discussed how some theorists critical of the 'new surveillance' and risk paradigms sought to retain a focus on the material and ideological aspects of policing and surveillance. Indeed, for a number of these writers, the development of public–private surveillance networks have emerged within a wider political and economic restructuring of the late twentieth-century city, understood as 'entrepreneurial' (Hall and Hubbard, 1996) or 'neoliberal' in character and resulted in changes to the local state within which social democratic and representational governance has diminished (Harvey, 2005: 47). This kind of urban state assemblage has buttressed business and corporate interests in urban governance generally and the management of crime and deviance in particular (Coleman, 2004). Moreover, in these newly 'revitalised' cities it is 'the privatisation of the architectural public realm' that has led to 'an unprecedented tendency to merge urban design, architecture and the police apparatus into a single comprehensive security effort' (Davis, 1990: 224). For Davis, both public and private policing practices have intersected in the latter part of the twentieth century to produce 'fortress cities, brutally divided between fortified cells of affluent society and places of terror where the police battle the criminalised poor' (Davis, 1990: 224). Indeed, for some writers, the rise of 'defensive' urban spaces in the form of gated communities, access control points, alcohol-free zones, business improvement zones and privately owned and secured leisure and consumption areas, attest to the continuing interrelationship between policing and surveillance and the control of working-class activity and space (Coleman, 2009b).

As we saw in Chapter 3, one of the central and recurrent concerns of policing and surveillance into the early twentieth century was the control of the streets. From its inception, the 'new' police surveillance has rarely operated on its own and formed close working relations with other bodies brought into the state assemblage to engage in local governance as well cultivate intelligence gathering exercises with acquiescent communities (Gatrell, 1990; Coleman, 2004). In terms of contemporary entrepreneurial city building, some scholars have observed how the need to manage and maintain competitiveness in local urban economies has dovetailed with security and surveillance partnerships geared towards controlling petty offences and clearing city streets of human detritus and related 'obstructions' to the desired image of a crisis-free civic order. 'Visibility' in this kind of cityscape has become important in partnership-based policing strategies, raising questions concerning whose visibility and whose behaviours are deemed problematic. Youth cultures, signs of poverty (in the presence of the homeless, for example) and behaviours associated with non-consumption have been singled out for surveillance attention by networks of 'new primary definers' (Coleman and Sim, 2000; Coleman, 2005). It is these primary definers – including economic developers and business leaders – who have joined with older definers of urban order (the police and local authorities) to both reconstitute the local state and demarcate 'new' standards of behaviour in increasingly commercialised urban space. Here, the centrality of image management in promoting cities as 'desirable destinations' has underpinned local elite concerns to 'reclaim the streets' and buttressed spatial restrictions on movement, coupled with a consensus around ideas of 'civility' and 'order' within and across public and private security domains. In this context, contemporary street policing and the kinds of partnership forms of surveillance they have spawned have reflected and reinforced order-maintenance or zero tolerance approaches to crime control, as witnessed in the networked policing of 'petty nuisances' associated with begging, vagrancy and street trading (Coleman, 2004). Underpinned by academic theories such as the 'broken windows' thesis, many of these urban policing partnerships have justified their work upon the idea that serious crime results from the unchecked low-level disorder of poor street people – those 'disreputable ... unpredictable people' (Wilson and Kelling, 1982, who have turned the contemporary city into a 'frightening and inhospitable jungle'. This model has intensified order-maintenance policing in which crime and disorder become increasingly blurred and in which sovereign control over territory is aggressively maintained. This approach has encouraged the intensification of disciplinary classification that began in the first decades of the nineteenth century and was aimed at lower-class subjects. It is the 'risks' they are thought to pose that are targeted for policing as a first line of defence to the ideals concerning 'quality of life' in contemporary cities. The category of lower-class disorder 'breaks down the lines between minor infraction, minor disorder and major offence' (Harcourt, 2001: 149). As Harcourt has argued, twenty-first-century order-maintenance policing frowns upon and reinforces the disorder of street people and ignores the 'disorder' of tax evasion, insurance fraud, insider trading and police corruption (2001: 17). This bias in the formulation of 'risk' has been observed in terms of surveillance strategies designed to support vengeful street cleansing (Smith, 1996) and 'purification' (Sibley, 1996), and the more or less explicit strategy of spatial exclusion of the socially and politically marginal as a result of a reordering of the 'public' realm under conditions of urban regeneration (Harcourt, 2001; MacLeod, 2002; Mitchell, 2003; Coleman, 2004; Wacquant, 2009). In this sense, networked forms of punitive policing have also heralded a 'return' to aggressive and heavy-handed policing and surveillance of poor and disadvantaged groups that we noted as a historical feature of policing in Chapter 3. This is crucial in that surveillance strategies aimed at normalising subjects (or indeed rehabilitating them in a welfare sense) have always been patchy and contradictory regarding some of society's most vulnerable social groups. Thus, as Brown (2005) has indicated, theorists in the field have usually over-stressed *both* the 'return' of punitive strategies *and* the 'decline' of welfare or more democratic forms of control. However, at the punitive end of the spectrum, a re-emphasis on public order policing has raised questions concerning 'public belonging' and the right to the city in relation to poor, racialised minorities in particular (Coleman, 2009b; Wacquant, 2009). This has also led to increases in complaints concerning police corruption and violence aimed at the least powerful (Harcourt, 2001). While 'plurality' regarding institutional sites and policing tools may have been stressed by some, others have retained an analysis that focuses upon the ideological and structural levels of coherence across policing networks. First, on a material level and in terms of encouraging an 'extended police family' through public–private partnerships (Home Office, 2003: 54), many have argued that it is not that states are becoming less important (or ceding power through 'hollowing out'), but that they are subject to ongoing 'reorganisation' (Peck, 2001: 447). Secondly, on an ideological level, public–private alliances (constituting a state assemblage) have reinforced historically prevailing definitions of 'crime', 'risk' and 'harm' as 'emanating solely from powerless and disaffected people' (Coleman, 2004: 227). We shall further explore the social impacts of these differentiating surveillance practices in Chapter 6.

However, contemporary urban management strategies and associated policing schemes are subject to local variation. Global prescriptions of change, whether formulated in terms of a 'risk society' or a 'new punitiveness' have failed to connect supposedly global transformations to the level of local expression regarding the emergence of policing and surveillance partnerships in specific places. Indeed, and once again, as we already stressed, these 'new' targeting practices are best seen as mediated by 'existing' social relations and local cultural traditions. For instance, empirical research has shown that 'front-line' practitioners in criminal justice agencies and security networks continue to be guided by the 'old' concerns of 'welfare' and 'reform' (Kemshall and Maguire, 2001). Research on the operation of CCTV systems in mass private property has shown that while some CCTV operators may use 'economic' forms of reasoning (Garland, 2001), choosing to monitor 'vulnerable' targets and 'time periods' rather than individual suspects, others continue to work with the old 'welfare mentality', empathising with the plight of local working-class youths (McCahill and Norris, 2003c). When asked by local police officers to remotely monitor a 'black' youth, for example, one CCTV operator in a South London shopping mall said: 'this Nicky Green needs a job man. He's gonna spoil himself, you know. If he had a job he'd be a nuisance to no one' (McCahill and Norris, 2003c: 29). In another study, it was reported that when low-paid, low-status, mainly working-class security officers found themselves using CCTV surveillance systems to monitor their own locales and neighbourhoods, they were not always willing to cooperate with the police. Thus, when 'wanted' persons were identified on the cameras at Housing Estate Mall, the security officers decided not to contact the local beat officer. As one security officer said: 'I wouldn't grass (i.e. pass the name of a wanted suspect on to the local beat officer) on Tommo 'cause he's all right, he's never given me any bother. Anyway, he's off the smack now' (McCahill, 2002: 199). This, of course, was why the nineteenth-century surveillance and police expert, Edwin Chadwick, suggested that policing should ideally be carried out by anonymous state officials, 'because it decontextualized policing from local, class, interpersonal and family conflicts' (McMullan, 1998b: 118).

Summary and conclusion

As we have shown in this chapter, the construction of surveillance networks is blurring the boundaries of the 'public–private' divide along the 'sectoral', 'geographical', 'spatial', 'legal', and 'functional' dimensions (Jones and Newburn, 1998), giving rise to a *plural policing continuum*. At the *state-power* end of the continuum, central state actors ('geographical'), publicly funded out of taxation (sectoral), with a legitimate monopoly of coercive powers (legal), use surveillance systems to monitor public space (spatial), with the aims of identifying, apprehending and punishing known offenders (functional). In contrast, at the *private-justice* end of the *plural policing continuum*, private security officers sell their services in the free market, armed only with the powers of ordinary citizens, and use surveillance systems in a 'proactive' way to enforce the internal rules of the organisation, rather than state-based norms of apprehension and punishment. Within this continuum there is, of course, enormous scope for diversity and complexity in the policing of 'public' and 'private' space. For instance, policing activities in many cities across the UK now mirror those of the shopping mall, with open-street public space CCTV systems being used by 'state' and 'non-state' actors in a 'pre-emptive' way to monitor and exclude undesirables from the new spaces of consumption.

However, while drawing attention to 'empirical complexity', we would also suggest that there are some broader political and structural processes shaping the actions of those involved in the operation of 'plural policing' networks. As Kevin Stenson (2005: 280) has argued, it would be 'naïve to present state agencies as simply operating on a common plane of security provision alongside the commercial sector'. Indeed, as we saw in the case of policing 'domestic extremists', the police (often working closely with government departments and commercial interests) have accelerated and intensified 'new surveillance' techniques in order to monitor and contain threats to the 'national interest'. Thus, with their symbolic power, legitimacy claims, huge command over resources and information, and key position as a 'back-up of last resort', it would be 'implausible to reduce state organizations ... to the status of equivalent nodes in the market for security' (Stenson, 2005: 273; Crawford, 2006: 459). We should not be surprised to find, therefore, that while the expansion of surveillance systems may often be driven by 'beyond-the-state' interests of 'loss prevention', 'risk management' and 'commercial image', these systems can be easily and routinely co-opted for traditional policing. Thus, while the 'public' police may increasingly find their actions shaped by the actuarial concerns of compliance-seeking institutions (Ericson and Haggerty, 1997: 49), it could equally be argued that in reacting to the 'crime control' requirements of central state actors, 'private security' officers have added the goals of 'crime fighting' and 'law enforcement' to their central concerns of 'private justice' and 'loss prevention'.

The developments discussed here have cast critical light on the development of contemporary public–private partnerships involved in the business of surveillance and policing. We have questioned the idea of 'paradigm shifts' in both conceptual terms and in terms of understanding surveillance and policing practices as they occur on the ground. We have stressed that these developments in public/private surveillance should not be seen as polar opposites but as constituting complexly entwined policing strategies within a constantly evolving state assemblage. Thus, it is not the case that state (public) authority and power is on the decline and that commercial (private) power is increasing (or vice versa). On the contrary, the alliances and interrelationships between these two arenas (along with the tensions and contradictions within and between them) point to a rescaling and re-legitimation of surveillance practice and its concern with the 'governance of crime'. This not the same as a wholesale break with past practice. Indeed, many have argued that when exploring the 'new' urban spaces of the twenty-first century, questions concerning *who* and *what* constitutes problematic and criminal behaviour *across* the policing spectrum has remained broadly unchanged. Thus, while new surveillance technologies have continued to be inaugurated alongside 'turf wars' concerning inter-agency responsibility, these points of change and conflict have to be placed alongside the broader ideological convergence across contemporary surveillance networks within a state assemblage that remains a hub from which 'crime' is defined and pursued. In relation to the 'new urban spaces of consumption', there is little or no evidence of a 'paradigm shift' concerning the categories of plural police property, which continue to be drawn in terms of those crimes, misdemeanours and foibles of the relatively powerless – the homeless, street nuisances, petty criminals and disorderly youth (Coleman and Sim, 2005).

STUDY QUESTIONS

1 What evidence is there to support Johnston and Shearing's (2003) claim that recent years have witnessed a paradigm shift from a 'punishment' mentality towards a 'risk' mentality'?

2 Is surveillance best thought of as a 'dispersed assemblage' (Haggerty and Ericson, 2000) or as a 'widening net of state power'?

3 In the advanced capitalist cities of the west, what are some of the wider political and economic factors thought to be driving surveillance and policing? What constitute their targets, and why?

FURTHER READING

Coleman, R. (2004) *Reclaiming the street: Surveillance, Social Control and the City*, Cullompton: Willan (see Chapters 4, 5, and 7).

Coleman, R. (2009b) 'Policing the working class in the city of renewal: the state and social surveillance', in Coleman, R., Sim, J., Tombs, S. and Whyte, D. (eds), *State, Power, Crime*, London: Sage.

Crawford, A. (2006) 'Networked governance and the post-regulatory state? Steering, rowing and anchoring the provision of policing and security', *Theoretical Criminology*, Vol. 10, No. 4, pp. 449–479.

Johnston, L. and Shearing, C. (2003) *Governing Security: Explorations in Policing and Justice*, London: Routledge.

Jones, T. and Newburn, T. (1998) *Private Security and Public Policing*, Oxford: Clarendon Press.

Norris, C. and McCahill, M. (2006) 'CCTV: beyond penal modernism?', *British Journal of Criminology*, Vol. 46, No. 1, pp. 97–118.

Stenson, K. (2005) 'Sovereignty, biopolitics and the local government of crime in Britain', *Theoretical Criminology*, Vol. 9, pp. 265–287.

5

Globalisation, Surveillance and the 'War' on Terror[*]

CHAPTER CONTENTS

Questioning the 'new terrorism': surveillance before
September 11   92

The globalisation of surveillance   96

The 'global integration' of discrete surveillance systems   99

The limits of global panopticism   101

Bringing the war back home   104

Summary and conclusion   108

Study questions   110

Further reading   110

*An earlier version of this chapter appeared in McCahill, M. (2007) 'Globalisation, Surveillance and the "War" on Terror', in M. Mullard and B. Cole (ed.) *Globalisation, Citizenship and the War on Terror*. Cheltenham: Edward Elgar Publishing, pp. 212–232.

OVERVIEW

Chapter 5 provides:

- An historical overview of the relationship between 'terrorism' and 'surveillance'
- An examination of the 'global diffusion' of surveillance and the integration of discreet surveillance systems
- A focus on the limits of 'global panopticism', which argues that the rapid diffusion of new surveillance measures is unlikely to have the desired impact on 'global terrorism'
- A look at how surveillance measures introduced to prevent 'terrorism' are being deployed to monitor the wider civilian population

KEY TERMS

- Biometrics
- Bringing the war back home
- Globalisation
- Immigration

- New terrorism
- Patriot Act
- Pre-emptive surveillance
- Racial profiling

This chapter aims to explore the relationship between 'globalisation', the 'war on terror', 'surveillance' and 'citizenship'. First, in keeping a critical focus on 'continuity' as well as 'change', this chapter aims to show how the rapid increase in the use of 'new surveillance' technologies has been driven by wider global trends which pre-date the 'war on terror'. Secondly, following the attacks on September 11 in the USA, the chapter traces intensifications of these developments as the 'rush to surveillance' has become a 'global' phenomenon (see Ball and Webster, 2003; Lyon, 2003a). Thirdly, the chapter draws upon theoretical debates on 'panopticism' and 'post-panopticism' to argue that the rush to a 'technological fix' may not have the desired effects in terms of preventing 'global terrorism'. Finally, we argue that the 'globalisation' of surveillance may have serious unintended consequences which threaten civil liberties and community cohesion.

Questioning the 'new terrorism': surveillance before September 11

Surveillance discourses around 'terrorism' have been central in framing responses to political violence. A key discursive construction at work here has been the commonsense assumption that following the attacks in the USA on September 11

2001, 'everything changed'. This view was lent support after the terrorist attacks in London in 2005 when the then British Prime Minister Tony Blair stated that 'the rules of the game have changed' (*Daily Telegraph*, 16 September 2005). In this climate, government spokespeople, security experts and media narratives have increasingly sought legitimacy and wider public support for a range of new surveillance and security measures framed within a discourse of a 'new terrorism'. It has been argued that this 'new' discourse 'is not simply extending into national policies about immigration, detention, identity cards, policing and surveillance; it actually appears to be driving them' (Mythen and Walklate, 2006: 129). Within this discursive framework, it is argued, 'exceptional' circumstances call for 'exceptional' measures, hence the rapid introduction of new legislation (e.g. The Patriot Act in the USA), 'new' practices (e.g. detention without trial, 'shoot to kill' policies and developments in paramilitary policing), and the deployment of powerful technologies (CCTV, biometrics, message interception, data mining, etc.). These kinds of measures, deployed in the 'new' surveillance landscape, have been characterised as following a 'pre-crime logic' (McCulloch and Pickering, 2009) similar to Bogard's ideas of pre-emptive surveillance found in Chapter 2. The aim of 'pre-empting the threat of terrorism through disruption, restriction and incapacitation' are also evident in restrictions on association with groups defined as terrorist and 'the criminalization of a wide range of conduct, not necessarily linked to any violent act' (McCulloch and Pickering, 2009: 633). For Ericson (2007b), this has shifted surveillance and policing to a logic dominated by prevention at all costs and promoted practices that undermine the maxim of 'innocent until proven guilty' enshrined in due process.

However, the rapid introduction of new legislation and surveillance practices in response to 'terror' is not an entirely new phenomenon. Consider the UK reaction to Feinian bombings in 1883, for example, when Parliament introduced the Explosive Substances Act, or the introduction of new legislation and surveillance practices in response to the 'troubles' in Northern Ireland during the 1970s. The Prevention of Terrorism (Temporary Provisions) Act (PTA) 1974 was subject to a mere 17 hours of debate in the House of Commons before its new powers were approved. In this instance, 'Parliamentary debate was driven by the public outrage caused by the Birmingham pub bombings which resulted in the deaths of 21 people and the injury to a further 180' (*The Guardian*, 11 September 2002). As Paddy Hillyard (1993: 2) has pointed out, the British state's response to the 'troubles' in Northern Ireland during the 1970s constituted 'part of a much longer line of exceptional measures directed against Irish people'. Indeed, measures such as the PTA consolidated a much longer historical trajectory in constructing the Irish community in Britain as 'a suspect community' and 'subject to wide powers of examination, arrest and detention' (1993: 257). Thus, as McCulloch and Pickering have argued, it is important to connect the policing and surveillance strategies indicative of a 'new terrorism' with the latter's 'historical antecedents'. Pre-emptive strategies of containments, disruption and aggressive policing connect 'to the long established history of liberal democracies to deny rights to identifiable groups both at home and in "their" colonies on the basis of a wholly imaginary inferiority or dangerousness' (2009: 639). Similarly, Brown (2002) has argued that strategies of excessive and 'exceptional' surveillance and punishment date from the nineteenth-century colonial context (in British-controlled India, for example), and connect to contemporary strategies in that 'severe, repressive penal practices sustained by images of the "criminal other"' remain 'central to modern states' *development*' (2002: 419, emphasis in original). Furthermore, as Hillyard (1987: 307) has pointed out, exceptional measures (or aspects of them) can and do become normalised into 'ordinary' criminal justice and legislative practices so that these 'exceptions' find expression in 'circumstances for which they were never intended'.

Furthermore, as Norris et al. (2004) have pointed out, the first large-scale public space CCTV surveillance system deployed in the UK was erected in Bournemouth in 1985 when the town was hosting the annual Conservative Party Conference. This followed an attempt by the IRA to assassinate the Prime Minister (Margaret Thatcher) and her cabinet by blowing up the conference hotel in Brighton at the previous year's conference (Norris et al., 2004: 111). These developments accelerated during the 1990s when 'new' surveillance technologies were introduced in a number of major cities in response to 'terrorist' attacks. The original catalyst for CCTV expansion in central London, for example, came in 1993 in response to the IRA's terrorist attack on Bishopsgate (Norris and McCahill, 2006). In 1995, CCTV was deployed throughout urban public transport networks in Tokyo following attacks by followers of the Aum Shinrikyo cult using sarin nerve gas (Sorensen, 2003: 3). In the same year, laws governing the use of surveillance in public places were significantly relaxed in France amidst fears of urban unrest and terrorist attack (Anon, 1994).

The measures introduced in the Patriot Act in the USA in 2001 (e.g. wiretapping, widening government access to data held by Internet Service Providers, etc.) are not entirely new either. As Haggerty and Gazso (2005) point out, the FBI and the National Telecommunications and Information Systems Security Committee had a long list of desired surveillance-related measures long before the events of September 11. These included legal enhancements to their wiretapping capabilities and provisions for governmental agents to compel Internet Service Providers to provide information on their customers. As Haggerty and Gaszo (2005) have explained, these measures were recycled from earlier legislative efforts which were said to be essential for the international 'war on drugs' or 'money laundering'. Following the attacks on September 11, these measures were quickly introduced by the government against a background of widespread fear among the general population over the potential threat of further terrorist attacks.

The 'war on terror' is, for some writers, bound up with wider transformations in 'penality' which has been taking place for a number of years. David Garland (2001), for example, has argued that over the last two or three decades there has been an increasing recognition on the part of central state actors in western societies that they are unable to exercise sovereignty over the problem of crime, particularly as it takes on characteristics associated with globalisation ('money laundering', 'international drugs trade', 'terrorism', etc.). The government response to this predicament has resulted in a series of policies that are highly contradictory. Garland notes that on the one hand the state appears to be attempting to reclaim the power of sovereign command by the use of phrases like 'zero tolerance', 'prison works', 'tough on crime', and 'three strikes'. However, at the same time there has been an attempt to face up to the predicament and develop new pragmatic 'adaptive' strategies, including the shift towards 'risk management' and attempts to devolve responsibility for crime control to the private sector and the wider civilian population. As Norris and McCahill (2006) point out, however, it seems clear that one of the main reasons for the rapid increase in the use of 'new surveillance' technologies in recent years is because they manage to straddle these conflicting discourses on crime control: 'on the one hand, the "sovereign state" approach with its "expressive" gestures and "punitive" sentiments, and on the other, the "adaptive" strategies with their emphasis on "prevention" and "partnership"' (Norris and McCahill, 2006: 100).

Such adaptive strategies are consistent with the 'pre-crime logic' mentioned earlier, and are evident under the US Patriot Act of 2001 which aims to 'pre-empt' crime through 'message interception'. The same can be said of the Computer-Assisted Passenger Prescreening System (CAPPS), which performs a 'risk assessment' and assigns a score to passengers entering the USA. Other 'pre-crime' or 'adaptive measures' include 'responsibilisation' strategies, which are increasingly addressed not to central state agencies such as the police, 'but *beyond* the state apparatus, to the organisations, institutions and individuals in civil society' (Garland, 1996: 451; O'Malley, 1992). In the United States, a whole range of 'watch programs', such as 'CAT Eyes' ('Community Anti-Terrorism Training Institute'), as well as more diffuse campaigns of 'citizen awareness', encourage members of the community 'to be alert for "anyone who does not appear to belong"' (ACLU, 2004: 7). These developments are mirrored in the UK with the launch by Scotland Yard of the Life Savers campaign, which asks people 'to consider whether the behaviour of those they encounter, through work or socially, gives them any reason to think they night be planning terrorist attacks' (*The Guardian*, 22 March 2004). As Peter Clarke, the Deputy Assistant Commissioner of the Metropolitan Police put it, 'all communities have a role to play in tackling the terrorist threat' (*The Guardian*, 22 March 2004). Further evidence that crime prevention today involves a whole range of agencies 'beyond-the-state' was also evident in the aftermath of September 11 when central state authorities quickly compiled data from a whole range of 'private' surveillance systems and databases to track down those involved in the attacks (Haggerty and Gaszo, 2005).[1]

---

[1]Once again, we can question the novelty of these developments because there is a long history of cooperation between central state actors and private-sector surveillance programmes. For instance, during the Cold War US telegraph companies (Western Union, RCA and ITT) provided the government with copies of cables sent to or from the United States everyday (ACLU, 2004).

At the same time, however, government responses to the threat of 'terrorism' also reflects the 'sovereign state' approach, with its 'expressive' gestures and 'punitive' sentiments. As David Lyon (2003b) points out, these include the 'swashbuckling words' used by politicians which 'go hand-in-hand with a willingness to place suspects in a Cuban prison camp' (2003b: 103). Similarly, the network of surveillance cameras known as the 'ring of steel', which was introduced in response to the IRA's terrorist attack on Bishopsgate to monitor the entrances to the City of London, could be seen as a 'symbolic gesture' designed to reassure international finance about the security of the city (Norris and McCahill, 2006). Moreover, in the 'global media age', 'expressive gestures' and 'punitive sentiments' send messages to those beyond the confines of national borders. As Baker and Roberts (2005: 123) have argued, the political slogans associated with the 'new punitiveness' (e.g. 'three strikes and you're out', 'life means life', etc.) travel easily across national borders and have become familiar features of the penal landscape. It could be argued that a similar process has occurred with the global 'war on terror', which, like the 'new punitiveness', arises in response to exceptional cases, becomes highly mediatised and gives rise to a number of control measures in different national jurisdictions (Baker and Roberts, 2005: 133). The rapid dissemination of 'ideas', 'images' and 'news' via the mass media means that 'distant events' can have significant 'local impacts'. The power of synoptic surveillance is pertinent here too in promoting the surveillance agenda. For example, the way 'dominant media representations of radical Islam have de-humanized and demonized in equal measure' has been used as a means of 'encouraging the public to accept a separation between rational western citizens and a monstrous terroristic Other' (Mythen and Walklate, 2006: 131). Simplistic and emotive synoptic representations that construct problems of 'crime', 'deviance' and 'terror' not only have the power to transcend time and space but – as noted in Chapter 2 – also have the power to facilitate panoptic expansion in surveillance technology and integration. In this respect, the images of September 11 that were constantly displayed on television screens throughout the world and the subsequent use of slogans with global currency like the 'war on terror', has taken the 'new punitiveness' on to a wider stage as the intensification of surveillance has become a 'global' phenomenon.

The globalisation of surveillance

The principal legislative response to the attacks of September 11 was the legislation entitled 'Uniting and Strengthening of America to Provide Appropriate Tools Required to Intercept and Obstruct Terrorism Act of 2001' (USA PATRIOT Act).

The legislation was introduced by House Judiciary Committee chairman, F. James Sensenbrenner on 2 October 2001 and became law 24 days later (*The Guardian*, 11 September 2002). The new powers introduced through this Act include expanded powers to require businesses to turn over records to the FBI and Internet Service Providers (ISPs) to preserve all data specific to a client or for a specified period of time. The Act also included proposals that require college and university administrators to provide authorities with any information on foreign students suspected of being involved in terrorism and proposals to make medical records of suspects available to investigators.

Following the lead shown by the USA Patriot Act, anti-terror bills that restrict freedom of expression have been introduced in Indonesia, China, Russia, Pakistan, Jordan, Mauritius, Uganda and Zimbabwe (Hamilton, 2002). To further tighten internet controls in Saudi Arabia, all service providers are now required to keep records of all internet users in order to track access to forbidden websites. Several European countries have also extended the length of time web users' data can be held by ISPs. In the UK, the Anti-Terrorism Act 2001 required ISPs and phone companies to retain traffic data for up to a year. In November 2001, the French parliament voted for a law forcing ISPs and telecoms companies to retain traffic and locations data for a maximum period of one year (*The Guardian*, 12 September 2002). The French parliament has since extended this to up to three years, and new procedures will give police access to them without the permission of an investigating magistrate (*The Guardian*, 28 July 2005). Germany had one of the strictest data protection laws in the European Union before September 11, but in October 2001 the government voted to require telecoms providers to install tapping technology for the police and security services. In Spain, since September 11 anti-globalisation protestors have complained of monitoring by security forces, who equate them with 'terrorists'. Plans being drawn up by Europol, the police and intelligence arm of the European Union, propose that telephone and internet firms retain millions of pieces of data, including details of visits to internet chat rooms, and of calls made on mobile phones and text messages. The information retained about emails will include who sent the message, where the email went, its contents and the time and date it was sent (*The Observer*, 9 June 2002). Furthermore, in response to the July 7 attacks in London in 2005, the Italian cabinet endorsed a package of measures including the easing of restrictions on surveillance of the internet, giving investigators broader access to telephone records and clearing the way for DNA samples to be taken without consent (*The Guardian*, 28 July 2005).

Since September 11 2001 there has been a rapid increase in the use of 'biometric' surveillance systems. Biometric systems rely on having access to various physical characteristics (gait recognition, fingerprint and palm print recognition, facial recognition and iris recognition) and then on algorithms that enable the verification process to be automated (Introna and Wood, 2004). An example is the 'iris recognition' system installed at Schipol Airport in Amsterdam a month after September 11 (Lyon, 2003b). As Introna and Wood (2004) have pointed out, within a few weeks of the terrorist attacks of 2001 almost 17 bills were introduced in the United States Congress, including measures to allow tax benefits to companies that use biometrics. As Bennett (2005) has pointed out, the use of biometric systems at borders in the USA began well before September 11 when, in 1997, the Computer-Assisted Passenger Pre-screening System (CAPPS) was introduced. In a typically pre-emptive manner, the CAPPS system looked at a traveller's overall flight history to flag potential security risks for more detailed baggage checking (Bennett, 2005). In 2001, the Aviation Security Bill introduced a new version (CAPPS II) which was to include all passengers, not just those with checked baggage. On 5 June 2002, the National Security Entry-Exit Registration System (NSEERS) was introduced. This system captures and archives biographic data and images of the faces and fingerprints of select foreign nationals visiting or residing in the United States on temporary visas. On 5 January 2004, this was replaced by the United States Visitor and Immigrant Status Indicator Technology program (US-VISIT) which collects biometric identifiers, fingerprint scans and digital photographs of foreigners entering and exiting the US (Bennett, 2005). This was soon followed by Secure Flight, which includes a 'passenger threat index' which evaluates the threat each passenger poses.

A number of other countries are issuing, or planning to issue, biometric passports to their citizens and biometric visas and residence permits to third-country residents. The European EURODAC system, for example, authorises the fingerprinting of all individuals aged over 14 who apply for asylum in an EU country, or who are found illegally present on the EU borders and in the EU territory. Ass (2006) has pointed out that 'the Norwegian government has made it standard procedure to X-ray photograph the hands and teeth of young asylum seekers in order to verify their age' (2006: 147). As Hayes (2006) has noted, from 2007, all EU citizens will have to be fingerprinted to get a passport and 'with some member states pushing for the introduction of biometric ID cards as well we are now fast approaching a time in which everyone in the EU will be registered and fingerprinted by the state' (Hayes, 2006: 30).

Since September 11 there has also been an expansion in the number of countries planning to introduce CCTV surveillance systems. As Norris et al. (2004) point out, while a national survey conducted in 1997 revealed that only 13 police departments in the USA were using public-space CCTV surveillance cameras, by 2001, 25 cities had installed public-space CCTV systems. In Chicago alone plans were announced in 2004 to install more than 2,000 surveillance cameras in public places (Norris et al., 2004: 111). Following the attacks in New York and Washington DC, 'industry officials predicted that the sale of CCTV surveillance cameras in the U.S. could soar to nearly $5.7 billion by the end of 2001' (Nieto et al., 2002: 32–33; cited in Norris et al., 2004: 115).

Other countries planning to introduce CCTV surveillance systems after the September 11 attacks (and fears of domestic terrorism) include India, which introduced CCTV surveillance in at least five airports (Norris et al., 2004: 118). What is more, despite being the most (visually) surveilled country in the world with around 4.2 million surveillance cameras in operation (Norris and McCahill, 2003), the response to the July 7 bombings in the UK from the mayor of London, Ken Livingstone, 'was to double the number of CCTV cameras on London's tube network and ensure there were cameras on both decks of every London bus by the end of the year' (*The Guardian*, 14 September 2005). Impressed by the speed and relative ease with which the London bombers and suspects were identified using video surveillance, the French government announced plans to install CCTV cameras in every Paris bus and metro corridor before the end of 2005 (*The Guardian*, 28 July 2005). The July 7 bombings in London also prompted the German parliament to call for increased surveillance of airports, train stations and underground networks (*The Guardian*, 28 July 2005).

The 'global integration' of discrete surveillance systems

The integration of discrete surveillance systems across different national jurisdictions is not a new phenomenon. For example, Europol was established in 1993 as an agency for intelligence exchange and gathering between European states' criminal intelligence services, such as the National Criminal Intelligence Service (NCIS) in the UK. This agency included analysis files covering drug trafficking, illegal immigration and 'Islamic extremist terrorism' well before September 11 (*The Guardian*, 10 September 2002). Similarly, the Schengen Information System (SIS), set up in the early 1990s, created a widespread network of police cooperation, data registration and surveillance across Europe (Mathiesen, 2000). The Schengen Agreement also introduced the Supplementary Information Request at the National Entries, otherwise known as SIRENE. Through SIRENE, police authorities in one country who have arrested a person who is registered in the SIS by another country, may require supplementary information, not stored in the SIS, from the latter country (Carerra, 2005). There are also plans to introduce an updated SIS II which will have a greater capacity to hold more information, including biometric information (Mathiesen, 2006: 106). Recent reports suggest that in 2007 the details of 895,000 individuals and over 17 million objects were held on the SIS central database (Mathiesen, 2006: 103). Long before September 11 2001, the 'spy system' named *Echelon*, which captures global telecommunications data, involved close cooperation between the USA, Britain, Canada, New Zealand and Australia (Mathiesen, 2006: 112).

Once again, these developments have intensified since September 11 as the construction of new forms of information-sharing and 'interoperability' has increasingly connected discrete surveillance systems across different national jurisdictions. It is reported that data on two of the hijackers involved in the September 11 attacks already existed on different databases as suspected terrorists and yet no authoritative response was mobilised (Levack, 2003). Stung by this, the US authorities set up the Total Information Awareness program (later changed to Terrorist Information Awareness), as yet another attempt at surveillance integration and governmental collaboration. As Sam Cava, director of the Department of Defence's Biometrics Fusion Centre in West Virginia has stated, 'It doesn't do to have 50 systems that don't cooperate' (*The Guardian*, 18 June 2004). Since September 11 there have been several other attempts to open up existing systems to new users. Canada and the USA, for example, have introduced Databank Integration, which aims to integrate Police, Customs and Immigration databases both nationally and internationally, including the integration of immigration, customs and visa data between Canada and the USA at foreign locations (Haggerty and Gazso, 2005).

It could be argued that for a network of relationships to be considered 'global', it must include multi-continental distances, not simply regional networks between the USA and Canada or between European partners. It has been reported that British police will be given access 'to US intelligence databases containing DNA samples, fingerprints and digital images of thousands of foreign nationals seized around the world by the USA as terror suspects' (*The Guardian*, 18 June 2004). The same newspaper reported that Canada already has direct electronic access to such FBI databases and that discussions with the UK are taking place through PITO (the Police Information Technology Organisation), about whether they should have (direct) access to US systems (*The Guardian*, 18 June 2004). Furthermore, soon after September 11 the European Union struck a deal allowing the USA to obtain personal data from the Europol law enforcement agency on suspects (*The Guardian*, 20 December 2002).

The integration of discrete surveillance systems looks set to increase in the future. One of the central aims of the EU Security Research Programme (ESRP), for example, is to achieve 'interoperability and integrated systems for information and communication', shorthand for linking national and international law enforcement databases and information systems (Hayes, 2006: 33). The ESRP is also seeking the 'principle of availability', under which all data held by a law enforcement agency in one state should be automatically accessible/ available to all the others (Hayes, 2006: 33–34). New measures proposed include widening access to the Eurodac database of asylum applicants' fingerprints from immigration authorities to security agencies. The Commission is also engaged in attempts to link national DNA databases and, in the longer term, proposes a European criminal Automated Fingerprints Identification

System (Hayes, 2006). Moreover, the Prum Treaty has opened up the prospect of 'reciprocal access to national databases' between Europe partners 'containing DNA profiles, fingerprints and vehicle registration data' (Mathiesen, 2006: 117). As Mathiesen points out, at the level of 'policy' and 'parliamentary sanction', these developments are increasingly 'de-coupled' from the nation state, giving rise to the possibility of 'global control without a state' (2006: 120). We will critically explore these developments in the next section.

The limits of global panopticism

As David Lyon (1994) has pointed out, the sociological response to the general issue of surveillance has been dominated by images of the panopticon. As we saw in Chapters 2 and 3, Jeremy Bentham's late eighteenth-century ideas concerning panoptic architectural systems of social discipline provided the momentum for the development of modern systems of social discipline applicable within prisons, factories, workhouses and asylums. As Foucault (1979) argued, the architectural design of the panopticon created a state of conscious and permanent visibility that assured the automatic functioning of self-control and self-discipline. The 'disciplinary' practices found in the institutional setting of the prison are situated at the 'sharp end' of the panopticon spectrum (Lyon, 2006b) and clearly had resonance for the 70,000 detainees (Amnesty International, 2005: 4) that were held in Guantánamo Bay, Bagram and Kandahar, Camp Bucca and Abu Ghraib, and other institutions that make up the 'global archipelago of exceptionalism' (Neal, 2006: 45). As we have already indicated earlier in the book, Foucault thought that disciplinary power was not confined to the institutional setting of the prison. Instead, he argued that the principles of panopticism served as a model for understanding the operation of power in modern societies and that these principles would 'seep out from their institutional location to infiltrate non-institutional spaces and populations' (Smart, 1985: 88).

As many writers have argued, the advent of time-space transcending technologies has reflected this dynamic, extending the disciplinary potential of the panopticon to non-institutionalised public space. Thus, while historically the 'direct supervision' of individuals was limited to the enclosed and controlled spaces of modern organisations (Giddens, 1985: 15), the development of CCTV systems in public spaces means that the 'direct supervision' of the subject population is no longer confined to specific institutional locales, nor does it require the physical co-presence of the observer. In this respect, the power of the panopticon has been dramatically enhanced by technological developments which have allowed the disciplinary gaze to extend further and further across the entire social fabric. Furthermore, the emergence of powerful computers and telecommunications networks has allowed for the systematic categorisation of whole populations and, as discussed earlier in Chapter 2, Gandy (2007) referred to this as a 'panoptic sorting'. Here, individuals – in their daily lives as citizens, employees and consumers – are continually identified, classified and assessed and the information garnered from this is then used to coordinate and control their access to goods and services. As Lyon (2003b) has pointed out, in the aftermath of September 11, the 'panoptic sort' was quickly co-opted by central state actors who used marketing devices such as Customer Relationship Management (CRM), datamining and data-warehousing to tackle 'terrorism'. The central aims of the Pentagon's Total Information Awareness (TIA) Office, set up in 2002, for example, was to create new algorithms for mining, combining and refining data that would allow them to successfully pre-empt and defeat terrorist acts (2003b: 91).

However, while the expansion of surveillance described in the previous section could be interpreted as a 'global dispersal of discipline', there are a number of problems with the ideas of 'panopticism' and 'dispersal of discipline' in relation to the 'war on terror'. First, as Haggerty (2006: 34) points out, in Foucault's work:

> The movement of panoptic principles into new settings is presented as entirely frictionless. Surveillance appears to proliferate because it represents a self-evident increase in the functionality of power. Entirely missing from this account is any sense of a surveillance politics.

We should remember, for example, that 'globalising' forces are always filtered through domestic politics. For instance, while research conducted on the rise of surveillance in Europe by the Urbaneye project found a general diffusion of CCTV throughout European society, the growth of open street CCTV systems has been restricted in a number of countries due to the legal/constitutional environment. In Germany, for instance, the Constitutional Court has declared that 'the knowledge of being under surveillance, why and by whom is crucial for a democratic society and the autonomy of its citizens' (Töpfer et al., 2003: 11). Similarly, 'in Norway ... there is a strong data protection regime that has explicitly concerned itself with regulating CCTV through a licensing requirement' (Wiecek and Rudinow-Saetnan, 2002: 11). Changes in political administrations can also reverse or halt practices and policies derived under previous political arrangements. Barack Obama's presidency in the USA in 2009 began with his intention to close Guantánamo Bay, along with the banning of torture and an end to 'extraordinary' rendition. Similar concerns arose within the political elite in Britain in 2009 with questions being raised as to the efficacy of 'the war on terror' and its implications for due process and 'normal' criminal justice functioning.

Secondly, the construction and operation of 'global' surveillance networks is shaped by the competing organisational and occupational concerns of control agents operating in different national jurisdictions. For instance, an internal note of a meeting between European and American officials in Dublin on 'the new transatlantic agenda' revealed 'that the FBI prefers to deal with individual EU states rather than Europol' (*The Guardian*, 25 March 2004). It has also been reported that even the former head of the US Department of Homeland Security, Tom Ridge, may not have had 'proper access to intelligence even from within his own country' due to the tendency of the CIA and the FBI 'to hold on to their intelligence and secrets' (Stephan, 2004).

Thirdly, while 'panopticism' and ideals of 'omniscience' may help us understand the appeal of surveillance systems for control agents, Foucaldian notions of 'anticipatory conformity' and 'normalisation' can also be questioned. As Haggerty and Gazso (2005) have argued, terrorists themselves are aware of the different configurations of surveillance and security that surround particular targets. It has been reported that Dhiren Barot and his co-conspirators went to great lengths to avoid surveillance by not using phones and sending coded emails (*The Guardian*, 7 November 2006). Similarly, in a foiled al-Qaida plot to hijack an airliner and fly it into the US Bank Tower in Los Angeles, Khalid Sheikh Mohammed recruited Jemaah Islamiyah for the mission 'because it was thought that south-east Asian hijackers would be less likely to arouse suspicions than Arab Muslims' (*The Guardian*, 10 February 2006). As Vincent Cannistraro, former director of the CIA's counter-terrorism centre explained, 'this was going to be the follow-up to September 11 [and] we weren't looking in south-east Asia. We were looking at the stereotype of Arab Muslims' (*The Guardian*, 10 February 2006).

Fourthly, as a number of writers have pointed out, Foucaldian notions on the connection between 'visibility' and 'power' can also be questioned, especially when people 'want to be seen' (Yar, 2003; Koskela, 2006). As Anne Marie Oliver has pointed out, portraits of dead suicide bombers in the West Bank and Gaza are plastered all over the walls and videos of their last interviews are on sale on street stalls (*The Guardian*, 14 July 2005). In relation to the July 7 bombings in London, she suggests that we should not underestimate the 'star factor' and the acquiring of glory that could have motivated the 'Yorkshire bombers'. Furthermore, 'it does not matter whether it is Britain or Syria or the West Bank, they are highly romantic figures ... and the fact that they carried with them credit cards and other personal ID suggests *they wanted to be known*' (*The Guardian*, 14 July 2005, emphasis added).

A final point relates to the observation that while information technologies may extend the surveillance capacities of the central state and modern organisations, it has also increased the global reach of terrorist groups, such as al-Qaeda, who can use computer and telecommunication links, email, cellular and radio networks to conduct operations over long distances while minimising the need for fixed physical presence (Paul, 2005). On 24 October 2006, in an interview, a former radical who had a self-revision process claimed that more than half of young Saudis who were recruited to embrace radical ideology were recruited through the internet. He revealed that there were more than 5,800 sites for radicals on the internet.[2] The rapid proliferation of surveillance systems may, not therefore, have a significant impact on the reduction of 'global terrorism'. However, in the following section we want to consider another issue: that once surveillance systems are introduced to monitor 'external' threats posed by 'terrorists' and other serious 'criminals', they can soon be used to monitor the behaviour of the wider civilian population.

Bringing the war back home

As pointed out earlier in this chapter, long before the so-called 'war on terror' and during an earlier phase of 'globalisation' through colonialism, new surveillance systems were often tried and tested in a colonial setting before being imported to the 'mother' country (Zureik and Salter, 2005). Zureik and Salter (2005) point to the work of Timothy Mitchell (1988), who noted that Jeremy Bentham's visit to Egypt in the nineteenth century was prompted by his desire to assist the Turkish ruler of Egypt at the time to instil obedience and discipline in the Egyptian population through surveillance techniques. Thus, Bentham's 'panoptic principle was devised on Europe's colonial frontiers with the British Empire, and examples of the panopticon were built for the most part not in Northern Europe, but in places like colonial India' (Mitchell, 1988, quoted in Zureik, 2001: 8). Similarly, in Southwest Africa early in the twentieth century and in the course of its domination of colonial populations, the German government developed a number of the techniques later applied against the Jews during the Nazi period of rule between 1933 and 1945 (Torpey, 2005: 157).

Global politics continued to shape surveillance practices during the twentieth century when external threats to the British state became inexorably entwined with internal threats to capitalism (Higgs, 2001). As Higgs (2001) has noted, with the establishment of communist regimes in the USSR and China, many of the international threats to the British state can be seen as meshing with internal opposition to capitalism posed by trade unionists, peace activists and other 'left-wing' groups. Throughout the twentieth century, paramilitary style policing and surveillance tactics have been perfected in colonial contexts

---

[2]The authors would like to thank Ibrahim Al-haidar (PhD student) for this reference.

and applied in domestic public order situations, and signalled a shift from ideas of 'minimum force' towards an emphasis on more routine levels of extreme force along with the construction 'of people as enemies, rather than suspects' (McCulloch and Pickering, 2009: 637). In the course of the twentieth century, and particularly during the Cold War, the resources and surveillance technologies at the disposal of the security forces and Special Branch in the British police were increasingly used to target dissidents and protesters as 'the distinction between geo-politics and internal class politics [became] blurred' (Higgs, 2001: 191). As Norris and Armstrong (1999) have pointed out, following the end of the Cold War, surveillance of the civilian population increased when global security companies sought to expand their operations into civil rather than military markets. Furthermore, 'Racal-Chubb, GEC-Marconi, and other high-tech companies, with their origins as defence contractors', expanded into the civilian markets of CCTV, electronic tagging for convicted offenders, intelligent scene monitoring and integrated database management (Norris and Armstrong, 1999: 33). Like current determination to employ DNA databases (Wallace, 2009) and the political desire to promote particular forms of industrial expansion (see the previous chapter on the policing of protest), many developments in surveillance and policing, purported to be in the interests of 'public safety' and 'security', are in fact part driven by economic considerations and a correspondence between commercial and government interests. Indeed, such developments have become a common feature in many advanced capitalist urban landscapes, such as the involvement of businesses in the financing and management of CCTV (Coleman, 2004), 'electronic monitoring' used in the UK to track offenders (Nellis, 2003) and 'intelligent scene monitoring' introduced on the London Underground (Heath et al., 2002).

Furthermore, the 'global war on terror' has provided a political and ideological platform to intensify these developments and led some commentators to identify the emergence of a 'security-industrial complex'. Hayes (2006: 3), for example, has argued that 'the traditional boundaries between external security (military) and internal security (security services) and law enforcement (policing) have eroded'. As part of the EU Security Research Programme, EU officials have promised Europe's biggest arms and IT companies substantial funding to ensure that they can compete with US multinationals (Hayes, 2006). Arms companies have also been joined in the emerging 'security-industrial complex' by the IT sector and its large multinationals, the IT revolution having thrown up novel possibilities for the surveillance of public and private places. For Stephen Graham (2004), the blurring of 'external' security and 'law enforcement' is becoming visible at the urban level 'as globe-spanning, geostrategic concerns blur into very local, urban spaces, [and] all of a sudden it seems normal for Western cities to face a palpable militarization previously more common in cities of the global South' (2004: 12). Police chiefs in Liverpool, for example, are planning to use unmanned aerial vehicles (UAVs) similar to those used by the CIA to assassinate 'terror suspects' and innocent villagers in Afghanistan (Hayes, 2006), 'to hover over problem estates as part of plans for Britain's first "yob squad" to tackle anti-social behaviour' (Lusher, 2006). These developments had already taken off in the USA when in April 2006 police used unmanned 'surveillance drones' to monitor a large gathering of bikers in Charles County, Maryland (Lusher, 2006). As Graham (2004: 264) states:

> Here we confront the latest stage in a long history where disciplinary devices are developed to try and assert control and dominance for colonizing powers within colonized cities being later transmuted back into 'homeland' cities by military and political elites.

The use of surveillance systems to monitor the wider population has been greatly facilitated by the broad legal definition of 'terrorism' in the 'anti-terror' legislation. The European Union's 'Framework Decision' on combating terrorism, which came into force on 1 January 2003, has a definition that includes activities designed to seriously 'alter political, economic, or social structure(s)' (Lyon, 2003b: 50). In the UK, for example, anti-terror laws are being used to arrest people protesting peacefully against arms fairs and neo-liberal globalisation. Section 44 of the 2000 Terrorism Act, which allows police to stop and search anyone in a designated area, has been used to obstruct demonstrations against the Iraq war, global capitalism and arms fairs and even those who heckled speakers at a Labour party conference in 2005 (*The Observer*, 22 January 2006). Similar concerns have been voiced by American civil liberties groups who have denounced the FBI for using new counter-terrorist powers to spy on anti-war demonstrations (*The Guardian*, 24 November 2003).

Furthermore, there is also evidence that information on a number of individuals is being stored in global 'anti-terror' databases or what we might call *just-in-case databases* (Lyon, 1994). After September 11, the EU embarked on an extension of the Schengen Information System (SIS) and proposed four new categories of people to be included: 'violent troublemakers' such as protestors and suspected football hooligans; terrorist suspects; people to be prevented from leaving the EU; and people whose visas have expired, who would be subject to arrest and expulsion (*The Guardian*, 10 September 2002). As Mathiesen (2006) has pointed out, in 2007 33,000 people were entered on the SIS database for so-called 'discreet surveillance', which holds that 'the person in question may commit a crime in the future' (2006: 104). In Canada, it has been reported that a recently constructed 'anti-terrorist' database will be used to help monitor tax evaders and catch domestic criminals (Haggerty and Gazso, 2005). Also, the photographic database of the facial recognition system in Tampa, Florida contains a list of people 'who might have "valuable intelligence" for the police' (Stanley and Steinhardt, 2002: 1). Introna and Wood (2004) have described a case at the Fresno Yosemite International Airport when 'a man *who looked as if he might be from the Middle East'* triggered the alarm of a facial recognition system and (although clearly a 'false positive') was detained and questioned by the FBI 'just in case' the system saw something they did not see. The authors wondered 'if these false positives may be stored in a database "just in case" and become targets for further scrutiny' (2004: 234).

Finally, 'bringing the war back home' is being filtered through public participation strategies which reinforce long-standing and fairly circumscribed definitions of social harm. As Andrejevic (2007) has argued, the 'war on terror' has implications for the wider process of responsibilisation (Garland, 2001) and reinforced broader trends in surveillance over criminals and disorderly individuals and groups. This is demonstrated in the various schemes designed to enlist citizens for participation in surveillance and to be 'the eyes and ears' of policing agencies (through neighbourhood watch, community safety programmes, using hotlines to report welfare benefit fraudsters, and using mobile phones to capture images of wrongdoers, etc). As noted earlier in this chapter, responsibilisation has been conjoined with 'wars on terror' and 'wars on crime' and bid 'us to do a portion of the state's safety work not only in keeping ourselves safe but also in evaluating the conduct of others' (Mythen and Walklate, 2006: 136). These ways of sharing in, and conjoining with, the act of surveillance do point to a widening responsibilisation for 'risk management'. At the same time, however, such a widening of responsibility continues to reinforce some fairly narrow definitions of the 'risks' and 'harms' to be watched out for. In terms of such developments, Andrejevic (2007: 176) has argued that:

> Entrusting members of the public with surveillance technology will encourage them to internalize the norms of state surveillance and policing: they will identify the problem the same way the police do, thanks, at least in part, to having been accorded the role of an agent of the state.

In this sense it is not only the experts who have a role in surveillance: surveillance becomes embroiled in notions of 'civic duty'. This is particularly the case in a climate of generalised fear and suspicion. One only has to think of such climates embroiled in 'wars' on 'terror', 'crime' and 'anti-social behaviour' where invitations to 'participate' unfold, raising questions about who is 'participating', who is to be monitored and with what effects upon social inclusion and citizenship? We shall explore such questions in the next chapter, but for now we can observe once again that 'new surveillance' technologies are not simply to be understood for their rationalistic or instrumental components, but instead for how they intersect with processes of moralisation (*who* and *what* is to be targeted and cast as the suspicious 'other'). As this process unfolds, further research will be required on the relationship between the encouragement of citizen vigilance and the coercive surveillance powers of the state which, as discussed in historical terms in Chapter 3 and in the previous chapter, have been targeted most heavily upon already marginalised and relatively powerless groups.

Summary and conclusion

The rapid growth in the use of 'new surveillance' technologies over the last two decades has been driven by social, political and economic forces which pre-date the 'war on terror'. McCulloch and Pickering (2009) have urged us not to see the 'war on terror' and its associated surveillance developments as isolated from the wider material and ideological developments found in both historical and contemporary criminal justice practices. They argue that both arenas have influenced, and continue to influence, each other in both international and domestic settings. They urge scholars to see connections between forms of policing directed towards marginal groups in the urban context (see Chapter 4 of this book) and international 'policing' when they ask: 'is the continued occupation of Iraq entirely different from the aggressive and militarized policing of African-American neighbourhoods in the United States or indigenous peoples are communities in Australia?' (2009: 639). This reiterates Paddy Hillyard's point made at the beginning of this chapter, in that surveillance practices developed in one context can have consequences for, and find practical application within, another seemingly unrelated one. The 'war on terror' and the manner in which it has been politically communicated reflect longer historical trends in surveillance practice and targeting. As we have seen in this chapter, since the attacks of September 11 these developments have both 'intensified' and 'globalised'. But more pertinently, they have also pointed to how the 'intensification' of surveillance has not fallen evenly on all social groups. In the immediate aftermath of the attacks on September 11 in the USA, it has been reported that up to 5,000 men, aged between 18 and 33, from Middle Eastern countries were rounded up for questioning in what was been described as 'a dragnet based on ethnic profiling, not evidence' (*The Guardian*, 22 June 2002). In the UK, Ministry of Justice statistics showed 'stop and account' powers were used by police on 2,353,918 occasions in 2007/08, with twice as many stops and searches of Asian people per head of population than of white people. Furthermore, black people were almost three-and-a-half times more likely than white people to be stopped on the street and questioned. Stop and search rates for the same period resulted in arrest in only 1% of cases (*The Independent*, 1 May 2009). Evidence such as this raises questions as to whether surveillance of this kind is, in its own terms, 'effective' in reducing 'risk' and targeting 'the right people'. However, focused on here have been the detrimental social impacts of such measures upon already existing social divisions.

In fact, outside the UK, ID cards have become associated with police abuses and repression of minority groups. Mouloud Aounit, the secretary-general of the French anti-racism group MRAP, argued that the cards 'aren't in themselves a force for repression, but in the current climate of security hysteria they facilitate it'. He also stated that 'young people of Algerian or Moroccan descent are being checked six times a day' (*The Guardian*, 15 November 2003). In relation to the use of automated surveillance systems at border controls, Lyon (2003b) has argued that 'racial profiling' is being coded into the software and has given rise to a new category of suspicion – 'flying while Arab' (2003b: 99). For more affluent, low-risk populations, on the other hand, the same technologies used at airports and borders, actually speed up their travel through various fast-tracking programmes for frequent travellers. In Amsterdam, frequent travellers can purchase a fast pass called Privium, which utilises 'iris recognition' technology to allow them to enter the country through a kiosk turnstile without talking to an immigration officer. For the cost of membership and a short interview, Privium members may check in late at close parking facilities, enjoy increased velocities through security and immigration checks and enjoy VIP lounges with air-side access to their flights (Adey, 2004). Thus, while 'low-risk' passengers enjoy all the privileges of 'speedy global-local citizenship', others may have to endure the indignity of being taken out of the queue for a more detailed examination in the form of 'more direct forms of scrutiny, such as strip searches, interrogation, incarceration, and deportation, and more sustained forms of immobility' (Adey, 2004: 207). In the context of the 'war on terror', airports have become experimental sites in 'new surveillance' and it is important to think of the impacts of surveillance here as reinforcing broader political and economic restructuring through which consumer-based notions of citizenship, individual 'choice' in mobility and consumption are being redrawn. Thus, 'inequalities evident in airport security are reflective of wider societal changes to sort or differentiate movement into fast- and slow-moving groups' (Adey, 2004: 207) in a way that reflects and reinforces wider patterns of social discrimination.

Empirical research on the 'social construction of suspicion' in the post-September 11 environment is ongoing, but research has began to unpack its likely contours and subsequent impact on wider social and community relations. If 'new surveillance' technologies are used to target disproportionately many innocent individuals because they fit the profile of 'terrorist', further alienation is likely to occur as ideological 'fence sitters' begin to take sides and loose collectivities become more cohesive groupings whose unwarranted targeting reinforces the view that they do not 'belong'. In both its synoptic and panoptic aspects, the 'war on terror' (like that of the 'war on crime') presents a danger in being oriented towards an intensified punitiveness though which practices designed to pre-empt all possible threats fail, not only on their own terms, but in terms of their failure to 'challenge the assumption that exceptional times with exceptional risks make the unacceptable acceptable' (Hudson, 2009: 721). Surveillance and penal excess in these circumstances shift the meaning and practice of justice, posing new risks in blurring distinctions between rule by law and rule by terror (2009: 711). In this sense, as many have argued, the war on terror and kinds of surveillance this has encouraged present a danger in corroding liberties and rights for innocent and guilty alike, and in which state and non-state actors conjoin to undermine democratic principles and 'thereby do the terrorists work for them' (Grayling, 2009: 57). Divisive and simplistic representations that depict 'Us' and 'Them' may only fuel illiberal, divisive and controversial practices – from Control Orders to such practices as stop and search and fast- and slow-tracking controls on mobility. Furthermore, increases in racial violence aimed at Muslim groups have been reported in the context of 'the war on terror'. Indeed, this relatively hidden impact of the 'war' has been compounded by underreporting in a context where Muslims perceive the police to be 'anti-Muslim' (Institute of Race Relations, 2007). It is these kinds of under-explored, relatively hidden and divisive social impacts of surveillance which we consider in the next chapter.

STUDY QUESTIONS

1 Draw up a list of the surveillance measures that have been introduced since 9/11. Is the introduction of these surveillance regimes a 'new' phenomenon or an extension of existing trends?

2 Which theoretical perspective(s) within the field of 'surveillance studies' best accounts for the intensification of surveillance that followed the 'terrorist' attacks in the USA on September 11?

3 In what ways can it be argued that the contemporary surveillance of 'terror' poses mores risks to democratic values than terrorism itself?

FURTHER READING

Haggerty, K.D. and Gazso, A. (2005) 'Seeing beyond the ruins: surveillance as a response to terrorist threats', *Canadian Journal of Sociology*, Vol. 30, No. 2, pp. 169–187.

Hayes, B. (2006) 'Arming big brother: the EU's security research programme', Transnational Institute, TNI Briefing Series, No. 2006/1.

Lyon, D. (2003b) *Surveillance after September 11*, Cambridge: Polity Press.

McCulloch, J. and Pickering, S. (2009) 'Pre-crime and counter-terrorism: imagining future crime in the war on terror', *British Journal of Criminology*, Vol. 49, pp. 629–645.

6

Surveillance, Power and Social Impacts

CHAPTER CONTENTS	
'New surveillance' and the 'usual suspects'	113
The 'racialisation' of surveillance	117
The 'gendered' gaze	120
The impacts of informal surveillance	120
The impacts of formal surveillance	123
'Us' and 'them': the 'synoptic' gaze	124
The social impact of 'light touch' surveillance	129
Surveillance over the corporate realm	130
Surveillance over policing	135
Summary and conclusion	140
Study questions	141
Further reading	142

OVERVIEW

Chapter 6 provides:

- An introduction and overview of the social impacts of surveillance
- An exploration of the contextual and contingent nature of surveillance and its relationship to power
- An illustration of how the impacts of surveillance are differentiated across the social order
- A consideration of how the context of surveillance impacts on prevailing definitions and responses to crime and deviance

KEY TERMS

- Light touch surveillance
- New surveillance
- Social divisions

- Surveillance reach
- Synoptic gaze
- Usual suspects

The previous two chapters on policing and terrorism have already highlighted evidence concerning how surveillance, whether 'new' or 'old', is not a blanket exercise applied uniformly across the social terrain. This evidence challenged some of the assumptions found in Chapter 2, where some writers had spoken of the emergence of a 'new surveillance'. Some aspects of the 'new surveillance' literature are problematic not least in terms of ideas concerning the 'automation' of surveillance leading to a 'non-discriminatory' rationale for monitoring. As Lianos and Douglas stated, 'we have the opportunity to experience forms of control that do not take into account any category of social division' (2000: 266). In this chapter these arguments will be further scrutinised by continuing our focus on 'continuity' alongside 'change' in thinking about the practice of surveillance. Indeed, 'new surveillance' technologies and practices reinforce existing social divisions along the lines of class, ethnicity, age, gender and sexuality. First, it is argued that in the context of criminal justice and policing, the gaze of 'new surveillance' technologies continues to fall disproportionately on the 'usual suspects' and in doing so reinforces conventional and commonsense notions of crime, criminality and deviance. Secondly, far from reducing 'victimisation' and 'insecurity', the precise use of these new technologies within particular social settings can actually exacerbate existing insecurities for vulnerable groups. Thirdly, and in contrast to the monitoring of marginal groups, the quality and the quantity of surveillance over 'the powerful' also has social impacts in terms of the ability of the latter to elude processes of categorical suspicion and forms of disciplinary surveillance found in relation to other less powerful social groups.

This chapter will develop these points and explore the differential social impacts of surveillance while remaining focused on its uneven social reach. We wish to emphasise here a continuum of surveillance practice, beginning with those targeted at the formal and routine end of this spectrum (the power-less) before moving on to those targeted at a more informal, or what we call 'light touch', end of the continuum (the powerful). From whichever end of this spectrum that surveillance is undertaken, social impacts are evident on the life chances of those surveilled in terms of access and control over particular spaces, goods, services and upon particular working practices. Social impacts emanating from surveillance are also evident in terms of how societies come to understand, frame and respond to 'the crime problem' as well as the prob-lem of 'victimhood'. These impacts may be intended or unintended and reflect and reinforce relations of power that shape the habits and life chances of both 'the powerless' and 'the powerful', with distinct consequences for these groups not least in terms of whether or not we come to see them as 'criminal', trustworthy or suspicious and therefore deserving of particular kinds of surveil-lance. Thus, 'regardless of the domain, new surveillance systems often amplify existing social inequalities *and* reproduce regimes of control' (Monahan, 2008: 217, emphasis added) concomitant with the status and political-cultural capital held by particular social groups.

'New surveillance' and the 'usual suspects'

Gary Marx (2002) has noted that whereas the 'old' surveillance involved 'close observation, especially of a suspected person', the 'new surveillance' targets whole groups and populations. A perfect example of this phenomenon is the emergence of 'blanket DNA testing' of entire communities where everyone in the town or village is treated as a 'suspect' until the 'risk profile' proves other-wise (McCahill and Norris, 2003b). Similar arguments can be made in relation to the emergence of 'dataveillance', with reports suggesting that, in the UK, information is held on each citizen on approximately 700 databases (*BBC News*, 13 July 2006). However, while 'new surveillance' technologies clearly expand the potential for surveyors to monitor or collect data from large numbers of people, there is a growing body of empirical research which suggests that monitoring does not fall equally on all members of the population. This dis-proportionality has an historical lineage and, as discussed in Chapter 4, a relationship to the operation of plural policing and surveillance networks in contemporary urban contexts. In this section, we can begin to unpack the social impacts of these differential control measures. For example, in their observational study of open-street CCTV surveillance cameras, Norris and Armstrong (1999) illustrated how the operation of these systems leads to the over-representation of young, working-class males. Teenagers, for example, while accounting for less than 15% of the population, made up nearly 40% of those singled out for targeting by CCTV operators (1999: 109). Moreover, the targeting of this group was prompted 'not because of their involvement in crime or disorder, but for "no obvious reason" and on the basis of categorical suspicion alone' (1999: 197). Norris and Armstrong concluded by suggesting that the disproportionate targeting of the socially and economically marginal means that open-street CCTV systems 'rather than contributing to social justice through the reduction of victimisation ... may become a tool of injustice through the amplification of differential and discriminatory policing' (1999: 201).

As research on the use of CCTV surveillance systems and 'private security' in shopping malls has shown, the security officers target 'known criminals', 'suspected drug addicts', and those 'wanted' for the breach of bail conditions (McCahill, 2002; Wakefield, 2003). The use of CCTV cameras by private security to disproportionately target and exclude 'marginal' populations from the 'new spaces of consumption' draws our attention to competing definitions of risk and safety. Many of those who support the introduction of CCTV surveillance systems have made special reference to how such systems create a safer environment for women and children (see Coleman and Sim, 1996: 17). The managers of one mall in a northern city, for example, worked closely with the police on a Safe Child protection scheme which encourages children who become detached from their parents to go to a member of staff in any of the shops displaying the Safe Child sign in their windows. However, the management and security team had also implemented a formalised exclusion policy which aimed to keep school children out of the mall during school hours. This 'raised the question of whether school children were being excluded from what could be seen as a relatively safe environment (a busy shopping mall full of other people and patrol guards) to the "less-safe" spaces of public streets' (McCahill, 2002: 147). Furthermore, the use of exclusionary practices in shopping malls situated on deprived housing estates raises other questions. For instance, 'how do those who are banned from the semi-public space of the shopping mall gain access to basic public goods and services (Job Centre, health centre, etc.) which are provided on private property from which they are denied access?' (McCahill, 2007: 14).

In the context of 'criminal justice', 'new surveillance' technologies also fall disproportionately on marginalised groups. It has been reported that 40% of black males have their profiles stored on the UK's National DNA Database, compared with 9% of white males (McCahill, 2007: 12). Some estimates suggest that by 2010 over half of all black men will be on the database (*The Observer*, 27 May 2007). As a number of writers have pointed out, these practices are likely to reinforce inequalities in the criminal justice process. In relation to violent and sexual crime, the Canadian writers, Kubanek and Miller, have argued that:

> A DNA databank could only be effective if most violent crimes were committed by convicted repeat offenders. But most sex offenders have never been convicted. Men with the most privilege in society are even less likely to have been convicted. However, we know from the experiences of women, that those men are not less likely to have offended. At present, Native men, men of colour and poor men are jailed in Canada at a rate far out of proportion with Canadian demographics. Because their DNA would dominate the DNA databank, using such a databank to identify perpetrators of crime would reinforce and even promote more inequality in our justice system. (Kubanek and Miller, 1997, cited in McCahill and Norris, 2003b:133)

In other areas of criminal justice, it has been reported that over half of those subject to the surveillance practices of the Intensive Supervision and Surveillance Programme (ISSP) (e.g. electronic monitoring, drug testing, voice verification and face-to-face monitoring by probation officers) are unemployed with poor literacy skills (Youth Justice Board, 2006). While the 'new surveillance' is often said to indicate a shift away from the old 'normalising' strategies of social control, many of these practices are pervasive and retain an emphasis on transforming the behaviour of individual offenders. Norris (2007: 154), for example, has argued that the surveillance practices incorporated in the Government's Persistent Offender Strategy (GPSOS), including early intervention programmes, counselling sessions, treatment regimes and drugs detoxification, are all 'embedded in deeply disciplinary regimes, aimed directly at "training the soul"'. The increasing possibility of combining remote forms of electronic monitoring with GPOS, meanwhile, is likely to extend the 'temporal range' of surveillance by providing 'round the clock knowledge of an offender's location' (Nellis, 2007: 11). In terms of 'social impact', it has been reported that electronic monitoring (EM) and 'home curfew' systems can exacerbate 'family tensions in already unstable homes for juvenile offenders' (Paterson, 2007: 324). As the field officer in one study explained:

> The amount of domestics that were caused and things like that was unbelievable, and then you've got to go into the middle and try and sort it out. A lot of people when they argue, want to get away from each other and when you don't have that option you're pretty restricted, aren't you? (Paterson, 2007: 324)

The last decade or so has also witnessed the introduction of a whole range of 'community initiatives', including 'acceptable behaviour contracts', 'Anti-Social Behaviour Orders (ASBOs)', 'dispersal orders' and 'parenting orders'. As Crawford (2006) has argued, these measures have seen the British state become 'engaged in ambitious projects of social engineering' and once again these strategies fall disproportionately on working-class communities. In his research on the use of ASBOs, for example, Campbell (2002) found 'that more than 60 per cent of the ASBOs examined in the survey were associated with people manifesting very obvious social or mental problems, chiefly linked to drug or alcohol abuse' (in Hughes, 2007: 127). According to Rodger (2008), many of the strategies used as part of 'community safety' and 'civic renewal' programmes rest upon a major paradox in that while the central aim was 'to build social capital and trust in communities beleaguered by anti-social behaviour' (2008: 167), the strategies for doing so (CCTV, ASBOs, Community Wardens) actually aroused 'a sense of suspicion', placed 'neighbour against neighbour', and divided the community 'between "established" and "outsider groups"' (2008: 167).

Over 30 years ago, Damer (1974: 203) warned how the inhabitants of extremely deprived housing estates (living in what he called a 'dreadful enclosure') can often collude with their own negative label and 'retreat into the womb of their houses whence they view the outside world of their neighbours with fear and suspicion' (see also Taylor, 1999: 118). In the context of community initiatives involving the introduction of 'new surveillance' technologies, Monahan (2006) has written about the 'feelings of fear, anxiety, and discomfort' expressed by those monitored by surveillance systems in 'low-income housing projects' (Monahan, 2006, in Cunningham and Noakes, 2008: 188). Furthermore, in one deprived housing estate in the UK which had introduced a communal television aerial system to allow the tenants to watch the images displayed by the CCTV cameras on their own TVs, the surveillance infrastructure only served to exacerbate existing social problems. As the CCTV control room staff explained:

> 'Some of the residents with "mental problems" will sometimes sit and watch Channel Nine (the tenants communal television aerial system) all day and scare themselves to death thinking someone's gonna come and get them'.

> 'What's happened in the odd block is some people sit and watch Channel Nine all the time, find out who's going out and then go and do [burgle] their flat.' (Cited in McCahill, 2002: 172)

In focusing on this research, we have begun to deconstruct the manner in which the social impacts of surveillance often fall disproportionately upon already vulnerable groups. In many instances, then, the impacts of surveillance on such groups are highlighted in the form of exclusions, emotional or psychological instability, or through having a disruptive and disorganising impact on lives and life chances. Typically, these kinds of impacts derive from situations in which surveillance is developed through a 'top-down' approach or even where it is imposed upon subject groups with little or no space for negotiation in relation to a surveillance regime.

The 'racialisation' of surveillance

Over the last 200 years, surveillance practices have fallen disproportionately on members of ethnic minority communities. As we saw in Chapter 3, the development of surveillance within the social relations of capitalist modernity took place alongside concerns to regulate and control poor mobile populations. In Republican France in the latter half of the nineteenth century, 'gypsies' and 'nomads' were subjected to intensive surveillance through the use of ID cards, anthropometry, and mobile police squads who took photographs of any 'nomads' or 'romanies' travelling the countryside (Kaluszynski, 2001). As Kaluszynski (2001: 131) has pointed out, here for the first time we saw the collection and collation of dossiers 'based on categories attached to "racial characteristics"'. The surveillance of 'mobile populations' was also a concern of the British authorities in 'colonial' India where British conceptions of criminality and racist evolutionary ideas combined to criminalise the activities of 'nomadic traders', 'gypsies' and 'pastoralists' (Cole, 2001: 96). As Cole points out, 'the empire served as a laboratory in which criminological theories and techniques were discovered, developed and tested for eventual application on the common criminal back home'. This included the British system of fingerprint identification which 'was rooted in colonial governance' (2001: 96). As Mark Brown (2005) has argued, the legacy of colonial forms of rule is still evident in contemporary surveillance and punishment practice. This is particularly so in relation to the use of imprisonment and zero tolerance forms of policing which, in targeting 'suspect communities' (for example, Blacks in the USA and UK, and Aborigines in Australia), exclude subject groups from civic and political participation. In this sense, targeted surveillance of whole communities is not only disproportionate but has the impact of suspending – temporarily or permanently – the extensions of liberty to particular groups.

These historical accounts on the 'restrictions of movement' continue today through the use of surveillance and screening at 'borders', which 'often disproportionately impact upon ... non-white travelers' (Finn, 2008). As Cagatay (2006) has shown in his study of the surveillance regimes used to monitor Turkish migrants living in Germany, the surveillance and policing of 'global migrants' is pervasive. Drawing upon the work of Bigo (2005), Cagatay shows how this surveillance includes 'administrative networks' of 'customs officers, immigration officers, consulates, private transport and security companies, national police forces and gendarmes'. The 'global migrants' in his study are also subject to various forms of 'interface surveillance', including computing, video-surveillance, genetic tests, fingerprint identification systems, and biometrics. A whole range of 'files' and 'dossiers' are also stored in local residents' registers, central foreigners' registers, central employment registers, central work permit registers. Finally, they are subject to various 'ordeals' (Nock,

1993), including medical examinations, practical examinations, loyalty declarations, compulsory integration courses and conscience tests (Cagatay, 2006).

However, it is not just 'global migrants' who are subject to intrusive levels of surveillance. In the UK, the disproportionate surveillance of minority ethnic groups by police officers using 'stop and search' powers has been well documented. As Phillips and Bowling (2007: 434) have pointed out, the highly discretionary powers enshrined in the 'sus' law were 'used extensively and often arbitrarily against black communities'. While 'sus' laws have since been abolished, the 'ethnically coded' statistics on the use of 'reasonable suspicion' have revealed 'a clear picture of disproportionality' which 'persists to this day' (2007: 435). The authors point out that in 2004 'black people were 11.5 times more likely to be stopped and searched than white people and Asians twice as likely' (2007: 435). The statistics on searches under The Criminal Justice and Public Order Act (see section 60 which allows a search 'without suspicion' for some serious crimes), reveal that in 2001/02 'black people were 28 times more likely to be searched and Asian people 18 times more likely to be searched than their white counterparts' (2007: 435–436).

Given these figures on the use of police 'stop and search', it is not surprising to find that the electronically mediated gaze leads to disproportionate targeting. As Norris and Armstrong (1999) have shown, CCTV operator targeting practices lead 'to the over-representation of men, particularly if they are young or black' (1999: 196). In one of the three case studies in their observational research, it was reported that 'the selection of Black youth was not just a matter of operator discretion but a deliberate matter of policy' because the control room shifts were told that 'the priority target was ... black youths and the priority crimes drug-dealing and street robbery' (1999: 125). Disproportionate targeting on the grounds of 'race' have also been reported by Benjamin Goold (2004: 157), who found that black people were four times more likely to be targeted by CCTV operators than we would expect from their number in the total population.

Following the terrorist attacks in New York on September 11 2001 and in London on July 7 2005, surveillance of minority ethnic groups has intensified (see Chapter 5). The bombings carried out in London on July 7 2005 were immediately followed by intense media and political attention which focused on the potential 'radicalisation' of British Muslim youth. In 2007, the Muslim Council of Britain warned that a whole 'generation of young Muslim men is being criminalised' (Spalek and Lambert, 2007: 12). Indeed, before the attacks of 2005, police statistics of stop and searches under counter-terrorism legislation revealed that in 2002/03 'the number of stops and searches of Asians had increased by 302 per cent in a year compared to a rise of ... 118 per cent for whites' (Spalek and Lambert, 2007: 12). This uneven impact of surveillance became 'writ large through the seven-fold increase in the number of Asian people stopped and searched by the British Transport Police following the

July 7 bombings' (Mythen and Walklate, 2006: 132). The powers of 'stop and search' have been applied during street encounters between the suspect population and the police and decisions have often been heavily influenced by the historically evolved discretionary powers and subjective evaluations of the latter. However, many contemporary surveillance practices have been conducted not by human agents but by the use of biometric devices, computer profiling and other 'automated' surveillance systems. As Lianos and Douglas (2000) have suggested, the proliferation of 'automated socio-technical systems' has meant that subjective evaluations and discretionary powers are becoming much less significant as 'deviants' and 'law-abiding citizens' are replaced with efficient users of 'the system'. But 'is it possible that subjective evaluations can be inscribed into an algorithmic formula?' (McCahill, 2002: 192). As we have argued already, empirical research had found that discriminatory practices can become an in-built feature of some automated surveillance systems. Indeed, in their research on facial recognition systems, Givens et al. (2003: 2) examined a data set of 2,144 images (two images for each of 1,072 people) and concluded that 'white subjects are harder to recognize than Asian, African-American or other subjects, even when the system is trained with racially balanced data sets'.

What impact is the intensification of 'racialised' surveillance and the ensuing 'culture of suspicion' likely to have on community relations? In mid-twentieth century America, J.H. Griffin (1960), in his book *Black Like Me*, described black people's experience of a 'racialized' surveillance when he spoke of the widespread use of the 'hate stare' directed at them in the American South (in Haggerty and Ericson, 2006: 14). As Finn (2008) has shown in her research on the experiences of young South Asian women living in America post 9/11, the 'hate stare' has recently returned to the United States. Many of the young women in this study spoke not about databases or ID cards, but about the feeling of being watched or 'stared at' by their fellow Americans. The 'culture of suspicion' post 9/11 is increasingly evident in a number of countries and is compounded by government campaigns designed to mobilise 'active citizens' to play a part in the 'war on terror' (Chan, 2008). As Chan (2008) argues, campaigns concerning the 'imminence of terrorist attacks' increases levels of 'intolerance' and 'prejudice', developments that cannot be regarded as totally unrelated to the recent increase in 'racially motivated' attacks in many countries, including Australia and Britain. For Chan, these developments suggest that 'the culture of suspicion has in fact developed into a culture of hatred' (2008: 234). Mechanisms of formal surveillance, then, can feed-off and reinforce wider processes of racialisation. This has been documented in relation to how policing and surveillance can fuel social prejudices and create 'no-go areas' along with a landscape of fear and immobility for those targeted. In this way, 'otherness' is reinforced through the creation of barriers to full social participation (Gifford and Bundey, 1989).

The 'gendered' gaze

As outlined in Chapter 2, feminist perspectives have explored how surveillance operates differently for women and girls in terms of the kinds of technologies used and the spaces (both formal/public *and* informal/private) within which surveillance operates. This can be illustrated in practice, in terms of the targeting of women and how this targeting impacts upon already existing gender inequalities. In 1998 Sheila Brown argued that the relationship between 'gender', 'surveillance' and 'security' did not receive much attention in some of the early debates on electronic surveillance. Brown pointed out that men and women's experience of 'public space' and 'surveillance' was likely to be very different. For many women, Brown noted, 'feelings of extreme visibility in public space are created by the masculine regulation of the public domain' (1998: 218). In her study of women's experience of public space in the North East of England, for example, '45% had been "stared at", and 38% had been "shouted after" by men in the previous 12 months of the survey, in ways which made them feel "uncomfortable"' (1998: 212). This 'gendered' perspective on women's town-centre use led Brown to argue that CCTV surveillance cameras were likely to have very few 'benefits' for women. This is because women already police and regulate themselves by avoiding male-dominated public space, and the introduction of CCTV simply means there will be 'more men sitting in front of camera screens' adding to the 'exaggerated visibility' experienced by women.

The impacts of informal surveillance

One of the concerns expressed by the respondents in Brown's (1998: 217) study was the use of cameras in public space for voyeuristic purposes. Such informal processes of surveillance and social control have been referred to by McCahill and Norris (2003b) as the 'misappropriation of personal information' which takes place when information gathered about people 'is used in ways that are inappropriate or not in accordance with stated aims and objectives' (2003b: 134).[1] The most common form of 'misappropriation' has been reported when 'crime fighting' cameras are used to monitor women for voyeuristic purposes. As Norris and Armstrong (1999: 129) have shown in their observational study of three open-street CCTV surveillance systems, 'ten per cent of all targeted surveillances on women ... were for apparently voyeuristic reasons'. The use of

---

[1]The 'gendered' nature of 'misappropriation' has also been reported in other contexts. Holtorf (1998), for example, has stated that the Washington DC police department 'admitted that it routinely subjected urine specimens taken for drug tests from female police officers ... to pregnancy testing without their knowledge or consent' (1998: 51).

CCTV cameras to voyeuristically monitor women in 'public space' has also been reported in the USA. In Tuscaloosa, Alabama, CCTV operators used traffic surveillance cameras 'to zoom in on several college-aged women's breasts and buttocks as they walked down the street', images which were then displayed on a cable channel (Gargis, 2003). In 2004, a police officer working in the CCTV control room of San Francisco International Airport used the cameras 'to focus on women's breasts and buttocks' (*Bay City News*, 2005).

Other reports have suggested that CCTV operators have used 'public space' cameras to voyeuristically watch women in the 'private spaces' of their homes. In Liverpool, two council-employed CCTV operators used CCTV cameras to watch a woman in her home as she undressed and used the bathroom (*BBC News*, 13 January 2006). Similarly, security officers monitoring the images displayed by the CCTV cameras at the Welsh Assembly buildings 'were caught turning CCTV cameras onto nearby homes and hotels' (*BBC News*, 3 July 2007). Elsewhere, police officers in New York used the night-vision capability of surveillance cameras on a helicopter to secretly watch a man and women as they shared an 'intimate moment' on a rooftop (Dwyer, 2005). In China, CCTV operators trained a public space CCTV surveillance camera on the window of a private household for 59 minutes and 41 seconds as a woman took off her clothes and entered the bathroom (*Southern Metropolis Daily*, 10 May 2008). Voyeuristic surveillance of women in 'public space' also takes place through so-called 'up skirting' (a term used to describe taking photographs up an unsuspecting woman's skirt using a mobile-phone camera). Although it is not possible to judge how many women have been victims of 'up skirting', a cursory internet search displays hundreds of sites with many thousands of images of 'upskirted' women taken on the street, escalators, shopping centres, public transport, schools, workplaces and nightclubs. The normalised objectification and circulation of these amateur surveillance-come-pornographic images is emblematic of the cultural perception that women's bodies are public (men's) property – and is reinforced in many elements of tabloid representations of women (Saner, 2009).

Other examples include video voyeurs using 'covert' surveillance techniques to monitor women 'as they change their clothes, perform natural functions or engage in sexual activities' (Simon, 1997: 884). Examples of 'covert' cameras being used voyeuristically have been reported in Tennessee when 14 Nashville Kats cheerleaders were secretly videotaped in a dressing room (Loggins, 2002); in Atlanta, Georgia, when a woman reported that she had been filmed in a Toys R Us toilet (*Associated Press*, 11 July 2003); in Pittsford, New York, when 12 female students were filmed in a restroom (Orman, 2003); and in Adrina, Michigan, when the owner of a 'tanning room' was arrested after the police found a hidden camera (Pelham, 2004). Hillie Koskela (2000) has also illustrated these practices in relation to CCTV operators in an Australian casino who 'videotaped women in toilets and artists' changing rooms, zooming in on the exposed parts of their bodies and editing the video sequences on to one tape that was shown at local house parties' (Koskela, 2000, quoted in McCahill and Norris, 2003b: 134).

The impact of voyeuristic surveillance can have serious social and psychological consequences. From his consultation with a number of victims of covert videotaping, Simon (1997) suggests that there are four major overlapping areas of psychological damage. These include 'the development of psychological symptoms and disorders, distrust in relationships, fear for personal safety, and shame and humiliation (narcissistic injury)' (Simon, 1997: 886). In one case:

> Sexual intercourse with a co-ed was covertly videotaped by her then boyfriend using a miniature black and white TV camera mounted in a smoke detector at a fraternity house. The videotape was shown over and over to fraternity brothers, creating a sensation on campus. The sexual encounter was surreptitiously transformed into a porno flick to the horror of the victim, when she later discovered the existence of the videotape. The victim became severely depressed and suicidal, requiring psychiatric hospitalization. (Simon, 1997: 885, quoted in McCahill and Norris, 2003b: 134–135)

The information (i.e. images) produced by 'new surveillance' technologies like CCTV cameras are also *controllable and not subject to the messiness or unruliness of time* (Simpson, 1995: 158). This allows images to be 'stored' in electronic spaces (on a computer file or videotape), ready to be 'lifted out' at some future, as yet unspecified, time and place (McCahill, 2002). This 'temporal' flexibility of 'new surveillance' technologies means that these forms of voyeurism are not experienced as a one-off event or incident. As long as the recordings exist, the 'victim' of voyeurism can be 'victimised' over and over again as the videotapes, discs and images circulate freely among a wide range of potential viewers (particularly over the internet). In this respect, electronically mediated voyeurism becomes a relatively hidden yet pernicious and socially damaging element in the data flows that may arise in 'rhizomatic' fashion. As Simon (1997: 886) has argued, the 'fear of commercial distribution of the videotape may stay with victims over a lifetime' (quoted in McCahill and Norris, 2003b: 143). One victim, for example, reported how several nights a week she 'wakes up in a cold sweat with two unanswered questions on her mind ... "What has he done with those videos, and who else is he showing them to?"' (Aziz, in McCahill and Norris, 2003b: 135).

The 'gendered' nature of surveillance is also evident in relation to issues surrounding the 'informal surveillance' used predominantly by male abusers of women within intimate relationships. The advent of new technologies accessible to the population at large (such as camera phones and web-based forms of monitoring) can be used to coerce those targeted by them. Within the 'continuum of intimate partner violence', the 'degree of "surveillance" of battered women by their (primarily) male partners is extreme and their danger severe' (Campbell, 2000: 718). In these situations, perpetrators of violence against women use 'all the sophisticated electronic equipment available', such as those associated with monitoring email and phone calls in an attempt to 'never leave their partners alone with professionals' who may be seeking to help them 'or strangers' (2000: 718). Such an informal regime of surveillance can have the effects of inducing coercive psychological control as well as presenting a means of countering 'progressive' surveillance by researchers and authorities concerned with women's safety in abusive relationships. This kind of 'unseen' surveillance then can be, and is, used by mostly male perpetrators of serious social harms in order to further their sense of power, control and intimidation over their victims. As a form of controlling surveillance it also operates as a basis for opposition to other forms of surveillance enacted – at least on the face of it – by authorities concerned to protect the interests of abused women.

The impacts of formal surveillance

If perpetrator surveillance serves to undermine the autonomy of victims of domestic violence, what about formal surveillance undertaken by authorities to 'protect' such victims? A further difficulty is evident when we consider how authorised criminal justice surveillance of domestic violence is enacted under the umbrella of 'crime prevention'. Viewing domestic abuse as 'just another crime' belies the uniqueness of this form of social harm from the viewpoint of its victims and the role that formal surveillance can perform. In both the USA and the UK since the early 1990s, a process of victim recognition has taken place along with practices of criminalisation and arrest, marking a change in rendering this form of harm more visible and as a property of criminal justice and surveillance systems. However, it has been reported that as a result of official surveillance in this area, organised as part of crime prevention generally, an increase in women's insecurity can be discerned because surveillance increases the level of publicity and prosecution aimed at perpetrators (see Chesney-Lind, 2006). In this sense, the initiation of official scrutiny of domestic violence can leave women under greater threat from 'partner' abuse as the latter may become more aggressive in asserting their control. With increasing official scrutiny, victims themselves have become more likely to be arrested by police for resisting or 'fighting back' against violence (Chesney-Lind, 2006). Moreover, the application of criminally oriented surveillance and forms of state intervention that follow raises the issue of muting, through 'which the voices of the women themselves, and what they might want from the criminal justice system (if anything), is lost' (Walklate, 2008: 43).

Indeed, many women report that they want something other than what official surveillance as criminal investigation can offer: while wanting violence to end, they may not want relationships and families to be broken up by state intervention (Welsh, 2008). In the UK, for example, surveillance and preventative measures have often been used to 'lock out' abusers from homes whereby the residence of the victim becomes fortified as a 'panic room' in which the victim is imprisoned and rendered immobile under the notion of 'protection' (*Dispatches*, Channel 4, 2007). As we have seen in other contexts, surveillance has the effect of 'individualising people' (Monahan, 2006a: 12), and in the case of domestic violence this works for both perpetrators and victims. Therefore, in the case of violence against women, surveillance – as an adjunct to conventional crime prevention approaches – presents a danger in marginalising the broader issues concerning the generation of violent harms against women. By attempting to isolate, contain and criminalise male violence, a series of questions remain for how the surveillance responses of the state 'understands' and renders 'visible' the problem of domestic abuse as a gendered issue. Individualising strategies of surveillance, coupled with a criminalisation agenda, may bring some benefits in some circumstances (Chesney-Lind, 2006) but do less to address longer-term cultural and structural issues in terms of being able to offer 'either a challenge to the development and dynamics of the locations in which male power is most operationalized – the home and family – or the model of masculinity, parenting and husbanding that is learned by boys and teenage men in such locations' (Welsh, 2008: 244). The social impacts of surveillance in this area highlight limitations in our expectations of what surveillance can do in terms of recognising the needs of acknowledged 'victims' – not only in terms of potentially exacerbating their plight, but also in terms of undermining a wider appreciation of the causes of violence against women and what should be done about it.

'Us' and 'them': the 'synoptic' gaze

You will recall from Chapter 2 how the project of the panopticon (where the few observe the many) has become interrelated with synoptic processes (where the many observe the few) (Mathiesen, 1997; Boyne, 2000). The proliferation of media technologies has allowed the wider society to scrutinise the activities of the powerful, supposedly fuelled by a 'rhizomatic' levelling or 'democratising' of surveillance (Haggerty and Ericson, 2000). As we saw in Chapter 2, however, this idea is not as straightforward as might first appear. In this section, we develop this argument to show that while moves towards 'synopticism' are clearly evident, 'synoptic' and 'panoptic' regimes often combine in novel ways to perpetuate and reinforce the monitoring and surveillance of 'marginalised' groups. As we saw from Chapter 3, negative portrayals of 'working-class youth' and the 'degenerate poor' in the mass media date back at least as far as the early nineteenth century when stereotypical accounts of the 'Great Unwashed' dominated in Victorian England (Pearson, 1983). The twentieth century also witnessed a whole series of 'moral panics' in relation to 'working-class subcultures', which led to calls for more intensive policing and surveillance of these populations (Cohen, 1971). It was noted in Chapter 3 how the middle classes were more likely to come across the 'criminal classes' in newspapers and periodicals than on the street. Early media constructions of the crime problem depicted the latter as a uniquely lower-class phenomenon and deserving of punitive responses. These trends have continued in recent media portrayals of 'new surveillance' technologies which have often deployed a discursive strategy of 'positive self-presentation and negative other-presentation' (van Dijk, 1998: 61). We can illustrate the use of this discursive strategy by examining, first, media coverage of crime and deviance and, secondly, coverage of 'visual surveillance', particularly CCTV.

We can begin here by considering the production of 'reality' TV shows that offer a synoptic window on 'the problem of crime' (as found in *Crimewatch UK*, *America's Most Wanted*, *Police, Camera, Action*, etc.). Do these kinds of TV show present us with a detached knowledge regarding 'the problem of crime', who commits it and where? What kinds of messages do such programmes relay about the powerful – in this case the police and forces of law and order? The programmes draw upon official surveillance technologies and experts (police, security personnel and crime profilers). The resulting narrative and imagery depicts crime in a particular way: through atypical and individually murderous events, or interpersonal violence and petty offences focused on the publicly visible aspects of the street. In this way, the medium of television encodes events and people in ways that supposedly reflect commonly held social values. This is achieved through over-typifying some behaviours and activities as the source of socially harmful behaviour (typically 'street crime'), while, underplaying other social harms. For Doyle (2006: 221), reality TV does not present an innocent or disinterested picture, and ties a particular visual spectacle (the synoptic) about 'the problem of crime' to moral discourses about what should be done (the panoptic). For example, in shaming particular bodies and activities, synoptic surveillance TV is 'emotive, embodied, and voyeuristic in a way that may connect it with identification with powerful authority'. Furthermore, media attention to particular crimes and individuals influences criminal justice, making it more likely that media-profiled crimes will be 'prosecuted and punished with extra vigour' (2006: 220). The social impact of this mass medium highlights the processes through which we are encouraged to 'see' – or, using Foucault's phraseology, how the 'soul' is disciplined to perceive in moral, emotive, political and cultural terms – different segments of the population through the mass media in a way synonymous with powerful and state-led definitions of 'order' and 'disorder'. The media reliance on official sources for information about crime or the 'war on terror' is productive of

Figure 6.1   How are the police watched and represented in media terms? This satirical caption highlights the incongruous idea of developing a 'Policewatch' TV programme in the same format as the BBC's Crimewatch
Source: www.guardian.co.uk/media/cartoon/2009/apr/20/benrik-pitch, accessed 20 April 2009

a surveillance discourse that relays a heightened sense of disorder and fear throughout the body politic (Altheide, 2009). A further impact results from how these fear-inducing tales of criminality and terror are often the basis for establishing the expansion of real-world panoptic surveillance, implicitly endorsing calls for more street cameras, more prisons, more data checks, and greater police powers. However, in principle, there is nothing within this technological medium to prevent police malpractice being brought into view in terms of wrongful arrest, verbal abuse and unwarranted use of violence (see Figure 6.1), but such issues have remained largely invisible and difficult to envisage as a focus for prime-time television. The police remain very much in the 'Us' category in reality TV depictions, which raises further issues concerning how the police are watched in panoptic terms outside the media. This issue is highlighted later in the chapter.

The social impact of the uses of surveillance in a synoptic medium has an effect of turning its intended targets into the category of 'other' – annulled subjects to be replayed on popular crime shows as the victims of what Foucault called 'dividing practices' (1994b: 326). Here, surveillance 'objectivises' and separates 'the mad and the sane, the sick and healthy, the criminals and the "good boys"' (1994b: 326), more often than not for the titillation, fear and entertainment of the 'law-abiding' audience. As already indicated, while synoptic surveillance relies on a diet of the 'usual suspects', reinforcing common-sense ideas of 'crime' and 'social harm', it is also skewed by what this medium renders silent and leaves relatively invisible. A further example would be how corporate wrongdoing or 'crime', committed in pursuit of legitimate goals, along with the negative and socially harmful consequences of a range of corporate action, hardly features in synoptic terms. As we shall indicate below, whether in terms of the few observing the many or the many observing the few, harmful corporate actions (deaths at work, unsafe working conditions, environmental pollution, etc.) scarcely figure in comparison to other arguably less harmful activities, such as conventionally defined crimes (Tombs and Whyte, 2007). Furthermore, the world of the private domestic sphere, where two women are murdered each week in the UK, receives little or no attention in reality media, yet it is here where feminist writers have argued that violence is endemic (Bindel, 2008).

The second issue to consider here is the manner in which 'synoptic' and 'panoptic' forces can also work together in media portrayals of visual surveillance such as CCTV. The regular media usage of CCTV footage often results in an intensification of 'panoptic' regimes directed at the poor. Government-initiated 'responsibilisation' strategies, for example, encourage the majority of 'law-abiding citizens' to watch and report on the activities of the deviant 'other' and the 'outcast' (McCahill, 2003). In the UK, television and newspapers have played a major role in these developments by attempting to encourage citizen involvement in the area of crime control. For instance, television programmes like *Crimewatch UK* and *Crimestoppers* contain Photocalls asking viewers to identify suspects from CCTV footage. In some areas, local newspapers have teamed up with *Crimestoppers* in an attempt to encourage citizen involvement in crime prevention activity. One local newspaper, for example, published 'mug shots' from video surveillance footage that was designed to encourage 'active citizens' to phone in with information as to the whereabouts of local villains (McCahill, 2002: 64):

> In one article, a local newspaper printed pictures taken from CCTV footage of a young mother and her two children with the headline: 'MOTHER FAGIN'S YOUNG HELPERS'. The newspaper reported that a mother and her two young children had been captured by a local supermarket's CCTV system 'carrying out a Fagin-style raid' in a local market town on the outskirts of a northern city. The article encouraged people to phone in with the names of the suspects who, as the newspaper put it, 'spoke in a rough Northern City accent'. The description of the woman as Mother Fagin also depicted her as 'other' and conjured up Dickensian images of the 'dangerous classes'. (McCahill, 2002: 64–65)

But it is not just 'thugs', 'binge drinkers' and 'prostitutes' that are singled out for mass media scrutiny in 'synoptic' displays of 'out-groups'. On some occasions, whole sections of what the press perceive to be aspects of 'working-class' culture are portrayed negatively and in ways that leads to a further intensification of 'panoptic' regimes directed at the poor. Thus, while it is often suggested that 'synopticism' has reversed hierarchies of surveillance by turning the 'surveillant gaze' on 'elites' and 'celebrities', even here media portrayals have a 'class-bias' which serves to reinforce existing social divisions. As Hayward and Yar (2006: 14) have pointed out, the mass media have recently turned their attention to so-called 'chavs' and 'celebrity chavs' (e.g. David and Victoria Beckham, Jade Goody, Daniella Westbrook, Coleen McLoughlin). The term 'chav', the authors explain, is a derogatory term applied to members of the working class who are perceived by 'superordinate classes' to be *aesthetically impoverished* due to their 'vulgar' and 'excessive' consumption habits ('designer sportswear', 'chunky' gold rings, 'excessive' make-up, 'sun-bed tans', etc.) (2006: 14, emphasis in original). This demonisation of working-class culture, they go on to argue, results in a 'cruel irony' as attempts by young working-class people to recreate (through dress and other symbols) the life-style of the 'celebrity chav' leads to further strategies of social control and exclusion:

> Street level attempts to mobilise cultural capital based on overt displays of designer clothing have instead inspired a whole new raft of bizarre micro social control mechanisms, including everything from town centre pubs and night-clubs refusing entry to individuals wearing certain brands within their premises (no Timberlands or Burberry) … to the recent zero tolerance policy imposed on 'designer hoodies' and baseball caps. (Hayward and Yar, 2006: 22)

As McCahill and Finn (2010) have pointed out, the interplay between 'working-class identity' and the introduction of 'micro-strategies of social control' has been noted by other writers. Rodger (2008), for example, draws upon the 'cultural toolkits' approach developed in the work of Bourdieu (1977) to suggest that cultural and class identities 'become inscribed not only on the mind … but also on their bodies' (Rodger, 2008: 67). Rodger refers to the work of Nayak (2006), who has argued that the 'body capital' of young working males (such as the 'charver' in Newcastle) has led to their exclusion from clubs and bars in the city centre (2006: 64). Nayak refers to how the 'charvers' 'hold their head' and 'arch their backs when walking' (in Rodger, 2008: 64). The targeting practices of open-street CCTV operators in UK cities are also said to fall disproportionately on those who practise the 'scrote walk' (Norris and Armstrong, 1999). As some of the CCTV operators explained, this included those who looked 'too confident for their own good' or who had their 'head up, back straight, upper body moving too much', or those who were 'swaggering, looking hard' (1999: 122). As McCahill and Finn (2010) argue, for these young, working-class males the body becomes both a 'performance' *and* a 'straitjacket' (Shilling, 2003) as the 'subcultural' attire and demeanour designed to convey resistant impressions leads to fur-ther surveillance and exclusion from the class-based behavioural perfor-mance criteria associated with the 'new spaces of consumption' managed by public-private security networks (see Chapter 4; Coleman, 2005).

As a number of writers have shown, mass media reporting on CCTV cameras has been almost unanimously supportive of the introduction of this new technology (Norris and Armstrong, 1999; McCahill, 2002; McCahill and Norris, 2002). The CCTV revolution in the UK began in 1993 when, following the tragic murder of the toddler Jamie Bulger and the ensuing 'moral panic' about 'persistent young offenders', politicians 'claimed that CCTV was a "friendly eye in the sky" that will "put criminals on the run"' (Norris and McCahill, 2006). Similarly, in the regional press, CCTV stories were dominated by local elites who used the newspapers to emphasise the positive aspects of CCTV. In his study of CCTV reporting in a recession-hit northern town, for example, McCahill (2002) found that only two (out of a total of 272) 'voices' cited in the newspaper articles were critical of the introduction of CCTV. On the other hand, newspaper reporting on other forms of visual surveillance, such as speed cameras, have presented the mass media with a problem. Because unlike open-street CCTV systems which target the deviant 'outcast', speed cameras target 'respectable citizens'. As McCahill and Norris (2002) have shown in their analysis of three English newspapers, journalists overcame this problem by suggesting that cameras that monitor 'Them' (e.g. thieves, robbers, muggers, etc.) are good, while cameras that monitor 'Us' (e.g. motorists, workers, etc.) are bad. Thus while open-street CCTV cameras were presented as 'silver bullets' that will 'crack crime' (Norris and Armstrong, 1999; McCahill, 2002), 'speed camera' stories revolved around ten 'critical' themes: speed cameras are about revenue not safety; deterrence should come before entrapment; speed cameras have no film in them; resisting speed cameras; the camera never lies, but speed cameras do; speed cameras can cause crime/accidents; speed cameras erode civil liberties; we need 'Bobbies' not cameras; speeding does not kill; and speed cameras do not target 'real' criminals (McCahill and Norris, 2002).

The social impact of 'light touch' surveillance

The examples we have looked at so far have been centred on intensive, routine and relatively normalising forms of surveillance. Those subject to such surveillance regimes are very much on the outside and in a relatively powerless relationship to the agenda-setting surveillance forums they are subject to – they have little or no influence upon it. This is in contrast to what we look at next, in the form of what we want to call 'light touch' surveillance. Light touch surveillance is most fruitfully applicable to more powerful social groups and institutions and is surrounded by different kinds of surveillance discourses and practices from those that we have examined above. It is 'light' in the sense that it has less enforcement power, less resources and less of a punitive gaze than the forms of intense and often heavy-handed surveillance we have looked at so far. This kind of monitoring was illustrated in Chapter 3 in the discussion of the historical development of surveillance over the workings of the factory system and the attempts to deal with fraud in the world of business. Light touch surveillance applies to powerful groups and institutions where it has an ambivalent role in delineating the terms 'criminal' and 'victim'; it appears less certain and assured in terms of its rules of engagement and has different consequences for powerful groups subject to it. In this sense, it appears less prescriptive than in our previous examples in this chapter and refers to situations where a less than robust gaze and punitive sanctioning regime prevails over powerful groups. Indeed, as has been argued elsewhere, the latter group have greater 'political, social, ideological and economic capital' at their disposal in order to legitimate their role as an 'inside player' with the cultural authority to shape the meaning and interpretation' of prescribed surveillance (Snider, 2009: 180). Light touch surveillance, therefore, is often 'light' because powerful groups are able to shape surveillance practice (from 'the inside'), and thus engender a 'light touch' upon how they are watched. Light touch surveillance nurtures cooperative, compliance-based and self-regulatory approaches in terms of surveillance over the powerful (Tombs, 2002) where regulators 'advise, educate, bargain, negotiate and reach compromises with the regulated' (Tombs and Whyte, 2007: 152). The reasons for why these approaches predominate are explored in the next chapter.

Importantly, as we shall see, the occurrence of light touch surveillance has substantive social impacts. This is so when we consider the role of light touch surveillance over corporate and state spaces and how such surveillance of these powerful domains may in fact fail to identity (or label as 'criminal') harmful behaviour, leaving much harmful activity relatively unchecked and outside a robust inspecting gaze. The fact that some places, people and institutions are subject to 'light touch' surveillance has implications for understanding the relationship between power, crime and mystification. As we shall see, the light touch conferred to some of the most powerful groups in modern society aids a process of under-emphasising some 'crimes' and victimising behaviours compared to 'those who are officially portrayed as "our" criminal enemies' (Box, 1983: 3). In this respect, then, surveillance in its lighter, less heavy-handed forms may obfuscate as much as it reveals *vis-à-vis* the relationship between power and crime.

Surveillance over the corporate realm

Corporations have been more successful in regulating the public than the public has been in regulating corporations. (Sutherland, 1983: 201)

Corporate crime refers to illegal acts or omissions resulting from deliberate decision-making or culpable negligence within a legitimate formal organisation. As such, acts and omissions correspond to the normative and cultural goals of an organisation and are intended to benefit it (Tombs and Whyte, 2006: 74–75). It is often implied that the massive expenditure and manpower devoted to surveillance of the 'criminal situations' found in the streets is warranted given the assumption that that is the space where society's most dangerous individuals and activities are located. It is well established, though rarely acknowledged in political, media and academic circles, that some corporate activities (whether legally sanctioned or illegal) promote some of the greatest social harms as measured in financial, social, economic and environmental costs. Indeed, these harms can and often do take on global proportions whether in environmental destruction or financial loss and injury, whose costs have been evaluated as dwarfing those incurred by conventional crime and met predominantly not by corporations themselves, but by the population at large (Reiman, 2007). Harms enacted here would include environmental devastation, loss of savings and income and deaths and injuries at work. Regarding this latter form of harm, even the officially compiled statistics in developed countries tell us that one is more likely to be a victim of lethal harm and non-lethal injury related to work than one is to be a victim of conventional crime – and that the overwhelming majority of these harms are related to violations of law (Tombs, 2007: 531). For example, in the UK for 2004–05 occupationally related fatality rates (which can be categorised as 'safety crimes') range from between 1,600 and 1,700 (excluding industrial illness and exposure). Homicide rates (as indicative of 'serious conventional crime') in 2003 were recorded at 1043, an eight-year high (Tombs and Whyte, 2007).

As we have noted, over the last 30 years there has been an explosion of interest in crime prevention discourses and practices across many countries and regions that have been underpinned by far-reaching developments in 'new surveillance' technologies. However, in the vast majority of instances there has been an absence of focus on corporate illegalities within crime prevention agendas, even though many of the new ideas and technologies currently being adopted seem suited to monitoring and preventing corporate wrongdoing (Alvesalo et al., 2006). Indeed, the expansive shift to situational crime prevention (with its three-part emphasis on disrupting criminal activity in 'place' through providing deterrence and capable guardians to surveil and report on wrongdoing) may be a case in point, as others have argued:

> If 'surveillance' and its associated technologies are often used to discipline the relatively powerless, there are conditions under which it can be progressive and ... conducted 'from below', and may be used to expose crimes of the powerful. (Alvesalo et al., 2006: 5)

Situational surveillance in the form of visual and documentary monitoring is perfectly feasible in corporate places. Law can serve the 'preconditions of corporate good-citizenship' if 'the credible means and commitment to enforce it' (deterrence) are apparent (Alvesalo et al., 2006: 6). What counts as a 'capable guardian' may be contested both in relation to street crime and particularly in corporate spaces, but the evidence suggests that a unionised workforce offers the most capable safeguard against injury and harm associated with the workplace (2006: 6). However, it has been argued that situational forms of surveillance would need – in order to be effective over the corporate realm – to be reconnected to questions of the social. In other words, the power imbalances that underpin the generation of corporate harm would need foregrounding along with 'a re-responsibilisation of the state' to take crimes of the powerful seriously as pushed for 'by local publics, worker groups and social movements' (Alvesalo et al., 2006: 9). The panoply of surveillance measures accompanying the huge growth in 'community safety' is another case in point. Urban safety partnerships, also involving local businesses, not only fund and manage surveillance projects, but are able to define 'business crime' as crimes *against* businesses and target surveillance accordingly (Coleman et al., 2005). Crucially, there may be no 'ontological reason' for situational and community safety surveillance agendas to be applied against corporate harms, but there is a palpable 'inability to re-imagine the legitimate targets of those agendas' that point to a lack of political will among policy-makers (Alvesalo et al., 2006: 2). Nor are the impediments to surveilling corporate crime to do with low-risk assessments associated with the production of harms in this arena (Croall, 2009).

Are the most harmful social events or activities subject to what we might call a 'proportionate' level of surveillance? Like the monitoring of conventional crime on the streets, one might expect a similar state orchestration of surveillance capacity geared towards corporate wrongdoing and harm – particularly in light of the costs these incur financially, socially and psychologically (Hillyard and Tombs, 2004). However, official surveillance in terms of health and safety at work displays quantitative and qualitative differences. For example, in the UK in 2007 there were around 1,000 inspectors employed by the Environment Agency and 1,600 by the Health and Safety Executive (HSE), compared to 16,000 community support officers – as adjuncts to the police – involved in the regulation and surveillance of street crime and other 'nuisances' (Whyte, 2007: 32). Consequently, on average and in terms of health and safety at work, workplaces in the UK can expect an inspection from the HSE once every 20 years.

Furthermore, and related to this, the visibility of work-based harm, compared to what we think of as conventional crime, is limited. In general terms there is a dearth of time spent on, and resources allocated to, surveillance in this area, together with the accruement of 'knowledge' about such social harms that surveillance may help bring into the public and political domain. If we return to synoptic surveillance, then, corporate wrongdoing or crime, committed in pursuit of legitimate goals (Tombs and Whyte, 2007), along with the negative consequences of a range of corporate action hardly features. As we have already seen, whether in terms of the few observing the many or the many observing the few, harmful corporate actions scarcely figure as prominently as other arguably less harmful activities. Synoptic media representations of corporate crimes tend to mollify 'the status of the businessman' and thereby do not promote 'the same organized resentment' (Sutherland, 1983: 60) that we saw in earlier examples of synoptic portrayals of lower-class and lower-status conventional criminals. For Sutherland, the power of the corporation to regulate public and governmental perceptions of itself should not be underestimated and the impact of such powerful portrayals is seen to undermine any moves to a culture where corporate crime is rendered visible and dealt with through robust surveillance regimes, due process and the rule of law.

More broadly, then, what are the social impacts of applying 'light touch' surveillance to powerful groups and spaces? First, light touch surveillance creates an uneven playing field for those firms seeking to comply with the regulatory guidance initiatives that do exist – even though these are becoming increasingly 'voluntarist' and 'self-regulating' in orientation (Tombs and Whyte, 2010a: 61). In terms of compliant corporations, they can be 'victims' of a surveillance regime characterised in general terms by uncertainty and under-enforcement: 'Good firms that invest in prevention and who give a greater priority to safety suffer a competitive disadvantage compared to those who only expend time and effort in the unlikely instance that they are caught' (O'Neill, cited in Tombs and Whyte, 2007: xvi). Accordingly, this kind of system encourages 'the good to be not so good and the bad to stay bad' (2007: xvi) with regard to safety in the workplace at both corporate and state levels. A light touch approach is increasingly aligned with self-surveillance for the majority of firms, which impacts upon the (in)visibility of corporate actions: 'Put simply, how are regulators to know about company performance if the latter are left to self-regulate, and thus able to distort or withhold evidence of noncompliance/poor performance from regulators?' (Tombs and Whyte, 2010a: 61).

Secondly, levels of surveillance have an impact on prosecution of corporate offenders. In 2004–05 the HSE prosecuted only 35% of all workplace deaths it investigated. This figure fell to just 8% in 2009 as lighter touch initiatives were instigated (Tombs and Whyte, 2010b). This has broader impacts as 'low levels of inspection, detection, formal enforcement and sanctions' in the corporate world 'ensure that safety crimes are regarded as less serious than other crimes of violence' (Tombs and Whyte, 2007: 205). And this has global dimensions in relation to the proliferation of harmful activities such as the exploitation of child labour, failing to pay a living wage, and the 'dumping' of unsafe waste products. Furthermore, it is estimated that such harms 'impact more severely on the most economically weak nations and within these on the poorest and most vulnerable workers' (Croall, 2007: 102).

Thirdly, and in developing the points made above, surveillance does not merely *react* to the problems of crime and deviance. Surveillance systems 'actively contribute to the creation of certain truth regimes (whether about innocence or guilt, trustworthiness or suspiciousness, value or liability)' (Monahan, 2008: 218) and actively construct target populations upon whom these categories can be legitimately pinned. Indeed, the surveillance assemblage that is applied to the powerful has a delineating impact in reinforcing a common perception that some forms of death and serious injury are in fact 'accidents' or 'tragic' aberrations rather than systemic processes or matters of criminal responsibility. And such a view is mirrored in cultural, media, legal and political pronouncements on the harms of the powerful (Tombs and Whyte, 2007: 71). Furthermore, 'the ideology of the accident can persist' because 'of the lack of scrutiny [and surveillance] of actual cases' – as we have seen in relation to the paucity in numbers of Health and Safety Inspectors – reinforcing how 'light touch' surveillance has the effect of representing major and often systemic social harms as one-off incidents (2007: 71). Thus, light touch surveillance of the powerful reinforces a widely held assumption that corporate crimes are accidents rather than being the result of knowingly negligent or reckless illegal activities. Applying a surveillant assemblage through the lens of 'accident' or 'unfortunate occurrence' has helped to 'obscure an inter-related set of issues around seriousness, criminality, fault, causation, and so on' (Tombs and Whyte, 2007: 72). It is not only that light touch regulation is ineffective as an impacter on corporate wrongdoing (particularly from the point of view of injured or maimed workers or members of the public) (Tombs, 2002), but also, moreover, the lack of surveillance of the powerful can lead to a situation where 'victimization is "hidden" by the construction of incidents ... as "accidents" or "disasters"' which have 'a more or less random effect, irrespective of class, age or gender' (Croall, 2007: 83). Indeed, this deficiency of surveillance in respect of corporate crime tells us very little about the processes of serial or multiple victimisation (relating to consumers, residents or workers) and how these impact on the least affluent (Croall, 2007).

This constitutes an important aspect of surveillance and relates to situations in which its 'light touch' signals a less than systematic, regular and routine form of inspection – shaped less by discourses of censure, discipline and control, as is the case with conventional crime, and more by a language of accommodation and compliance concerning the powerful. It also points to how states organise surveillance practices differentially towards crimes of the streets and crimes of the suites – each carrying different targeting strategies and messages in relation to the powerful and powerless, respectively. These differentials in surveillance and enforcement are profound for the way in which they impact upon common understandings and ideas about 'crime', 'deviance' and 'victimisation'.

Surveillance over policing

'Watching' or 'monitoring' police behaviour stems from concerns about the nature and use of police powers, and especially the effectiveness of remedies for the abuse of such powers. (Jefferson and Smith, 1985: 124)

Police forces remain one of the key surveillance institutions in the arbitration of crime and deviance. As we have already indicated in Chapters 4 and 5, police surveillance tactics have not been without controversy, raising questions as to whether they are doing more harm than good in relation to the fostering of 'good' community relations, or in respect to whether they have an impact upon levels of crime. Less attention has been directed at surveillance *of* the police, particularly in rendering their activities visible in moments of controversy (including deaths in custody, differential targeting and coercive public order tactics). Surveillance of the police and how much the public can see concerning what they do is bound up with issues of 'accountability' and 'oversight' relating to fair treatment of citizens, protecting civil liberties and human rights, and ensuring 'community safety'. However, across modern policing systems 'the modern state' has been and continues to be 'deeply ambivalent about the way in which the police should be held accountable' (Chan, 1999: 267). Ambivalence prevails in relation to if, *when* and *how* the police should be scrutinised by state and/or civilian bodies, raising questions about the limits about what the public can 'see' in relation to police work. Should the police be watched for 'wrongdoing', like other citizens? Should this watching be independent of the police themselves? Or should they just be trusted 'to get on with the job'?

These questions are thorny issues for the governance of the police institution, which has great power to shape its own representation in synoptic media characterisations thanks to the expansive public relations departments of police forces themselves (McLaughlin, 2007). Whether intended or not, such representations have a powerful effect in deflecting attention from the risks posed by state guardians to citizens in terms of deaths in police custody (over 1,000 in the UK in the 40 years up to 2006), and the 30 people shot dead by police in the 13 years up to 2005. In all these cases no officers have been convicted of causing any of these deaths (Sim and Tombs, 2008). Would greater surveillance of the police alter these harmful practices? Many of the friends and families of victims of police violence may think so, although the progressive impact as a result of watching the police appears limited. A key criticism of investigations into controversial and deadly police practices is geared around the impenetrability and information closure of the police body (see inquest.org.uk). There is an argument that poorly maintained or non-existent surveillance and regulation of the police allows spaces for crimes and misdemeanours to occur. As a charitable body that monitors deaths in state custody, INQUEST has been working with the family and lawyers of 47-year-old Ian Tomlinson, who died in the context of the heavily policed G20 protests in London on 1st April 2009 while he was walking home. For INQUEST, the incident:

> could have been swept under the carpet and the cause of his death dismissed as being from 'natural causes' without the benefit of the video footage and photographs that entered the public domain to challenge directly the police version of events. (INQUEST, 2009: 2)

INQUEST stated bluntly that:

> After working with families bereaved by deaths following police contact for 30 years it comes as no surprise to INQUEST that the initial reports of the death of Ian Tomlinson were at best partial and at worst an attempt to deflect attention from the potential wrongdoing of police officers. (2009: 8)

Surveillance of the event and potential evidence of police wrongdoing came from members of the public and *not* from official CCTV or mobile police cameras located in the city of London. Unofficial surveillance showed police striking and pushing Mr Tomlinson to the ground. Other footage showed police violence against a range of protestors and how many officers on the day where evading surveillance by the public through hiding their identification numbers and faces. This kind of surveillance operated opportunistically by the public is often referred to as 'sousurveillance', meaning 'inverse surveillance in response to surveillance by the state' (Coatman, 2009: 18) or where surveillance is lacking by the state. A good example of where this comes into its own is the policing of public order. Images from the G20 protests circulated across media outlets and had a huge impact in raising public debates about coercive policing tactics, the ambivalent role of the Independent Police Complaints Commission in investigating the police and how the police have privileged access to the media in order to construct in synoptical fashion a version of the events – which, as INQUEST notes, are often highly misleading in cases such as these. But as INQUEST and others have also noted, these debates were not the result of official surveillance footage which stayed strangely silent in relation to police behaviour. The cultivation of a public debate was a result of sousurveillance that arose to challenge official 'knowledge' of the event and was reflected in police attempts at media management. This form of *ad hoc* surveillance by the public of the police can have important social impacts in bringing debate and change to key events and institutions, but its role remains limited as it is divorced from a systematic judicial oversight of policing (Coatman, 2009). The issue of counter-surveillance will be picked again in the next chapter.

In another context, it has been argued that a regime of supervision over state guardians offers potential safeguards to police detainees. In the UK, for example, police officers have a legal responsibility to protect the health and well-being of suspects. Surveillance in this area has been seen as something with which to counter community mistrust of police officers (Newburn and Hayman, 2002). While noting some advantages in a London police station equipped with CCTV in the cells for police detainees, Newburn and Hayman (2002: 166) go further in specifying the potential in surveillance in this usually out-of-bounds area. With CCTV in custody suites, the 'possibility of "real time" independent scrutiny' exists: 'the public can watch the police'. Presently, having cameras in police cells does not reverse the power relation here – the prisoner cannot watch his or her guard in 'real time' nor have a say in the day-to-day management of such a system – which remains a police function. While a camera in a custody suite 'might provide some credible means of accountability', it 'can only be a comfort to detainees if it watches the space occupied by custodians and is tamper-proof' (2002: 164). In principle, 'the cameras could be monitored by someone other than the police'; in practice, however, 'so unusual would the suggestion be that the "citizen" could watch the state that it appears almost illegitimate – almost impossible'. Yet, 'why should this be so', particularly in the light of high levels of community mistrust of the police? (2002: 166). Watching the watchers (in this case the police) has been a contested issue since the inception of the new police in the early nineteenth century and continues to be a heated topic that has occasionally provided a platform from where challenges have been launched to the ideological power of the police in delineating what counts as 'crime' and who counts as a criminal.

However, strategies aimed at watching and monitoring state practices and harms struggle to be developed in an ideological and political context in which state servants and corporate power-brokers are nearly always viewed as the victims and rarely as the victimisers (Sim, 2000: 27). Within the cultural parameters of contemporary surveillance it is difficult to imagine 'a police officer dying on duty, or losing a limb or sight, and this not being investigated' using a panoply of surveillance powers, while at the same time 'only a small subset of occupational fatalities, and only about one-tenth of major injuries, are investigated' and even known about through monitoring techniques (Sim and Tombs, 2008: 99). Technologies such as CCTV remain broadly focused on particular kinds of spaces, crimes and criminals, and display an uneven relationship with power. As we have already noted, CCTV has been presented as imperative in solving some prominent cases (such as the murder of a child in public space). On the other hand, the same technology has been 'strangely, publicly, impotent' – for instance in the case of the police killing in London of an innocent man, Jean Charles de Menezes (Luksch and Patel, 2008: 32). It has been argued that the ability to 'see' policing in advanced democracies is being shaped by two conflicting trends. A kind of 'watching' has been established through the rise of an administrative state and managerialism, whereby computer surveillance systems and auditing oversee police adherence to rules and assess their performance in tackling crime. These kinds of managerial strategies, however, can be, and are, sidestepped in order 'to get the job done' (Ericson, 2007a: 394). On the other hand, many democracies have in the early twenty first century have developed forms of 'counter law' to the effect that police can operate more secretively and outside 'normal' oversight, and legal and work-based rules (as we saw in Chapter 5 in the 'war on terror'). The likes of Anti-Social Behavior Orders, unrestricted use of surveillance cameras, Control Orders and the working of the US Patriot Act, have fostered 'police power to target unfairly and promote injustice' (Ericson, 2007a: 389).

An appreciation of the broader context is important for understanding impacts arising from the surveillance of the powerful. Indeed, one such impact can be observed through a specific form of silencing that operates in relation to powerful spaces and activities. Indeed, as we have argued, a more ambiguous, though less penetrative and less forceful set of surveillance practices are evident both in and over the domain of the powerful. Here, harmful events occurring under the authority of a powerful body can, when subject to surveillance, be fragmented and 'reduced to a series of loosely connected, relatively minor details of an incident' that are 'often technical in nature' and devoid of a wider social context with little regard for the victims of state or corporate activity (Tombs and Whyte, 2007: 72). This form of silencing was evident, for example, in the coroner's court as the chief means of scrutiny brought to bear into the police shooting of an innocent man, Jean Charles De Menezes, in London in July 2005. On the face of it, this crucial means of scrutiny into some of the most powerful criminal justice and corporate institutions in the UK appear to hold powerful individuals and institutions accountable for their actions, in exploring 'unexplained' or 'suspicious' deaths in police 'care', in a prison or as an outcome of industrial accident or disease. However, coroners' inquests have been criticised by friends and families of those harmed and campaign groups (such as INQUEST) for, among other things, giving too much power to the coroner and not enough to the parties and the jury (in terms of seeing the evidence, arriving at verdicts, calling witnesses, obtaining legal aid, and addressing the coroner on key facts) (Ryan, 1996). Such inquests often rely uncritically upon police preparation of evidence in particular cases, sometimes impacting to limit how the police investigate themselves in controversial cases (Scraton et al., 1995). In bringing together a surveillance regime to scrutinise the police shooting of Jean Charles De Menezes, the coroner in London in 2008 instructed the jury to discount a verdict of 'unlawful killing' against the police. In keeping within a technical frame of reference, the coroner also drew a line that forbade the jury stating their reasons as to why an innocent man was killed. Instead, the jury were left to answer a series of 'yes/no' questions relating to whether the police had been 'reasonable' in their actions – including the suggestion they had been under pressure in 'the climate of fear' generated by a high state of terrorist alert.

A line was also drawn by the coroner in this case between what he saw as a 'deserving' and 'undeserving' victim in relation to the incident. This was framed by the coroner in terms of whose emotions counted when arriving at a verdict. Whereas the feelings of the mother of the deceased were marginalised as 'emotional responses ... and you are charged with returning a verdict based on evidence', the coroner asked the jury to remember that one of the police officers involved was a 'tough, fit, highly trained, mature man [who] broke down in tears' when recounting his experiences of the fatal day. He went on to state that 'this fact may assist you in assessing the depth of the emotional experience that he was going through' in relation to the events (The Coroner Sir Michael Wright, cited in *The Guardian*, 13 December 2008). The case points to the risks posed (albeit in extreme circumstances) to members of the public from state forms of surveillance and policing deemed 'exceptional' (see Chapter 5). The nature of the surveillance discourse constructed around this event was instructive as to how that event was detached from broader issues concerning institutional power and its more detrimental impacts. For example, while de Menezes was often described as an 'innocent Brazilian', within police, media and government vernacular the 'war on terror' in general and the police shoot-to-kill policy in particular were rarely the focus of critical scrutiny (McLaughlin, 2007; Hudson, 2009).

As we have indicated, surveillance over the powerful occupies a unique place within social relations. Deaths and injuries within the realm of powerful space poses questions for the credibility and legitimacy of the institution concerned and often expose to public view some damaging and extremely harmful institutional relationships and working practices. Not only is the legitimacy of powerful action often under question, but also the means by which a society holds its most powerful members to account (even render them 'responsible' or criminally liable). A focus on deaths of members of the public involving the police, for example, can potentially expose to public view a level of 'danger' and 'risk' associated with the peculiar legal wilderness and cultural context within which the police institution operates (and which are normally impervious to scrutiny). So the stakes are high when 'surveillance' is, by accident or default, brought to bear upon the powerful. Surveillance over those charged with the maintenance of order or those who manage key economic activities displays a qualitative and quantitative difference compared to the surveillance of the less powerful. Indeed, surveillance and regulatory agents have a unique relationship to the powerful and are often under great 'ideological pressure' to orchestrate a lighter touch that paves a heavy emphasis on justifying inspections, intrusions and sanctions against powerful players (Snider, 2009).

In relation to the powerful, light touch surveillance operates within and alongside different cultural sensibilities brought into play alongside the different legal rules and sanctions applied to powerful bodies that contrast sharply to those applied in the pursuit of conventional crime and the less powerful (Sim, 2009). In such cases, 'silencing' is more likely to come into play when dominant understandings of the world are upon a process of being destabilised, such as those understandings relating to routine police and corporate working rules and versions of events. In these kinds of surveillance scenarios the notions of the 'criminal' and 'victim' become problematic and fuzzy, seemingly more difficult to pin down in situations where powerful bodies and dangerous activities become fused in a manner that undermines established and commonsense understandings of how key institutions 'normally operate'. The forms of official surveillance and oversight enacted in these contexts attempt to manage controversial questions relating to state and corporate legitimacy (Burton and Carlen, 1979) and how such legitimacy translates into how societies define, pursue and sanction 'wrongdoing'.

Summary and conclusion

What we have touched upon in this chapter is how surveillance impacts differentially on the goals, values and cultural outlooks of both the powerless and more powerful groups. In relation to the powerful, there is an overlapping – or closer correspondence of interests – between surveillant authorities and the outlooks and working practices of the powerful. We explore this last point in the next chapter, but in terms of the arguments presented here, we have seen how this correspondence of interests can lead to *light touch* surveillance which impacts upon the tolerance shown in criminal justice terms towards particular harms, injurious events and dangerous practices. This can be contrasted to surveillance that differs markedly (in quantitative and qualitative terms) targeted at the powerless. As we have indicated, for relatively poor and politically marginalised groups surveillance can incur socially disconnecting effects, resulting in further criminal justice attention, criminal sanctions, social marginalisation and disruption of their life chances. However, these differences in the meaning and targeting of surveillance can be seen as two sides of the same coin. Thus, the relative lack of scrutiny over powerful groups, particularly in relation to corporate activities and the failure to mitigate harmful practices, has a disproportionate impact upon poorer communities in terms of the ill-health, economic costs and injuries that such harms bring (Hillyard et al., 2004).

In drawing attention to the social impacts of surveillance, we have at the same time retained a focus upon the reproduction of social relations and social divisions. We have maintained this focus to show how surveillance is a *dynamic process*, constantly shaping and reshaping the social world. The term 'new surveillance' offers great insights into how new technologies and rationalisations continually reshape how surveillance is practised and how its boundaries continue to unfurl. However, the term may overplay processes of change, and may even suggest clean breaks with past practice. So, by focusing on the impacts of many of these new technologies, we have seen how continuities have remained an equally important feature of contemporary surveillance, particularly in relation to its targeting *and* its role in shaping prevailing definitions of 'crime', 'deviance' and the 'victim'. This examination of the extent and limits of the reach of surveillance has, at the same time, widened the analysis towards the social ordering process and the normative rules, boundaries and sanctions in which surveillance is situated. Surveillance shapes these social orders *and is shaped by them*. To reiterate: The question of whether surveillance occurs, how it occurs and the extent of its inspecting and monitoring capacity all have to be explored in specific social relations and the kinds of power asymmetries these exhibit. So, as well as surveillance impacting upon aspects of social order and social divisions, the power relations inscribed in the latter also impact on surveillance. Surveillance shapes social order *and is shaped by it*. Exploring the social relations that constitute how surveillance is shaped, resisted and contested sheds light on how surveillance can be altered, modified and differentially experienced. We shall explore these processes in the next chapter.

STUDY QUESTIONS

1 In relation to CCTV monitoring in public space, outline the key social impacts on existing social divisions.

2 Illustrate the ways in which surveillance has unique impacts for women and girls.

3 What does synoptic surveillance tell us about 'the problem of crime' – in terms of the activities involved, where it is committed, by whom? How may synoptic surveillance reinforce or strengthen panoptic control?

4 In what sense is surveillance racialised?

5 What are the impacts of 'light touch' regulation and control upon how 'crime' and 'victimisation' are addressed in relation to powerful actors and institutions?

FURTHER READING

Croall, H. (2009) 'Community safety and economic crime', *Criminology and Criminal Justice*, Vol. 9, No. 2, pp. 165–185.

McCahill, M. and Norris, C. (2003b) 'Victims of surveillance', in Davis, P., Jupp, V. and Francis, P. (eds), *Victimisation: Theory, Research and Policy*, Basingstoke: Palgrave Macmillan.

Sim, J. and Tombs, S. (2008) 'State talk, state silence: work and "violence" in the UK', in Panitch, L. and Leys, C. (eds), *Violence Today: Actually Existing Barbarism*, London: Merlin Press.

Whyte, D. (2007) 'Gordon Brown's charter for corporate criminals', *Criminal Justice Matters*, Vol. 70, pp. 31–32.

7

'Contesting' and 'Resisting' Surveillance: The Politics of Visibility and Invisibility

CHAPTER CONTENTS

What is 'resistance'?   145

The 'everyday politics of resistance'   148

Ambiguities over resistance   153

Surveillance, 'performance' and 'display'   155

The 'Great Unwatched': power, surveillance and
invisibility   156

The role of the powerful in shaping surveillance
and 'risk'   161

Summary and conclusion   166

Study questions   167

Further reading   168

OVERVIEW

Chapter 7 provides:

- An exploration of the scope and meaning of 'resistance' and 'contestation' in relation to surveillance
- An examination of the politics of everyday resistance to surveillance
- A consideration of the ability of the powerful to shape and modify surveillance

KEY TERMS

- Counter-resistance
- Resistance
- Risk

- Surveillance conversation
- The powerful
- Visibility/invisibility

[W]here surveillance is perceived as or has the effects of control, the fact that its subjects interact and react with surveillance means that its effects are mitigated or magnified in part in relation to their involvement. (Lyon, 2007: 7)

At this stage of the book it may strike the reader that many of the theoretical perspectives we have considered have had very little to say about the 'surveilled' as a group of creative 'social actors' who may negotiate, modify, evade, deny, or take pleasure in surveillance practices. As John Gilliom (2006: 126) has stated, 'a tour of the field suggests that we have been particularly good at studying the watchers – the police, the CCTV operators, etc. – but not so good at the necessarily messier, less institutionalized, and exploratory but absolutely crucial job of studying the watched'. For instance, while studies on 'surveillance' and 'state bureaucracy' (Rule, 1973; Dandeker, 1990) have been 'marvellously suggestive for understanding the roots of contemporary surveillance', they tell us very little about 'those who are its subjects, the surveilled' (Lyon, 2007: 81). Similarly, Foucault's account of the use of 'disciplinary techniques' in penal settings was 'skewed towards the official representatives of the institutions – the governors, the architects, etc. – and not towards the voices and bodies of those being controlled' (Dews, 1987, cited in McNay, 1994: 101). Meanwhile, in 'post-panoptic' accounts of the 'data subject' (Bogard, 2006) there is a danger that 'real', 'living', 'monitored', 'tracked', 'tagged' or 'excluded' people may disappearing from the picture altogether. The ideals of 'privacy' and 'due process' have provided a powerful critique and avenue of resistance towards surveillance practices, but as Gilliom (2001) has pointed out, 'we still know relatively little about the *everyday politics of surveillance* as they are experienced and explained' both 'by those who are among the most closely watched' (Gilliom, 2001: 3–4, emphasis added) and those who are less closely watched in terms of their experience of 'light touch' surveillance.

We begin this chapter by clarifying the issues to be addressed by asking what it means to 'resist' or 'contest' surveillance. Next, we examine the 'politics of everyday resistance'. We go on to examine the ambiguities over 'resistance', before exploring the relationship between power, surveillance and the politics of (in)visibility. As Lyon has argued, surveillance is 'not a relentless or unyielding process' and in many settings 'it is amenable to modification' (Lyon, 2007: 163). The malleability and unevenness of surveillance are a consequence of the involvement of surveillance subjects and the tactics and means at their disposal to challenge or resist it. Thus, in the later part of this chapter, we focus on the varying abilities of actors to contest surveillance reach into aspects of their daily lives. What kinds of social actors and social spaces are resistive to surveillance *in a more systematic sense*? Who has the ability to contest and modify the agenda-setting *and* goal orientation aspects of surveillance systems and influence both the quantity and quality of a particular monitoring regime? Such questions will be examined in relation to powerful state and corporate actors and their capacity to temper both the meaning of surveillance *and* labels such as 'crime'.

What is 'resistance'?

As Hollander and Einwohner (2004: 534) have stated, 'everything from revolutions ... to hairstyles ... has been described as resistance'. Indeed, the concept of 'resistance' has become so widely applied that for some writers it is in danger of becoming useless as a meaningful social category. Hollander and Einwohner (2004) provide a useful starting point by suggesting that their review of the literature on resistance found two elements that were common to nearly all uses of the concept. These were, first, that 'resistance' usually involves some active behaviour (verbal, cognitive or physical) and, secondly, that 'resistance' nearly always involved a sense of 'opposition' or 'challenge' (2004: 538). However, this immediately raises the question of 'who' is doing the 'resisting' and 'who' or 'what' is being resisted? Resistance to surveillance, for example, can involve 'individuals' acting alone or 'interest groups' acting together in organisations such as Liberty, Privacy International, Statewatch and the American Civil Liberties Union (G.T. Marx, 2009: 296–297). Resistance can also go beyond the 'subject–agent relationship' and involve multiple actors working in 'surveillance authorities', 'commercial enterprises', and 'international governmental and non-governmental agencies' (Martin et al., 2009: 213).

Conceptually, resistance has been described by various authors as 'thin' (located in localised settings) and 'thick' (challenging structural power) (Raby, 2005). Others have contrasted 'resistance', as a challenge to wider power relations, with 'contestation', understood as those activities that undermine regulations and rules in a micro context (Aggleton and Whitty, 1985). Some believe the term 'should be reserved for visible, collective acts that result in social change and not "everyday acts ... that chip away at power in almost imperceptible ways"' (Rubin, 1996, citied in Hollander and Einwohner, 2004: 541). For Scott (1990), any definition of resistance should retain the 'everyday strategies' used by individuals or social groups. To dismiss these everyday strategies ignores the attitudes and behaviour expressed by many people in their everyday lives. Also, while 'everyday practices' may not challenge 'wider power relations', they can, as Gary T. Marx (2009: 305) points out, play an important part in the lives of 'subordinate groups' by 'meeting material needs and enhancing the individual's sense of dignity and autonomy'. Furthermore, 'acts of individual resistance' may be 'converted to the collective organizational responses of social movements' (G.T. Marx, 2009: 304).

As a number of writers have pointed out, surveillance is also a 'dynamic process', which means that resistance strategies are likely to involve a 'temporal' dimension with opposition coming at different stages in the surveillance process (G.T. Marx, 2009). We can use the example of CCTV surveillance cameras to illustrate the 'temporal' and 'dynamic' nature of resistance to surveillance. Empirical research, for example, has shown that resistance can take place at the level of 'adoption'. In one study on the construction of open-street public space CCTV surveillance cameras in the UK, it was found that local Labour councillors opposed the introduction of CCTV cameras because, as they put it, 'tax payers money should not be used to fund the security systems of private businesses in the city centre' (McCahill, 2002). In the same study, a successful Home Office bid by the council for a £50,000 grant to install CCTV cameras on a local industrial estate was eventually returned to the government because of disagreements over who should fund the system (McCahill, 2002). At the stage of 'data collection', resistance can come from 'subjects' who interrupt the flow of information from the body (Ball, 2005) and from 'agents' such as CCTV operators who ensure that the cameras are positioned so as not to capture specific events (McCahill, 2002). At the stage of 'analysis and interpretation', CCTV operators may choose not to report crimes observed or inform the police when 'wanted persons' are identified on camera (McCahill, 2002). Finally, in terms of the 'fate of the data' (G.T. Marx, 2009), tapes that contain footage of police misconduct may be removed (Goold, 2004) or go missing following deaths in police custody (Lewis, 2009b). We return to the issues raised by this last point towards the end of the chapter.

Defining the concept of 'resistance' becomes even more difficult when we consider the issues of 'domination' and 'resistance'. For instance, is resistance to surveillance a process that involves conflict between 'dominant' groups and 'subordinate' groups or is everyone involved in a complex network of 'power relations'? This, of course, is entirely dependent upon the theoretical approach that is adopted in relation to questions revolving around the nature of 'power' more generally. Raby (2005) makes a distinction between 'modernist' and 'postmodern' (or Foucauldian) theories on 'power' and 'resistance'. 'Modernist' theories, she explains, tend to view power as 'something that is possessed by the dominant group and wielded against the subordinate; the subordinate may, in turn, resist and attempt to seize power' (2005: 152). In contrast, with 'postmodern' approaches what is opposed is less clear because 'power is enacted by all' (2005: 162) and resistant strategies are more 'discursive', involving the 're-appropriation' of 'hate speech' or 'countering dominant definitions' with 'replacement discourses' (Raby, 2005: 154).

It is probably clear to the reader by now that our approach to the study of 'surveillance', 'power' and 'resistance' is what Raby (2005) would probably describe as 'modernist'. As we have argued throughout this book, despite some evidence of a 'rhizomatic levelling' of surveillance, the ability to conduct surveillance or to establish and legitimate a surveillance regime remains concentrated in the hands of 'dominant' groups. Moreover, as discussed in the last chapter, there is often an overlapping, or closer 'correspondence of interests', between the surveillant authorities and the 'powerful', evident in the greater tolerance and limited surveillance of the harms, injurious events and criminal activities committed by this group. This situation was contrasted to the surveillance practices targeted at the 'powerless', which resulted in further marginalisation, disorganisation and disruption of their life chances. This is not to say that official surveillance does not occur over the powerful or that 'marginalised groups' on the receiving end of surveillance are 'passive' subjects or 'docile bodies'. The 'surveilled' ('dominant' and 'subordinate') are a creative group of 'social actors' who may negotiate, modify, evade, or deny surveillance practices. However, any attempt to understand and explain the dynamics between 'surveillance' and 'resistance' has to remain sensitive to the workings of power and the different levels of social and political capital wielded by 'resistors'. Finally, while our approach might be described as 'modernist', it does not follow that we believe all activity at the 'margins' by 'resisters' is necessarily a 'good thing', as we shall argue shortly in the section entitled 'ambiguities over resistance'. Based upon our reading of the literature reviewed above, we would define 'resistance' to surveillance as follows: *Any active behaviour by individuals or interest groups that opposes the collection and processing of personal data, either through the micro-practices of everyday resistance to defeat a given application, or through political challenges to wider power relations which contest the surveillance regime* per se.

The 'everyday politics of resistance'

In his fictional novel, Nineteen Eighty-Four, George Orwell (1949) provided a 'dystopian' vision of a society in which citizens are monitored by Big Brother in their homes by a telescreen, a device which both projects images and records behaviour in its field of vision. Orwell gave the following description of this scenario in relation to *Nineteen Eighty-Four's* central character, Winston:

> The telescreen received and transmitted simultaneously. Any sound that Winston made, above the level of a very low whisper, would be picked up by it; moreover so long as he remained within the field of vision which the metal plaque had commanded, he could be seen as well as heard. There was of course no way of knowing whether you were being watched at any given moment. (1949: 4–5)

Despite this totalising vision of the power of surveillance, one issue that is often overlooked in commentaries on Orwell's book is how Winston Smith managed to engage in a number of 'avoidance' strategies to evade the gaze of Big Brother (see Marks, 2005). Winston was aware, for example, that 'by sitting in the alcove' of his room and 'keeping well back', he 'was able to remain outside the range of the telescreen' (1949: 7). These 'avoidance' strategies allowed him to scribble notes in his secret diary out of the view of the telescreen (1949: 82). Orwell's fictional novel also provided evidence of 'masking' or 'subterfuge', including when Julia, Winston's lover, wrote the words '*I love you*' on a folded scrap of paper and surreptitiously slipped it into Winston's hand (1949: 112). In public space, Winston and Julia chose to have their first meeting in 'Victory Square' to meld into the crowd and avoid the telescreens (1949: 119). Winston also adopted a 'social face' to avoid drawing the attention of the authorities. This took place during the state-controlled exercise regime that was monitored on the telescreen in his flat (1949: 39) and in 'public space' where 'to look round was to show guilt' (1949: 124). In the end, of course, Winston Smith's attempt to think for himself fails and he is crushed into conformity by the surveillance state. Nevertheless, Orwell was drawing attention to the possibility of the 'everyday strategies of resistance' (Scott, 1990) that might be carried out under the nose of a totalitarian state regime.

Resistance to centralised bureaucratic surveillance regimes has also been reported in the academic literature on surveillance regimes in a number of former communist countries in Eastern Europe. Pfaff (2001: 401) argues that despite the existence of 'panoptic' surveillance in the former German Democratic Republic (GDR), 'the regime apparently failed to produce genuinely disciplined subjects and unintentionally produced its own kind of deviance and dissent'. Pfaff (2001: 397–398) draws our attention to other research conducted on the former Eastern Bloc which has shown how a 'second society' developed in which 'people went along with official life, while ignoring its meanings, escaping into their own free time where they did as they pleased; getting drunk with colleagues at a state rally, knitting or reading the newspaper at mandatory political assemblies'. Similarly, in the context of the former 'Leninist' regimes in the USSR, Jowitt (1992) has spoken of the emergence of a 'ghetto political culture' in which people retreat from politics and the official sphere in order to minimise 'the "regime's interference in one's private life"' (Jowitt, 1992: 80).

'Everyday' resistance to state surveillance regimes has also been found in 'western' societies in the context of penal institutions and bureaucratic welfare regimes. Goffman (1961) found that even in the 'total institution' of the asylum the inmates managed to carve out 'free places' where they engaged in activities such as drinking alcohol or playing poker. Similarly, Sykes (1958) points out that despite the guns and the surveillance and the searches in New Jersey State prison, 'the actual behaviour of the inmate population differs markedly from that which is called for by official commands and decrees' (1958: 42). Gilliom (2001: 6), meanwhile, in his study of 'welfare mothers', has shown that while some groups may resort to the language of 'rights' and 'privacy', those at the sharp end of surveillance monitoring may engage in the 'quiet practices of everyday resistance and evasion to beat ... the powers of surveillance'. Gilliom (2001) argues that poor and underprivileged people often lack the resources to organise formal protests and resistance campaigns. Instead, they resort to *ad hoc* resistance techniques, including food stamp fraud and withholding information from the welfare administration.

Returning to our central concern, which is the use of 'new surveillance' technologies in the context of policing and criminal justice, we now want to focus on the following question: to what extent have the 'dialectics of disguise and surveillance' been transformed by electronically mediated power relations? To help us answer this question we turn to the work of Gary T. Marx (2003), who has come up with a useful typology of potential responses to surveillance. These include 'discovery moves', 'avoidance moves', 'piggybacking moves', 'distorting moves', 'blocking moves', 'breaking moves', 'cooperative moves', and 'counter-surveillance moves'. Those deploying 'discovery moves' and 'avoidance moves' attempt to find out if surveillance is in operation and then find ways of avoiding it. Examples of 'avoidance' include security officers using visits to CCTV control rooms to identity 'blind spots' on the ground so that they can avoid the managerial gaze when patrolling the mall (McCahill, 2002); 'homeless' people 'confining themselves to liminal spaces – the edges, the dark corners and the hidden recesses' (Doherty et al., 2008: 300); and young people in Glasgow arranging fights outside the CCTV cameras (Ditton, 1998). In some contexts, 'avoidance' strategies can become more 'organised' and 'collective'. As Monahan (2006b: 517) has reported, in the USA, the Institute for Applied Autonomy (IAA) has published a website called 'iSee' which provides users with street maps of Manhattan so that they can avoid public space CCTV cameras by mapping 'paths of least surveillance in urban areas'.

Those seeking to avoid surveillance may also choose not to 'raise the red flag' by changing any behaviour thought likely to trigger surveillance. In Sheffield, for example, groups of young black males explained how they would split up into smaller groups or travel separately 'rather than risk antagonising the police and receiving unwanted attention from other people in the Sheffield public' (Taylor et al., 1996: 218). Others may avoid interacting with 'known shoplifters' who are likely to trigger suspicion and targeting from CCTV operators (Ditton, 1998: 413). In contrast, 'piggybacking moves' (Marx, 2003: 377) aim to avoid surveillance by attaching oneself to a 'respectable' or legitimate' subject, perhaps arriving at a 'surveyed' space with 'non-deviants' or those thought unlikely to attract the attention of the surveyors.

Those deploying 'distorting moves' attempt to 'manipulate the surveillance collection process such that, while offering technically valid results, invalid inferences are drawn from a test or inspection of an attribute or behaviour' (Marx, 2003: 378). An early example of 'distortion' is provided by Joseph (2001: 171), who reports that in late Victorian Britain suspected criminals would 'curve their body to change their height (vaulting) or control their abdominal muscles (trickery) in attempts to fool people taking their anthropometric measurements'. In 1913 at Holloway Prison in the UK, suffragettes pulled funny faces or refused to keep still so that photographs taken by Scotland Yard 'would be ruined and no use for identification purposes' (www. notbored.org/suffragettes). Those subjected to surveillance by modern CCTV systems are also aware of the surveillance camera's constant gaze. In his observational research of the operation a shopping mall CCTV control room, for example, one of the authors reported how 'known offenders' would adopt a 'social face' in an attempt fool the CCTV operators:

> Dawn follows Sharon Brown on camera as she walks across the car park towards the estate. Sharon Brown turns and waves to her two friends but after walking a few more yards doubles back and starts to walk back towards the centre. (McCahill, 2002: 124)

Those deploying 'blocking moves' 'seek to physically block access to the communication or to render it (or aspects of it, such as identity, appearance or location of the communicator) unusable' (Marx, 2003: 379). As Hayward (2004: 187) points out, 'simply putting on a hooded jacket or balaclava can be an extremely effective precaution against CCTV surveillance – just ask any football hooligan or anti-capitalist rioter'. Similarly, strategies are deployed by internet users who use cryptography to curb the surveillance of their online activities or 'masking moves that are designed to feed meaningless data to monitoring tools' (Dupont, 2008: 257). These methods include downloading software (The Onion Router, Freenet, Psiphon, etc.) and using other strategies to 'thwart surveillance attempts by randomly routing the information their members want to send or receive through other members of the network, thereby making it impossible for supervisors to know who is effectively communicating with whom about what' (Dupont, 2008: 271).

The crudest form of neutralisation, as Marx has pointed out, are 'breaking moves', which simply aim to make surveillance devices inoperable or compromised in some way. In one study on the use of CCTV surveillance in the workplace, a security manager at a manufacturing plant 'described how some of the CCTV fuse boxes had been "tripped out" in suspicious circumstances' (McCahill, 2002: 165). The opposition to speed cameras in the UK, meanwhile, has led to cameras being destroyed by 'being pulled down by tractors, set afire with a fuel-filled tyre' and 'destroyed with shotguns and even dynamite' (Wells and Wills, 2009: 262). In Greece, it has been reported that 180 CCTV cameras have been burnt by radical groups (Samatas, 2008: 359). The previously mentioned Institute for Applied Autonomy have published on their website a document entitled the 'Guide to Closed Circuit Television (CCTV) destruction':

> The methods described are placing around cameras plastic bags filled with glue, affixing stickers or tape over camera lenses, shooting cameras with children's high powered water gun toys filled with paint, temporarily disabling lenses with laser pointers, cutting CCTV cables with axes or garden tools, and dropping concrete blocks on cameras from rooftops. (Monahan, 2006b: 521)

'Cooperative moves' usually involve collusion between the 'surveilled' and the 'surveyors' and have been reported in a wide range of contexts, from the 'workplace' to 'policing' to the former 'communist' regimes in Eastern Europe. As Rosenberg (1996) has pointed out, while dating a radical leader of the Student Solidarity group in Poland during martial law, General Jaruzelski's daughter used her 'chauffeur-driven car to transport clandestine Solidarity activists from one hiding place to another' (Rosenberg, 1996: 227). In the context of 'policing', Ericson and Haggerty (1997: 139) reported how police officers, worried about been filmed speeding, persuaded the installer of a video surveillance system in police cars 'to remove the speed display for the police vehicle, so that only the speed of the oncoming vehicle would be registered'. There is also evidence in the UK that some police officers manage to avoid the gaze of public space CCTV by giving a signal to CCTV operators to move the cameras away from potentially sensitive incidents (Norris and Armstrong, 1999). As Marx (2003) pointed out, 'collusion' is particularly characteristic of control systems where agents 'sympathise with those they are to surveil'. For instance, in one study of the use of CCTV in the workplace, the security officers were perfectly happy to ignore the activities of 'the lads', which involved 'lifting stuff over the fence', and 'nipping for a pint' during the night shift. However, the same security team were willing to spend over £2000 on covert surveillance equipment designed to catch the 'Vending Machine Thief', a white-collar worker suspected of stealing from a vending machine in the general office block (McCahill, 2002).

'Counter surveillance' involves turning the tables on those who do the surveillance. Steve Mann's 'Shooting Back' project, for example, utilises 'wear-able, high-tech surveillance devices to take video footage "shots" of security personnel and other workers in privately owned stores and shops' (Monahan, 2006b: 523). As Monahan points out, this counter-surveillance intervention is explicitly conceived as an art project that appropriates surveillance technolo-gies to challenge their dominant meanings and uses' (Monahan, 2006c: 524). The monitoring of the powerful has been facilitated by the proliferation of video cameras that allow the general public to tape instances of police brutal-ity (Haggerty and Ericson 2000: 618). The most infamous case took place on 3 March 1991 in the USA when George Holliday used a video camera to film black motorist Rodney King being battered by four white police officers of the Los Angeles Police Department. The resulting two-minute footage showed that King 'was hit 56 times with a baton, leaving him with 11 skull fractures, brain damage and kidney damage' (Wazir, 2002: 26). However, questions have been raised concerning the extent and effectiveness of such counter-surveillance and the cultural and legal capacity of police officers to evade or neutralise. We shall return to these issues at the end of the chapter.

Other forms of counter-surveillance include the use of information technology to propagate dissent and resistance to oppressive forms of government and/or harmful corporate conduct. These are important forms of counter-surveillance and, in the field of corporate watching, include *Hazards.org*, a web-based maga-zine concerned to get 'behind the company safety hype, and give answers ... to workplace problems' in using 'a global network of union safety correspondents' to provide information that corporations do not provide (see: //www.hazards.org/abouthazards/index.htm). Another example, is *Nocards.org*, whose 'efforts are directed at educating consumers, condemning marketing strategies that invade shoppers' privacy, and encouraging privacy-conscious shopping habits' (www.nocards.org/press/overview.shtml). Such forms of counter-surveillance may be fairly localised in their targets, but all stand outside, and in opposition to, official surveillance and information sources. They also attempt to 'empower' various public and community groups, not through state- and corporate-sponsored surveillance measures but in opposition to them. Another example of this kind of surveillance is www.fitwatch.blogspot.com/. Fitwatch was established in the UK to monitor and evade the surveillance activities of police Forward Intelligence Teams (FIT). Participating groups range from climate protesters to football fans who use the website as a resource to counter what they see as harassing and intimidating police surveillance within the public order situations we discussed in Chapter 4. Fitwatch encourages direct action against the police in the UK, 'making it harder for the police to film and gather intelligence' for their databases by blocking police photographers and photographing the police. These kinds of resistive surveillance measures destabilise official and media constructions of the 'public interest' in relation to surveillance and its uses. For those involved in these monitoring initiatives, the goals of surveillance are characterised as socially progressive in relation to the kinds of visibility they promote for workers, consumers and local campaigners, as is the case with *Scorecard.org*. As Monahan (2006a: 20) has illustrated, Scorecard 'collects and disseminates information about toxic releases in local neighborhoods' and 'assigns blame for environmental contamination' and aids the organisational support for local people concerned to monitor corporate activity in their area. In providing some level of amendment to asymmetries in official surveillance power and information brokering, such counter-surveillance has been defined as 'democratic, participatory, localized, and open to alteration' (Monahan, 2006a: 21).

Ambiguities over resistance

As Henry Giroux has argued, 'not all oppositional behaviour has radical significance, nor is all oppositional behaviour a clear cut response to domination' (1983: 285, in Raby, 2005: 157). Consider the case of opposition to speed cameras in the UK, for example. Opposition to speed cameras at the beginning of the twenty-first century involved a media-led campaign orchestrated by the conservative press and motor organisations. While the issue of 'resistance' is a very rare occurrence in reporting on open-street CCTV surveillance systems, there were several stories that have focused on this issue in relation to speed cameras:

> HOW TO BEAT THE SPEED CAMERAS (Headline: *Evening Standard*, 4 September 2001)
>
> Drivers are dodging controversial speed cameras by using a revolutionary device that alerts them in advance. ... The makers say the device gives the driver ample time to slow down gradually rather than slamming on the brakes at the last minute and risking an accident. (in McCahill, 2003: 42)

In the above article, speeding motorists were offered advice on how to beat the speed cameras by deploying camera detectors. In this story, speed cameras are described as 'controversial' while detectors, which allow motorists to break the law, are described as 'revolutionary'. This article also seemed to imply that the use of detectors is legitimate because detectors prevent accidents by allowing those who flout the law to slow down gradually rather than slamming on the breaks. The main objection to the use of speed cameras, however, was that cameras should not be monitoring 'Us' (motorists and 'respectable citizens'); rather they should be targeting 'Them' (thieves, robbers, muggers). In this respect, the resistance to speed cameras was highly individualistic and reinforced, rather than challenged, dominant discourses on surveillance and crime control. Summing up their research on the opposition to speed cameras in the UK, Wells and Wills (2009) have argued that:

> Resistance to surveillance should not ... be encouraged uncritically, nor viewed as necessarily a positive or empowering activity. For many, increased exposure to surveillance is not opposed on the grounds that it is intrusive or contrary to any notion of human rights or social justice. It can, instead, be a further manifestation of existing processes of discrimination and 'othering' as surveilled populations' resistant efforts are focused only on redirecting the surveillant gaze from themselves and on to other traditionally suspect populations. (Wells and Wills, 2009: 273)

Ambiguity can also be found in 'counter-surveillance' moves which, like the 'new surveillance' technologies to which they respond, also have 'unintended consequences' (Marx, 1981). As Huey, Walby and Doyle (2006) have reported, in 2002 local activists in Vancouver's DTES (Downtown Eastside) founded a Cop Watch program which aims to hold the police accountable by 'observing, recording and documenting police abuses' (Huey et al., 2006: 152). However, critics of Copwatch pointed out that while some Copwatch supporters are proponents of the decriminalisation of drugs, police officers have argued that the ability to use their discretionary powers and to 'turn a blind eye' to drugs offences was made much more difficult when their activities were being filmed. As one officer explained:

> The Cop Watch is ironic in itself because, if you see someone break the law, you can go 'If you leave the area, I'll just ignore the fact that I saw you doing something bad. But if I see you again, I'm going to have to arrest you'. But if you have someone here with a video camera following you around, as a police officer, for every little thing, you're going to get a ticket. (quoted in Huey et al., 2006: 157)

As Gary T. Marx (2009: 297) has pointed out, 'counter surveillance' or 'neutralisation' that the subjects of surveillance adopt can also provoke 'the *counter-neutralisation of agents*'. Motorists, for example, may 'neutralise' speed cameras with speed camera detectors, only for police officers to use the 'interceptor', a 'detector detector' that 'emits an alarm and flashing red light when it identifies a car using a radar detector' (2009: 300). Monahan (2006b: 528) has argued that while the beating of Rodney King in Los Angeles was captured on video camera and then displayed synoptically to the watching millions, 'this did not necessarily catalyze correctives to actions of police brutality, nor did it motivate greater police engagement with urban communities'. What happened instead, Monahan (2006) argues, was that the police learnt 'that they must exert greater control over the conditions where brutality occurs', as was the case in 1997 when a Haitian worker named Abner Louima was brutally beaten by the New York City Police in a police vehicle and in a police restroom away from unwanted scrutiny (2006: 528).

Surveillance, 'performance' and 'display'

As Koskela (2006) has pointed out, far from trying to 'contest' or 'resist' sur-veillance regimes, in some contexts people may actually embrace surveil-lance. She has argued that 'increasing numbers of individuals seem eager to expose intimate details of their private lives' through 'online diaries, reality TV, and web cameras in bedrooms' (2006: 5–6). For Koskela, the idea that surveillance can be experienced as 'fun' or 'liberating' challenges Foucauldian notions of 'panopticism' and the internalisation of control. But how far can Koskela's arguments be extended to other surveillance technologies and set-tings? Another group who seem willing to 'perform' in front of surveillance cameras, rather than avoid the 'disciplinary gaze', are the Surveillance Camera Players (SCPs). These are a performance-based activist-awareness group from New York who openly and critically engage in various public performances in front of open-street surveillance cameras, such as perform-ing Big Brother as a play in front of the cameras with placards designed to inform the crowd about what it is they're doing. Bill Brown, the founder of the SCPs, says that 'the one thing security culture thrives upon is secrecy. Secrecy is its oxygen. If you talk about it you're introducing carbon-monoxide into its oxygen and hopefully we can have it choke on being talked about' (Schienke and Brown, 2003: 361–362).

'Cultural criminologists' have also argued that surveillance may be welcomed by some groups. For these writers, 'traditional' criminology 'has neglected the emotional dimension of offending'. Indeed, 'if one is to fully understand trans-gression, one must begin with the passions, with the violent feelings which crime induces, both in offenders and victims' (Hayward, 2004: 147–148). In terms of how this approach might shed some light on the subjective experience and response to surveillance, these writers suggest that in a society character-ised by intensive surveillance and a 'culture of control' (Garland, 2001), 'risk-taking' is becoming more pervasive through the pursuit of behaviours ... which allows people 'to feel alive in an over-controlled ... world' (Hayward, 2004: 163). It is argued that 'new surveillance' technologies and 'situational crime prevention' measures may actually add to the excitement of committing crime rather than deter 'rational actors'. For instance, avoiding police surveillance may become part of the pleasure for those involved in 'football hooliganism', and 'twockers' who might see 'speed cameras as a challenge' (2004: 187). Similar arguments could be made in relation to political activism. For instance, while surveillance processes may have had a 'chilling' effect on some political activists, for others 'the costs incurred by repression are perceived as a solidarity-inducing benefit by a tight-knit activist core' (Cunningham and Noakes, 2008: 179). In a review of the literature, Cunningham and Noakes (2008: 179) reported how networks of activists within political movements 'can provide settings for activists' willingness to engage in "high-risk" activism, enduring jailings and physical harm for the sake of the cause'. These findings dovetail with a story told by Timothy Garton Ash in his book *The File: A Personal History* (1997), where he traces the 'file' kept on him by the Stasi when he travelled to the former East Germany as he worked as a journalist. On learning that the British security services had also 'kept tabs on him', Garton Ash expressed some irritation that they had not kept an 'adversarial file'. 'How much neater it would be', he says, 'if they could have had an adversarial file on me. Then one could say: "See, both the Stasi and MI5 were following me, what a fearless all-around dissident I must be!"' (Garton Ash, 1997: 218–219). Here we have the middle-class version of the Anti-Social Behaviour Order (ASBO), where the 'file' or label attached to the surveilled is regarded as a 'badge of honour' that reaffirms in a positive way the status and identity of the 'radical dissident' or 'outsider'.

The 'Great Unwatched': power, surveillance and invisibility

As the examples in the previous sections illustrate, the spaces of surveillance are disrupted in unanticipated ways and in everyday situations which point to a dialectical interrelationship between the surveilled and the surveillance regime, both playing off the other. But what about 'thick' forms of resistance? Here we are concerned with the ability and capacity to contest a surveillance regime and negotiate its rationale or modify its impact in terms of controlling those under surveillance. This kind of resistance is unevenly distributed across the social terrain, with differential consequences in terms of how and where surveillance occurs. As we saw in the previous chapter, some actors – because of social status or institutionally powerful position – are relatively under-scrutinised or subject to 'light touch' surveillance and this can be regardless of the reality of serious social harms and risks associated with powerful actors and institutions. In part, this has been the result of inherited institutional and ideological power relations that have facilitated *both* the flourishing of under-monitored spaces *and* the political and cultural capital of the powerful to influence their own surveillance through close proximity to surveillance authorities with whom a conversational dynamic is cultivated. The historical development of surveillance over crime and deviance discussed in Chapter 3 was underpinned by powerful social actors credibly articulating social problems and thereby influencing debates concerning where and how surveillance would take place. In this part of the chapter we develop these points by focusing on the contemporary reception of surveillance among the powerful and their capacity to shape surveillance and its social ordering properties.

In contrast to the examples earlier in the chapter where surveillance was contested from outside official surveillance regimes, resistance can occur *within* the heart of surveillance practice and discourse, creating room for those with greater economic and social capital to contest and negotiate the surveillance agenda and its goals. Proximity (in political, cultural and spatial terms) to the surveillance discourse is crucial in being able to influence it and metering its tone towards a conversational, as opposed to confrontational, framework. Those internal, or with a closer proximity, to surveillance discourses can foster a process of 'recognition' between themselves and the surveillance authorities, both of whom work together in formal and informal settings to construct shared assumptions concerning the aims and scope of surveillance. As we shall see, the cultivation of conversations in these settings is crucial to the process of fostering mutual identification as a means through which potential surveillance subjects come to be recognised as having legitimate voices on the part of surveillance authorities. The surveillance and policing of factory working conditions discussed in Chapter 3 led to surveillance arrangements between the state and the economically powerful as being characterised by a process of mutuality, whereby surveillance may be successfully defined (and even agreed upon) as disruptive to the normal functioning of certain economic assumptions and therefore deemed 'unnecessary' or 'burdensome'. In the contemporary world, however, it has been argued that 'the corporate world has become more visible and subject to regulation than ever before' (Ericson, 2007b: 7). Alongside this debatable point, it is also acknowledged that surveillance of corporate conduct at the most senior level is very much an internal affair based on a light touch form of surveillance or 'defensive compliance' in relation to corporate actors (2007b: 7). As we alluded to in the previous chapter, it is powerful state and corporate actors who are better placed to produce widely shared meanings as to surveillance norms as well as in shaping acceptable and appropriate surveillance solutions.

We begin here to examine how the fostering of communicative ties of mutual understanding and recognition in the surveillance process works in practice. For example, corporations may often be referred to as 'leaders' or 'beacons' in their field when the regulation of their activities through surveillance is being implemented. This can be illustrated with reference to 'policing' health and safety in the workplace. The protagonists in the conversation are usually powerful individuals and directors in the corporation and not those at the sharp end of their sometimes harmful practices (for example, workers or members of the public). Exploring who is involved in establishing the goals of regulatory surveillance, then, has profound implications for how harm is understood and responded to, as the example of the hazardous offshore oil industry makes clear. In this industry, 'where workers (the large majority of whom remain sub-contracted and causualized) have few bargaining rights' and have a limited capacity to pose alternative views, 'goal-setting' of regulatory surveillance has taken place between managers and regulators and 'effectively allowed the oil companies to dictate the terms of their own compliance to the regulator' (Whyte, 2006: 200). Indeed, practices of surveillance-as-regulation and law enforcement applied to the corporate sector in general are ensconced under the notion of 'compliance', whereby persuasion, education and bargaining underpin the conversational matrix between the watchers and the watched in this area. 'Compromise' is very often the *modus operandi* in this and other surveillance scenarios involving the powerful (Tombs and Whyte, 2007).

As we saw in the previous chapter, light touch forms of surveillance raise questions for how we think about, and respond to, corporate and state forms of harm and wrongdoing. We also saw how surveillance in these areas becomes embroiled in – and even compromised by – questions concerning the legitimacy and authority of powerful institutions. The close proximity of these institutions to surveillance discourses has had a bearing on the normative dimensions of surveillance into some of their practices. Indeed, as a result of this, there is evidence to suggest that surveillance in powerful domains also acts to manage dissent – in the form of discourses that undermine corporate decision-making – just as much, if not more, than bring to light fraudulent, criminal or unsafe practices within the corporate world. This in part reflects the political and economic pressures brought to bear upon regulatory agencies concerned with surveillance over the powerful and which produces a conversational surveillance dialogue that, more often than not, tempers a coincidence of interest between surveillant agencies and the surveilled. For example, surveillance agencies such as the Health and Safety Executive (HSE) in the UK, work on the communicative assumption of a 'common interest' between workers and managers with regard to workplace safety. In practice, the principle of 'common interest' works in favour of management. In the offshore oil industry bullying and other disciplinary tactics used by managers to harass and dispose of workers who raise safety concerns are routinely brought to the attention of HSE Inspectors. Yet this surveillance body 'has consistently refused to involve itself, preferring to maintain an artificial partition between "industrial relations" and "safety matters"' in referring all worker reported incidents back to management (Whyte, 2006: 198). This is because, in the words of one HSE Inspector, 'management have the most influence over safety in the workplace' (cited in Whyte, 2006: 198). In this state of affairs, trade union safety representatives report high levels of scepticism and mistrust with this kind of surveillance regime, which they identity as being firmly in the thrall of management (Whyte, 2006). It has also been noted that the safest places to work are those with strong worker organisation through trade union representation, through which to voice calls for enhanced regulation and surveillance over the right of management to manage with impunity. However, the creation of insecure tenures of employment and the wearing down of trade union rights over the past 30 years have eroded workers capacity to resist 'unsafe' managerial practices and engage meaningfully and credibly in surveillance discourses in this area (Tombs and Whyte, 2007: 48–49).

Similar issues are evident elsewhere in terms of how the development of light touch surveillance can neutralise criminal liability upon powerful actors. This can be illustrated in the supervision of the financial sector and, in particular, the mis-selling of endowment mortgages in the beginning in the 1980s up until the early twenty-first century. By the end of the 1980s, endowment policies accounted for four out of every five new mortgage contracts: a high-risk mortgage because there is no guarantee issued that an endowment policy will make enough money to eventually pay off the mortgage at its end point. The rise in popularity of this kind of mortgage can in part be explained by people not being informed of the risks involved and in being issued verbal guarantees that the endowment would eventually cover mortgage debt (Fooks, 2002). This is known as mis-selling, the 'systemic nature' of which 'would seem to suggest routine violation of the criminal law' by powerful financial agencies in placing people at a financial disadvantage (Fooks, 2002: 110). In the UK, the body responsible for overseeing this sector is the Financial Services Authority (FSA). Up until 2002 there had been no major criminal investigation into the practice of selling such policies and no prosecutions. The inconsistencies here are ensconced 'in the idea that corporations have a decisive, if mediated, influence on the form, content, and extent of publicly held and available information about their business' (Fooks, 2002: 106). From the outset the precise parameters of surveillance over business activity was limited in this example. Surveillance and oversight worked *not* towards criminal suspicion (although 'incompetence' and 'poor training' was often stressed). Instead, a momentum towards criminal suspicion was 'neutralized and deflected' by the interaction of legal constraints, professional concerns and cultural assumptions as to the nature of financial security and mis-selling of financial packages (2002: 115–116). The role of the FSA, even when acting on the basis of surveillance information where criminal violation was suspected, was compromised not least in terms of its 'statutory objective to maintain market confidence' (2002: 117). Again issues of the 'public interest' come to the fore and were problematised by the FSA's differential relationship with businesses on the one hand and the public on the other. Public dissent and some media scrutiny of endowment selling in the late 1990s did raise the prospect of understanding mis-selling within the conversational idiom of fraud and criminal liability within high-level financial decision-making. However, the response of the FSA was to manage public dissent by minimising the extent of victimisation and in attempting to restore public confidence in the industry. This was done along with the closing down of courses of public action against the industry and in pursuing a strategy that avoided 'both the question of criminal liability and its detection' and in a failure to tackle the corporate monopoly over information on financial practices (Fooks, 2002: 119).

As we saw in the previous chapter, calls for increased surveillance, regulation and 'policing' over corporate activities often occur alongside legitimacy deficits such as those driven by the spectacular frauds and market collapse associated with the banking system in 2007–08. The harms and risks generated under these conditions have been generated in terms of house price collapse and increased unemployment. It has been argued that these harms could have been offset much earlier had it not been for the light touch form of surveillance over powerful institutions and actors in the financial sector (Mattli and Woods, 2008). Over the last 30 years or so it has been argued in stark terms that the predominant form of surveillance discourse relating to financial services has been developed in a form through which 'bankers, earning millions, persuaded regulators, earning thousands, to opt for a "light touch"' mode of surveillance over financial services, effectively allowing some high-risk and fraudulent practices to go unseen and even normalised (Mattli and Woods, 2008: 23). For Mattli and Woods, the power of financial capital to resist and shape its own monitoring must be challenged if a clear and enforceable set of global rules is to be put in place, along with oversight powers over national regulators such as the FSA (who themselves would need monitoring given their lack of zeal in policing this area). Measures like these, alongside 'watching the watchdog bodies' found in non-governmental counter-surveillance we mentioned earlier, would contribute to an international court reminding all concerned of the duties of surveillance regulators in this area. At the moment these are just ideas whose fruition remains to be seen. However as ideas, they nevertheless cogently point us to the gaps that remain in surveillance provision over a segment of powerful actors in modern social orders.

The examples above have highlighted the different kinds of surveillance discourses that take place in specific contexts and which exhibit ongoing tensions in the governance of specific social spaces and over particular political and economic processes. Here, the 'public interest' served by surveillance, and associated forms of regulation and law enforcement, becomes embroiled within a kind of conversational matrix characterised by mutuality, negotiation and compromise, leading to unevenness in surveillance reach and controversies concerning whose interests a surveillance regime represents.

The role of the powerful in shaping surveillance and 'risk'

As indicated from the start of the book, there exists a broader material and ideological terrain where surveillance develops and within which some groups are problematized while other groups are not. Taking into account this broader terrain enables us to see that imbalances exist both in the resolve to apply surveillance resources to specific powerful sites and in the ability of powerful actors to modify the normative sanctioning power and outcomes of surveillance practice. Powerful groups, and their proximity to taken-for-granted assumptions concerning the priorities relating to economic and political interests and their greater command of resources and information, have greater affective power over the meaning and deployment of terms like 'public safety' and 'risk'. These categories, then, are not self-evident and are in fact shaped by powerful voices and interests that claim authority within surveillance discourses. How 'risk' is articulated and understood has implications for 'resistance'. For example, in the corporate sector, what is deemed 'risky' can have divergent connotations to do with how 'normal' business practice is sustained. As we have pointed to in the previous section, with recourse to a language of 'regulatory burdens' and 'red-tape', corporate actors have successfully articulated surveillance and inspection as 'harmful' and 'risky' to the business efficiency and the profitability of the corporate domain itself (Tombs and Whyte, 2007). Defining surveillance and regulation as a risk to 'good business' and as a destabilising yoke on the business enterprise provides a means to resist surveillance and shape its impact in the corporate world. In this area, light touch surveillance is couched in a vernacular that veils 'threats' to the public interest from corporate activity. The notion of the 'public interest' itself may be compromised by surveillance discourses that have a more conversational tone that works towards conciliation to business needs (Tombs and Whyte, 2007). In these cases, voluntary codes of compliance, self-regulation and surveillance in the corporate realm seeks to harness business acumen in shaping the politics of surveillance and visibility. Here a more accommodating relationship exists between surveillance and the surveilled. Surveillance is less imposed or demanded as an external force of inspection and is more a result of a negotiation process that denotes a degree of autonomy for the surveilled.

Far from surveillance having an easy relationship to risk, then, it is more useful to see how 'risk' is composed within social relations within which surveillance communicative discourse arises. In other words, 'risk' *vis-à-vis* surveillance is politically and differentially constituted. In the UK, the then Chancellor of the Exchequer, and soon to be British Prime Minister, Gordon Brown made this clear when he addressed the Confederation of British Industry on matters of surveillance and regulation of business:

> The better, and in my opinion correct, modern model of regulation – the risk-based approach – *is based on trust* in the responsible company, the engaged employee and the educated consumer, leading government to focus attention where it should: no inspection without justification, no form-filling without justification, and no information requirements without justification, not just a light touch but a limited touch. (G. Brown, 2005: 3, emphasis added)

What is deemed a 'risk' in this surveillance conversation with business leaders, relates not only to the surveillance of corporations 'and the enforcement of regulation, but also to the design and indeed to the decision as to whether to regulate at all' (G. Brown, 2005: 4). Even before 2005, the HSE had accommodated itself to this market-based strategy supported by a 33% reduction in inspections of businesses (Tombs and Whyte, 2010a: 55). The light touch results from shared assumptions as to the sanctity of key institutions across government and corporate stakeholders, in which maintaining 'healthy businesses' as central to the 'national interest' predominate. A more conciliatory and less combative surveillance discourse also applied in the UK when the Financial Services Minister, Lord Myners, reassured the financial industry when he stated that the 'the industry shouldn't worry' because 'I am not going to let it go the same way as our coal communities' (*Private Eye*, July 2009: 6). The identification of risk and the 'need' for surveillance do not speak for themselves but are products of communicative social bargaining between recognised and socially authoritative actors, with legitimate or even a corresponding interest between surveillers and surveilled. How to respond in regulatory terms to the risks generated by the financial sector through inflated bonuses, mismanagement and mis-selling remain debated issues within the parameters of surveillance discourse. According to some commentators, these parameters and the voices heard within them have already begun to shape a response. Between January and March 2009 Lord Myners held exploratory meetings with industry representatives, hedge fund managers, company directors, senior bankers and venture capitalists, who conjoined in the conversation regarding the best way forward concerning the monitoring and regulation of 'their' domains (*Private Eye*, July 2009: 6). It is precisely through these conversational settings that powerful 'insiders' employ 'power in ways that blue-collar criminals do not, through their ability to influence the form, shape and meaning of regulatory law' (Snider, 2009: 180). And these kinds of reciprocal communicative arrangements took place in a context where many banks in and outside the UK were bailed out by governments in 2008–09. In the UK alone this amounted to £141 billion in public sector debt (Office for National Statistics, August 2009: 5) to assuage what many have understood as the systemic corruption and malpractice at the heart of the financial system (Hutton, 2009).

The formation of surveillance discourses are important not only in muting criticism as to the risks generated by powerful activities, but also in shaping surveillant responses to these risks. But they are also important in redefining risks away from the harms generated by unchecked financial activity, and their remoulding into 'new' risks defined in terms of over-constraining surveillance and regulation of the business sector. The language surrounding a surveillance regime becomes important for the ways in which the surveilled gain an identity too (for example, as either 'cooperators', 'troublemakers', 'rule breakers' or 'criminals') and for the way in which problem activities are framed (for example, as 'accidents', 'aberrations' or 'crimes'). The monitoring of corporations and their regulation and inspection *vis-à-vis* normal business activities are decided upon within a balance of forces that take into account the workings of markets, the monitoring of 'sustainable' profitability and competitiveness. Here, governments may adopt the role as 'mediator' between pro-regulatory interests and representatives of corporations, but the balance of power between mediators, pro- and anti-surveillance groups is rarely or ever equal (Tombs and Whyte, 2007). The outcomes of surveillance discourse in this area are more likely to be in the application of 'voluntary codes' of practice, 'naming and shaming' and techniques of persuasion rather than full recourse to criminal sanctions, as was the case in the UK when the government introduced a 'voluntary code of conduct' for bankers in an attempt to stop them and their wealthier clients avoid tax (*The Guardian*, 27 June 2009). Even this voluntary form of self-surveillance was resisted by injunctions from top banks in order to stop information about their tax activities becoming public (June 2009). What seems clearer, then, from the examples discussed in this section is that the close proximity and greater cultural capital of corporate actors, in relation to both the surveillance discourse *and* the surveillance regime, has resulted in an ability to 'dispute the conventional meanings attached to their offences' [or harms] and in their ability 'to evade moral blame and legal culpability' (Cohen, 2001: 77). Indeed, the evasion of legal culpability, criminal labelling and the possibility of prison sentences in relation to corporate manslaughter in the UK has been buttressed in government forums where even raising these issues for discussion has been recognised as near impossible without the support of business leaders (see Sim, 2009: 92–93).

The form surveillance takes over the powerful is fundamentally decided upon not only in relation to the ability to articulate a political voice deemed *relevant* within a surveillance regime, but also by the powerful's capacity to both *use* and *shape* legal mechanisms. For example, governments can and do have the power to exempt themselves from scrutiny, as was the case with the Houses of Parliament in England, which voted to excuse its members from the

Freedom of Information Act (FOI) in 2007 (*The Guardian*, 19 May 2007). Seven government departments had been identified with refusing to give answers to more than half of all requests made by the public in the year up to December 2006 (*The Independent*, 28 December 2006). In the UK up until May 2009, Members of Parliament (MPs) had successfully fought off public scrutiny through evoking 'privacy' and 'security' – of their salaries, expenses and allowances accrued from taxpayers' money (some of which may be subject to criminal investigation). Although such scrutiny is theoretically allowable in the UK under the FOI, many MPs defended themselves against such scrutiny in articulating it as a 'risk' in that such 'transparency will damage democracy' (Brooke, 2009: 4). We can observe here how 'risk' and 'privacy' have a complex and not at all obvious relationship. Privacy as a defence against intrusion and surveillance has been and continues to be utilised differentially in that some individuals and agencies may be better placed to protect their privacy from surveillance than others.

Furthermore, the Protection from Harassment Act (UK, 1997), ostensibly provided protection against 'stalking', and has most successfully been utilised by corporations to limit and criminalise what they claim to be 'harassment' and 'victimisation' through forms of dissent and counter-surveillance enacted by protestors against aspects of their operations. According to Monbiot (2007), recourse to the Act has had the effect of stifling public dissent and nullifying the process of extending public information and awareness regarding sometimes harmful corporate activity. Indeed, Andrejevic (2007) has noted that corporations are best placed to successfully argue rights of privacy when claims are made on information they hold, particularly in relation to 'new media' holdings. This may be extended to the working of state legislation too, such as in the UK, which, on the face of it, provides citizens with legal safeguards in the form of the Data Protection Act (1998). The Act formalises a conception of privacy by limiting data transfers to 'interested' parties, including the general public. However, requests for data about oneself in relation to being captured in CCTV footage, through which a citizen may become a 'data subject', show gaps in the legislation which appear to favour state and corporate retention rather than public disclosure (Luksch and Patel, 2008). Reasons given for non-disclosure are varied and point to state and corporate discretion in what is disclosed and to whom. Such discretion is allowed under the legal framework. Reasons for non-disclosure include: cameras not working and tapes destroyed (sometimes against the guidelines stipulated in the Act); poor visual quality of the images so as to be 'useless'; the need to 'protect third parties' also present in the images; images embargoed by police in the course of another criminal investigation; informational data requested is not considered 'personal' by the data controller; and images not released where cameras are not operated remotely or controllers state that images are only given to police for unspecified reasons. According to Luksch and Patel (2008: 11), who reported these findings, the latter reasons for retaining surveillance information from the public illustrate 'a sorry litany of malfunctioning equipment, erased tapes, lost letters and sheer evasiveness' on behalf of state and corporate gatekeepers on information.

Finally in this section, we return to the discussion of counter-surveillance in relation to policing on the streets. We noted earlier in this and the previous chapter how the countering of official surveillance with citizen sousurveillance could bring into the public domain otherwise unseen controversies concerning police malpractice. This could involve blogging experiences of policing at public demonstrations and videoing events for uploading on the internet. As Clare Coatman (2009) has argued, although important, these counter-surveillance measures are not enough on their own. This has been because official bodies (concerned with police complaints, for example) do not normally draw upon citizen-led surveillance in their investigations of official malpractice. It has also been argued that 'sousurveillance can only be effective in a country where the media is free enough to air videos that challenge the official account of events' (2009: 19). And we could add that this effectiveness would be increased where the mainstream media was less ideologically skewed in favour of the forces of law and order in synoptic terms. Once again, though, structural limitations apply to the effectiveness of counter-surveillance in relation to policing. In the UK, under the 2008 Counter Terrorism Act, it is illegal to photograph a policeman. As the Act stated, this applies to photographs 'of a kind likely to be useful to a person committing or preparing an act of terrorism' (cited in Coatman, 2009: 19). Examples abound, however, where police officers have used their discretion to stop surveillance of them long before the Act came into operation and in situations more recently where the police have confiscated camera equipment where links to 'terrorism' were dubious at best (*The Guardian*, 11 September 2009).

More broadly, the ability to scrutinise policing practice whether through official or citizen-led means has to be placed within the structural asymmetries of power that accord the police a differential relationship to the politics of visibility within which police officers avoid a unwanted gaze. It has been noted that a reluctance exists on behalf of governments, quasi-legal and regulatory bodies to challenge the police institution's symbolic authority *vis-à-vis* the tropes of 'law and order' and 'safety' and the solidarity, sometimes intractability, of cop cultures when it comes to inspection and investigations concerning police malpractice (Chan, 2008). Police studies have long indicated how an insular 'cop culture' of the rank and file has played a major role in obfuscating scrutiny from both line managers and external bodies. Furthermore, the legal frameworks that exist to regulate and oversee police practice have at the same time buttressed an 'overall trend of increasing latent police power' (Sanders and Young, 2007: 278). For Sanders and Young, the effect of this has been that 'many police actions take place in a legal wilderness' so that in various instances 'police officers can roam at will without the restraint of the rule of law' (2007: 647). These kinds of structural constraints set a wider context for resisting scrutiny and in allowing powerful arguments that 'too much' surveillance may hamper legitimate work-based or institutional goals.

The examples discussed here have not been provided in order to argue that powerful bodies are, at all times, immune from scrutiny, but that such powerful bodies are better placed to evade, deny or obfuscate inspection as articulated in relation to a range of legitimate cultural, political and legal means and discourses. Differential access to such means points to how resistance to surveillance is asymmetrically distributed and deeply structured in prevailing relations of power. As we have indicated, a command of legal resources, coupled with ideological power, can influence the discursive dynamics of surveillance and provide a greater range 'in the inventory of denials available to the powerful' (Cohen, 2001: 280).

Summary and conclusion

As indicated at the beginning of this chapter, the limited amount of research attempting to explore the subjective experience and behavioural responses of those subject to surveillance monitoring gives rise to a number of unanswered questions. For example, to what extent have the 'dialectics of disguise and surveillance' been transformed by electronically mediated power relations? Do people ever think about their 'data image' and how the 'electronic trail' they leave behind may be stored, collated and used in ways that could have an impact on their 'embodied self'? Do those subject to monitoring by visual surveillance technologies, through demeanour and gesture, change their behaviour when in view of the cameras? Do they adopt a 'social face' designed to transmit information to those watching at a distance?

There is an extract in George Orwell's dystopian novel, *Nineteen Eighty-Four* (1949), when the book's hero, Winston Smith, tries desperately to adopt a 'social face' that he thinks Big Brother will find appropriate as he performs the state-controlled exercise regime (Physical Jerks) in his living room under the gaze of the 'telescreen' (1949: 39). Many of us may, on occasions, find ourselves, like Winston, adopting a 'social face' that we consider to be appropriate for the various (state and non-state) surveillance settings in which we find ourselves. Consider the shop worker, for example, who strains to adopt a 'social face' for the management who use surveillance cameras to monitor the minutiae of 'facial expressions' to ensure that staff are being 'polite' and 'friendly' with customers (McCahill, 2002). Or consider the political protestors who bring a change of clothes to the demonstration in a 'bid to confuse police video operators' (Hayward, 2004: 187). Or consider those entering the shopping mall who may decide to change their dress or appearance or reposition their bodies in a way that is conducive to the mall's consumerist ethic (McCahill and Finn, 2010). If this is an accurate account of the subjective impact of surveillance monitoring, does it matter? Well, maybe it does, because in each case the individuals concerned are made to feel as if they are under suspicion when they have done nothing wrong. This can only encourage a 'culture of suspicion' and a lack of 'trust' which provides further impetus for the intensification of a 'surveillance society'.

However, this micro-sociology of the 'dialectics of surveillance and disguise' needs to be situated in a much broader social, historical and political context by examining the relationship between surveillance, power and visibility/invisibility. The ability of the powerful to shape the surveillance of others as well as themselves has been documented in this book. Claims for the 'impartiality' of surveillance are undermined by the correspondence of interests between powerful economic, political and social actors/agencies and surveillance authorities. While in general terms greater visibility may now be obtainable through surveillance, this visibility remains contestable by powerful actors both ideologically *and* by their proximity to esteemed and established institutions. Surveillance regimes can therefore be modified by powerful social actors – perhaps in taking a conciliatory tone – through utilising their access to political representation, economic and cultural capital. States and corporations remain relatively under-surveilled spaces, not least in terms of the difficulties this gives rise to in 'unmasking the crimes of the powerful' (Tombs and Whyte, 2002), and in respect of access to information relating to powerful activities. Therefore the development of surveillance is not seamless in what it makes visible. The politics of visibility is uneven and differentially 'policed'. It is more useful to see 'visibility' as an arena of contestation involving political struggle and claims-making over the control of particular spaces, the meaning and application of law, and the means of cultural representation within which surveillance discourses are generated. In relation to the powerful, then, the ways in which surveillance operates creates what we might view as empty or unseen spaces in the sense that their visibility, and hence knowledge about them, is limited. This is particularly apt concerning the powerful and the quality and quantity of surveillance directed at this group and which, as yet, has brought a limited impact on curbing their 'crimes'.

STUDY QUESTIONS

1 What do you understand by the term 'resistance' to surveillance?
2 Have you, or anyone you know, ever 'resisted' surveillance?

3   What do the existing theories within 'surveillance studies' tell us about 'resistance'?

4   In what ways can the powerful neutralise surveillance?

5   Draw up a list, in order of credibility, of individuals and agencies involved in surveillance discourses around (a) city centre street crime and CCTV surveillance, and (b) deaths in the workplace and their regulation. In what ways might those involved in both discourses be able to affect surveillance in these areas?

FURTHER READING

See the special edition on *'Surveillance and* Resistance' in *Surveillance and Society* (2009), Vol. 6, No. 22, at www.surveillance-and-society.org.

Gilliom, J. (2006) 'Struggling with surveillance: resistance, consciousness, and identity', in Haggerty, K.D. and Ericson, R.V. (eds), *The New Politics of Surveillance and Visibility,* Toronto: University of Toronto Press.

Marx, G.T. (2003) 'A tack in the shoe: neutralizing and resisting the new surveillance', *Journal of Social Issues,* Vol. 59, No. 2, pp. 369–390.

Scott, J.C. (1990) *Domination and the Arts of Resistance: Hidden Transcripts,* New Haven, CT: Yale University Press.

Tombs, S. and Whyte, D. (2007) *Safety Crimes,* Cullompton: Willan (see Chapter 3 on obscuring safety crimes).

8

Deconstructing Surveillance, Crime and Power

CHAPTER CONTENTS	

Beyond 'what works': surveillance, the 'crime problem' and social harm 170

Surveillance as a social process: continuity and discontinuity 174

The state of surveillance 177

Contesting and resisting surveillance? 179

Surveillance and crime: contesting the 'public interest' 181

Summary and Conclusion 184

OVERVIEW

Chapter 8 provides:

- An overview and exploration of the key controversies surrounding surveillance and crime
- A discussion of the relationships between surveillance, social harm, resistance and the 'public interest'

KEY TERMS

- Power and social order
- Public interest

- Social harm
- The state

Beyond 'what works': surveillance, the 'crime problem' and social harm

This book has explored the relationship between surveillance and crime, not in terms of whether the former 'works' in a technical sense to prevent or reduce the latter, but in broader terms of how surveillance 'works' in respect of its impacts upon social understandings and responses to crime, *and* its role in facilitating and reproducing asymmetrical power relations within the social realm. However, before returning to this central point, it should be noted that surveillance has been critically debated in terms of its effectiveness in reducing 'crime', 'deviance' and 'terrorism'. Within crime prevention rhetoric and official social control talk, surveillance continues to be depicted as profoundly necessary and useful in the fight against crime and disorder. The assumption is that, at some level, it 'works' in bringing about greater security and safety for 'citizens'. Indeed, debates around surveillance couched in terms of whether it 'works' or not in 'preventing crime' has produced research findings that have questioned the ideological commitment and financial resources allocated to surveillance. For example, a review of 44 research studies on CCTV schemes in the UK by the Campbell Collaboration in 2009 found that they do have a limited impact on crime overall, but are most effective in cutting vehicle crime in car parks (*The Guardian*, 18 May 2009). In an earlier survey of research it was suggested that there 'is little substantive research evidence that CCTV works' as either a crime prevention or anxiety reducing tool (NACRO, 2002: 6). Although critical in evaluative terms, such studies have tended to limit their critique to managerial issues concerning where and under what conditions surveillance might prove to be effective in terms of, for example, using CCTV alongside improved street lighting and security guards, or applied narrowly at reducing vehicle crime in car parks (*The Guardian*, 18 May 2009). Similarly, the DNA Database in the UK has been critically scrutinised by independent monitoring groups such as GeneWatch UK, who have questioned government claims that the technology represents a panacea in crime fighting. For example, officials have claimed that keeping unconvicted people on the Database will serve as a roster with which to match crime-scene DNA collected by police, thus determining innocent and guilty individuals. It has been pointed out that 'matches are not the same as prosecutions or convictions – many matches occur with passers-by or are false matches' (Wallace, 2009: 3). Furthermore, from between 2004 and 2009 the Database has more than doubled in size, yet the proportion of recorded crimes detected using DNA has remained steady at 0.36% (2009: 3). In the interventions cited above, both CCTV and DNA monitoring and information-gathering practices have been questioned for how they 'catch' the innocent as much as the guilty in their data-nets and how these practices have undermined ideas of privacy.

These kinds of interventions are important in questioning the stated intentions of surveillance ingrained in crime prevention rhetoric. However, this book has focused less upon 'what works' in the narrow technical sense in order to focus on deeper questions concerning how surveillance reflects and reinforces (wittingly or unwittingly) unequal social relations of power. Indeed, developments in both CCTV and DNA can also be viewed as indicative of deeper changes in contemporary statecraft or how we are governed. Innovation in surveillance has been driven by wider changes, based not so much upon rational evaluation of crime prevention practice, but more upon wider political-economic developments such as privatisation and market-based solutions to social problems, the commercialisation of public life and the ongoing divisions between wealthy and poorer citizens. In these kinds of societies, surveillance emerges to secure and maintain particular kinds of socio-spatial relations and 'acceptable' behaviour within them. In these kinds of societies, the development, financing and ideological support for surveillance practices such as CCTV and DNA have emerged through a state-market nexus (Coleman, 2004; Wallace, 2009). Within this complex and unequal world, powerful ideas and practices continue to develop a form of statecraft forged out of contemporary social struggle and inherited practice, an analysis of which has provided a focus upon 'crime' as a contested object of surveillance power.

In this vein, then, the book's final chapter returns to the book's title, *Surveillance & Crime*, and to how surveillance not only reflects social relations but can also (through its targeting and impacts) produce them. In the proceeding chapters we have challenged a number of commonsense notions about the relationship between these two concepts by focusing upon surveillance as a medium of classificatory power. As we have argued, this power of surveillance only makes sense when situated within historically developing political, moral and technological processes involving deep-rooted social disorders of class, gender, 'race', sexuality and age. In developing this argument, the book has traced surveillance as *more than* a simple crime prevention tool – responding unproblematically to consensually based notions of 'crime' and 'deviance'. As stated at the beginning of the book, how we come to understand and perceive 'crime' is, in part, a result of surveillance practices in both panoptic and synoptic forms. Furthermore, surveillance, and the manner in which it responds to crime, both results from and contributes to struggles over the label of 'crime' itself. As we have seen throughout the book, there are a number of aspects to exploring this process.

First, those who use 'new surveillance' technologies play an important role in constructing the 'crime problem' by deciding who or what is regarded as socially problematic and should, therefore, be subject to surveillance practices. This process, involving classification, censure and normative judgement, continues to forge a politics of visibility which is differentiated between powerful and powerless subjects. Consequently, the surveillance gaze remains focused on 'the visible', while the broader, often invisible harms done to the society – state violence, deaths at work, environmental degradation, income tax evasion, corporate criminality, domestic violence – still remain on the margins of the governing class's consciousness (Sim, 2009).

Secondly, surveillance practices can, in some contexts, both reinforce and create 'new' social harms and deviant practices. Some writers, for example, have argued that the targeted collection and processing of personal and group information has created 'victims of surveillance' (McCahill and Norris, 2003b). Indeed, people can be 'victims' of surveillance when they are disproportionately targeted (for example, on the grounds of class, age, sex and 'race'); when the information gathered about them is used in a way that is inappropriate or not in accordance with stated aims and objectives; and when they are targeted by technologies that produce 'false' information that may have negative consequences for the individual concerned (McCahill and Norris, 2003b). As discussed in Chapter 6, the social impacts of surveillance over both powerless and powerful groups often fall disproportionately upon those already disadvantaged. Thirdly, as we saw earlier, surveillance can lead to a process of 'deviancy amplification'. This can occur when the disproportionate targeting of innocent people (for example, 'working-class youth', 'terrorist suspects') through 'panoptic' measures generates resentment among those who are treated as 'unwanted outsiders', and when 'synoptic' forms of surveillance can work to demonise 'out groups', leading to further deviant practices, such as an increase in racial attacks on Muslims (see Chapter 5).

Consequently, the relationship between surveillance and crime is not straightforward nor is it necessarily based on proportionality – where the extent, reach and intensity of surveillance operates in congruence with the magnitude, costs and injuries associated with a given social problem. Indeed, the most intensive, significantly resourced and far-reaching surveillance practices focus upon conventional definitions of crime (often petty offences focusing on public space concerning drug use, theft, vandalism, anti-social behaviour and offences of interpersonal violence. These crimes and misdemeanours, although clearly distressing and sometimes harmful, do not represent a high score on a scale of serious social harms (Hillyard and Tombs, 2004), but they do generate a significantly higher score in terms of spending and resources committed to tackling them. For example, in the UK in 2009 the Campbell Collaboration report stated that publicly operated CCTV is the single most heavily-funded crime prevention measure operating in and around the criminal justice system. Over the decade previous to 2009, CCTV accounted for more than three-quarters of total spending on crime prevention by the British Home Office, despite evidence suggesting its limited impact as a crime prevention tool. Indeed, it was also estimated that £500 million was spent in Britain on CCTV in the decade up to 2006 (*The Guardian*, 18 May 2009).

As we have argued in the book, rather than starting the analysis by focusing upon individual or group manifestations of 'crime' as a precursor to surveillance, we have focused upon the structural and cultural contexts that generate particular surveillance practices. Within these broader contexts, one of the key focal points we have drawn attention to are the networks of powerful institutional alliances and the interests they articulate in the process of configuring surveillance practices that reflect and reinforce prevailing ideological and cultural understandings of 'crime'. Indeed, in many instances, we have seen how surveillance reinforces long-standing 'ways of seeing' the crime problem. In this sense, surveillance is not immune from the social construction of crime and deviance but integral to it. Surveillance, when situated in social relations, opens up questions as to the nature of social order as a terrain which produces and reproduces the crime problem in selecting, cataloguing and classifying social harms judged to be 'criminal' and those which are not. Like the concept of 'crime', 'surveillance' is meaningless without an understanding of power.

Thus, the focus of surveillance power upon conventional crimes reinforces conceptions of state-led definitions of risk in which 'serious' crimes such as robbery and murder are amplified while the under-surveilled, yet socially costly, acts and omissions incurred in relation to workplace injury and avoidable 'accidents' are rendered negligible. The differential and partial nature of surveillance we have illuminated in the book omits and ignores the complexity in the 'the vicissitudes of life' and forecloses 'a more accurate picture of what is most likely to affect people during their life cycle' (Hillyard and Tombs, 2004: 21). Indeed, a reliance on officially sponsored surveillance and the utility of this, found in media reporting of crime, aids the production of a 'distorted picture of the total harm present in society' along with the perpetuation of particular notions of 'fear' associated with 'the myth of crime' (2004: 21). The production of discrete events, ideas and categories in relation to crime has perpetuated a situation in which less attention has been paid to the less visible but equally, if not more, damaging social harms associated with corporate, state and gender-based forms of injury and violence.

This means that as well as surveillance generating new risks as a consequence of its intended and unintended impacts, it also presents a skewed picture of the development and emanation (in individual and institutional terms) of some of the most serious social harms. Consequently, if we were to retain a narrow understanding of many of the surveillance practices that we have discussed in this book as merely 'crime' or 'risk' prevention tools, we shall miss some key social impacts of surveillance, particularly as it relates to the powerful and their activities.

Surveillance as a social process: continuity and discontinuity

General claims made by social scientists for understanding contemporary monitoring under the conceptual umbrellas of 'new surveillance', 'new penology' and 'new punitiveness' belie some of the nuances in surveillance practices. These nuances have been discussed in this book in relation to *the power of surveillance* and *the surveillance of the powerful* and the complex and multifaceted impacts surveillance can generate depending on the social relations that underpin and give meaning to surveillance practices. Whatever the conceptual umbrella applied to interpreting current developments, we have stressed the importance of the particular spatial context within which surveillant forms of control are enacted – *who* and *what* is being controlled, to what extent and for what purpose? To generalise from theoretical models presents the danger of explanatory globalism. It has been argued that such generalised conceptual frameworks 'can be sustained only if the reference points are the usual crimes of the usual suspects – the "conventional" offending of those populations and activities upon which and whom the criminal justice systems overwhelmingly concentrate' (Tombs, 2007: 546). Thus, as we saw in Chapters 6 and 7 in relation to the forms of surveillance applied to the powerful, concepts like 'punitiveness' rarely make much sense of what is going on in practice and are always in need of qualification.

Furthermore, with its focus on the shifting contours and parameters of social control, much of the criminological literature *over-emphasises* the *discontinuity* between different historical moments and *underestimates* the continuities and material and ideological connections between these moments. As Barbara Hudson has asked of the risk-oriented literature, 'What is new in all this?' (Hudson, 2003: 45). What is becoming clear is that notions of clean breaks with past practice, found in what Pat O'Malley calls 'catastrophic theorisations', assume rather than demonstrate the existence of a 'mass risk consciousness' (O'Mallay, 2004: 185) that supposedly infiltrates and guides the contemporary surveillance/crime control matrix. Over-simplifying processes of change has had the effect of marginalising an analysis of politics and history and, crucially, as in the case of new penological arguments, has foreclosed a consideration of developments in state surveillance and processes surrounding the *materialisation of order* (Mitchell, 2003). This refers to how, over time, assumptions, ideas and practices concerning the definition of crime, and the targeting of surveillance, become materialised within the day-to-day routines and working cultures of powerful institutional settings, especially with respect to state institutions. Accordingly, longer-term historical trends and shifts have been traced in this book in order to maintain a critical focus on how 'new surveillance' technologies continue to be shaped by and within 'older' governing values and practices.

Indeed, for Stan Cohen (1985: 37), developments in late twentieth-century surveillance and social control were complicated and contradictory, and subject to political, ideological and cultural shifts in emphasis (from 'state control' to 'community control', for example). However, for Cohen, 'the original patterns' of rationalisation, centralisation, segregation, and classification that we discussed in Chapter 3 have been subject to 'intensification, complication and extension', and not reversal. Similarly, for David Garland (2003: 63–64), talk of a 'crisis' in penal modernism that took root in the late nineteenth century has often been overblown. At the beginning of the twenty-first century Garland has argued that there are indeed 'new technologies of surveillance' and 'new forms of custody' but this 'is not an era in which new institutions and practices are being legislated into existence' as was the case in the transformative period we explored in Chapter 3. Furthermore, Joe Sim (2009: 3) has argued that a 'discontinuity thesis', purporting to explain change in penology, tends to rely on versions of history written 'from above', thus ignoring punitive practices on the ground that, in particular, have been integral to the prison since the end of the eighteenth century.

In their own ways, Cohen, Garland and Sim have questioned the linguistic labels used to denote change – such as the language of 'risk' associated with the idea of a 'new penology'. Again, the language used to describe practices may change along with innovations in technology, but this is not the same as saying that elements of the practice itself have been transformed or who the targets of these practices are. For example, as we have seen, the idea of criminality as a collective observable fact that requires special surveillance and control has a much longer history and traverses moral, scientific and risk-based discourses. Take the following two quotes separated by 129 years.

> Very great advances have been made of late years [sic]; we have in principle recognised the existence of a criminal class, and directed the operations of the law towards checking the development of that class ... bringing those who

belong to it under special control. (Edmund Du Cane, address to the Social Science Association, 1875, cited in Bailey, 1993: 246)

A hard core of prolific offenders – just 5,000 people – commit around 1 million crimes each year, nearly 10 per cent of all crime. *That's only 15 or 20 people* for each of our Crime and Disorder Reduction Partnerships. Yet they are wreaking havoc. The financial loss is estimated to be at least £2 billion a year. ... This hard core of offenders may include local gang leaders, drug dealers, vandals, car thieves and others whose prolific anti-social behaviour is causing most harm to local neighbourhoods. We will use the National Intelligence Model to help identification. *Once targeted, it will be possible for all of the Agencies concerned to focus, and bear down on, the same key group of offenders.* (Tony Blair, 2004: 3, emphasis added)

These quotations from senior political figures of their day point to *continuity* in the development of surveillance discourses as well as the supposed 'promise' of surveillance – to identify and then control the 'criminal element'. Striking also is the emphasis, then and now, on the *location* of criminal harm within the social order. We can identify changes in the language (from 'criminal classes' to 'prolific offenders') as well as changes in the technologies developed in response to the issue (from paper surveys to electronic databases). But we can also discern continuities in surveillance practices from these quotes – its disproportionate targeting *down* the social and political hierarchy both in normative terms *and* in practice (Coleman and Sim, 2005).

The disproportionate targeting of marginal groups predates 'new surveillance' developments but, as we saw in Chapter 6, the use of 'new surveillance' technologies continues this uneven practice. For many young, working-class and ethnic minority males, for example, surveillance continues to be 'hard' rather than 'soft' and surveillance power – in its disciplinary and normalising aspects – is more likely to be experienced in face-to-face confrontations with authority. For those on the Intensive Supervision and Surveillance Programme (ISSP) or Persistent and Prolific Offender (PPO) programmes, surveillance is still characterised by the 'old' disciplinary techniques of 'soul training' through therapeutic treatment and drug testing of the powerless (Campbell, 2006). Similarly, while the 'new surveillance' is 'continuous' and 'omnipresent', this is particularly the case for marginal populations, such as those who are subject to 'new' measures such as satellite 'tagging' programmes, which have the capacity to track individuals in 'time' and 'space'. The so-called 'new surveillance' may introduce new technologies, but once again these have disproportionate impacts, as is the case for many 'black' males who make up the majority of profiles on the DNA Database. Also, while the emergence of 'automated' surveillance systems may, for some, indicate the 'end of discretion' (Lianos and Douglas, 2000; see Chapter 2), empirical research reviewed in Chapter 6 suggests that some automated socio-technical systems have a built-in 'racial bias' that discriminate against minority ethnic groups. These more systematic aspects of surveillance, involving the targeting and designation of the 'criminal' or 'anti-social', not only have a long history but also a structure located in the politics and policies of state power.

The state of surveillance

To speak of a surveillance state is to focus on historically evolving institutional assemblages and correspondences of interests between governments, businesses and formal policing bodies engaged in surveillance. Indeed, rather than attempting to grasp the precise institutional boundaries of the state, the analysis in this book has implied a view of the state as 'catalytic' in the sense that it constitutes itself – and its ability to intervene in social affairs from a relatively structured 'centre' of power – through a process of 'constantly seeking power sharing arrangements which give it scope for remaining an active centre' (Weiss, 1997: 26). Thus, the 'centrality' of the state 'resides in the mobilisation of the social forces acting through it', while providing tutelage to the wider society with regard to mobilising ways of seeing and responding to crime (Coleman et al., 2009: 18). This leads to a view of surveillance that is less tied to a typology of strictly bounded 'criminal justice' institutions and more upon criminal justice as an interrelated but not wholly synchronised series of practices developed towards the production and perpetuation of social order.

The Joseph Rowntree Reform Trust published a report in 2009 that depicted the UK as a Database State with over 46 systems in operation at a cost of around £16 billion a year (Anderson et al., 2009). These findings buttressed the Information Commissioner's warning in 2006 that Britain had 'woken up' to a surveillance society in which 4.2 million CCTV cameras, number-plate recognition, Radio Frequency Identification (RFID) tags in shops, loyalty and credit cards, phone tapping and call monitoring, and internet surveillance all played a part (Surveillance Studies Network, 2006). In 2009 the Database State included the DNA Database, the National Identity Register, ONSET (that attempts to predict whether children will become criminals), ContactPoint (an index of all children in England and Wales) and the Treaty of Prüm Framework (a European-wide law enforcement sharing information system). The report highlighted that only six of the 46 databases should be allowed to operate on the basis that they were 'effective' and 'proportionate' and had safeguards against intrusions of privacy (Anderson et al., 2009: 6). Over half of these 'new surveillance' technologies had no clause to allow individuals to opt out. The report questioned the increasing reliance on 'coercive' surveillance technologies for delivering and assessing social needs and services (including responses to crime) (Anderson et al., 2009: 47). As one of its authors stated, 'Britain's database state has become a financial, ethical and administrative disaster which is penalizing some of the most vulnerable [in] society' (cited in *The Guardian*, 23 March 2009).

Andrejevic (2007: 7–8) has argued that one of the key features of contemporary surveillance states has been

> increased surveillance with diminished oversight and accountability – or, to put it another way, increasing asymmetry in the monitoring process: those who are increasingly subject to surveillance are prevented from learning about the details of the surveillance process itself.

For Andrejevic, it continues to be case that 'the watchmen don't want to be watched' (2007: 7–8). Thus, while transparency appears as an official goal of surveillance, the monitoring process itself is opaque and, indeed, relatively impenetrable to wider public scrutiny in terms of disclosure of information on individuals and the ability of those individuals to contest or reverse the surveillance gaze (see Chapter 7). In other words, there are serious issues of democratic accountability to be considered in relation to surveillance practices. This is the case in climates where secretive 'wars on terror' and where private companies (concerned with increased production and profitability) develop, fund and manage surveillance systems such as databases and CCTV, make public scrutiny and modes of redress obstructive.

Contemporary trends in the development of surveillance by states cannot be simply divorced from the core practices and ideological referents developed within the surveillance institutions and technologies of the nineteenth century, along with their differential impact on powerless groups within the population. Virginia Eubanks (2006: 90) has argued that the reasons for watching the relatively powerless 'have largely stayed constant' over the past 300 years. For her, these constants have been organised around the 'containment of alleged social contagion, evaluation of moral suitability for inclusion in public life and its benefits, and the suppression of working people's resistance and collective power' (2006: 90). In many respects, these constants have expanded and intensified in relation to the growth of poor and racialised prison populations in the USA and UK and the manner in which contemporary capitalist societies continue to be overshadowed by a 'hyperactive penal state' (Wacquant, 2005: 22). Many cities in the advanced capitalist west have variously adopted approaches in which the criminalisation of poverty (Wacquant, 1999) sits alongside a militarised surveillance landscape for the poor (see Chapter 4; Davis, 1990). The racialised, gendered and class nature of surveillance, and its relationship to criminal sanctions, have, for many writers, remained important issues in excavating the social forces and dynamics at work in 'the surveillance society'.

Contesting and resisting surveillance?

The relationship that surveillance has to different social groups varies. For some, it may be organised and perceived in a way that is non-burdensome or 'beneficial'; for others, it is bound up with a system of 'detection, judgement ... and punishment, aimed at limiting freedom and channelling behaviour' (Gilliom, 2006: 125). Thus, understanding both the structure and interface of surveillance requires that they should be socially and politically situated. As Gilliom has argued, how we understand surveillance needs to take account of 'how differently situated people – welfare mothers, prisoners, students, middle class professionals – speak of and respond to their various surveillance settings' (2006: 126). In reflecting and reinforcing wider social relations, regimes of surveillance are implicated in reinforcing existing social divisions along the lines of class, gender, 'race', sexuality and age. This can have the consequence of reinforcing Rieman's (2007) argument that 'the rich get richer and the poor get prison'. Allied to this, however, are the less visible but equally harmful consequences of surveillance for already vulnerable groups, associated with heightened punitiveness, psychological injury and the limiting of access to 'public' spaces, services and goods. These impacts are shaped by existing power relations within which 'dominant' groups, such as 'corporate actors', can and do 'work with government to build and implement technologies', allowing them to resist at the early stages of surveillance planning and implementation (G.T. Marx, 2009: 227). Resistance strategies pursued by 'powerless groups', in contrast, 'take place at the enforcement stage' during 'surveillance encounters' (Martin et al., 2009: 220). Thus, there is nothing necessarily fixed about how surveillance is shaped either at the planning stage or at the interface of practice. Processes through which surveillance can be shaped are also open to disturbances and moments of 'crisis' affecting the ground upon which surveillance can be contested and resisted. This can be illustrated further with the example of the surveillance of the powerful.

As indicated in earlier chapters, official surveillance *does* occur over the powerful and can lead to the exposure of some noxious forms of social harm. This, however, needs to be qualified. For example, such scrutiny remains inconsistent and varies in intensity, as witnessed by calls for increased oversight and policing of banks and financial institutions in the wake of the widespread 'disaster' of the capitalist market collapse of 2008–09. Furthermore, questions pertaining to *how* the powerful are watched usually arise in situations following major and high-profile policing 'mistakes', as witnessed, for example, after the broadcasting of violent images of policing (and the consequences that follow) in relation to protesters. Thus, the eruption of periodic legitimacy crises relating to powerful institutions do play a role in shaping surveillance discourses concerning powerful bodies and actions, and potentially open up political and media space whereby 'cultural permission' is allowed 'to pro-actively scrutinize the practices of dominant ... actors' (Snider, 2009: 180). In 2009, following public anger over bankers' bonuses and the inability (or reluctance) of the Financial Services Authority to regulate the industry, a former UK Director of Public Prosecutions (Sir Ken McDonald) opened up such a discursive space when he indicated that fraudulent bankers represent more of a risk to the public than 'muggers' or 'terrorists' (*The Times*, 23 February 2009). As is the case with conventional criminals, he argued for a surveillance regime that would instil 'fear' into financial authorities. He maintained that, 'if you mug someone in the street ... the chances are you'll go to prison'. However, he added that 'mugging someone out of their savings would probably earn you a yacht' (McDonald, cited in *The Times*, 23 February 2009). These kinds of interventions may be rare but they do contribute to a rupture in the surveillance discourse and bring the possibility of a move away from a conversational surveillance tone concerning the powerful to one couched in more punitive terms. We glimpse here also the contradictions and contingencies that exist in any state assemblage. However, these periods, in which a radical change in language appear in unexpected quarters, are often exceptional and, as Laureen Snider has argued, 'short-lived' in the popular consciousness. Indeed, such critical overtures in times of crisis stand in contrast to the 'paucity of cultural capital in "normal" times' that impedes sustained pro-surveillance debates over dominant social actors (2009: 180). Indeed, as we saw in Chapter 7, 'answering back' to a surveillance regime, and modifying any potentially systematising effects, is not equally distributed throughout the population. And this in turn reflects the tendentious nature of the cultural grammar of surveillance – containing assumptions to its 'normal' targeting and development – as it has been historically shaped by powerful social groups. In historical terms, decisions about whether surveillance is to occur or how it is to occur have been shaped by assumptions and inherited 'ways of doing things' that have become relatively normalised and taken for granted. Thus, we have seen how 'normalisation' works punitively towards the powerless, buttressed through a deep-seated range of legal and ideological censuring tools. Equally, however, 'normalisation' also occurs in a quite different configuration in relation to the less punitive tendencies shown towards the powerful, buttressed by discourses of mutuality and recognition constructed in mainstream political processes. In the case of the latter, legal and criminal justice agents can be, and are, persuaded against adopting a punitive surveillance regime on the grounds that it is not in the 'general', economic or 'public interest'. While we point to the importance of these trends in advanced capitalist social orders, these processes – along with both the form and extent of a surveillance regime, *and* the possibilities and means to contest it – are not globally uniform and will depend on different legal oversight measures, economic circumstances, political priorities, gender and 'racial' relations as they exist in different national jurisdictions (Lyon, 2007).

Elsewhere, Lyon has argued that the presence of faces and bodies will encourage 'data users to establish trust' (2003c: 27). However, as we saw in Chapter 7, many powerful groups – particularly the economically dominant – *have* always been able to rely upon this kind of close proximity, and more trusting, 'human-ised' face-to-face relationships to surveillance and policing authorities. As Chapters 6 and 7 have shown, this has had real impacts on how – and to what extent – they are surveilled. But symbiotic relationships cultivated between the powerful agents and regulatory surveillance regimes also have structural and ideological significance. We cannot explain 'light touch' surveillance, and the kinds of 'trust' and mutual understanding that have been borne out of this trust, in terms of the presence of the surveilled at the heart of the surveillance discourse alone, but as the result also of deep historical and ideological corre-spondences that have a structural significance. Alternatively, how can reintro-ducing 'the face' make a positive impact upon the policing of black communities, which have always been experienced as face-to-face and embodied, in the UK and USA, since plantation and slavery? Indeed, the presence of particular faces and the bodies (the black body or the body of the working-class youth, for example) have been and continue to be hugely symbolic and representative of disorder and criminality for state and corporate servants. Indeed, the real presence of such a 'body' and its signifiers continue to be sites for suspicion and surveillance as the precursor for exclusion, punishment and violence.

So although privacy may be a limited avenue for tackling the iniquitous, social sorting effects of surveillance, reintroducing the 'human' into surveillance discourses and practices should be tempered by the recognition of the cultural, economic, political and social processes that, over time, have institutionalised those groups that are recognised for their 'humanity' and 'reasonableness', such as the powerful, and those groups deemed less than 'reasonable' and therefore subject to vengeful retribution as a result of their being deemed 'lesser breeds outside of the law' (Gilroy, 1987: 72). In effect, can a humanised surveillance transform inequitable social relations or do we need to broaden the question to address ways of equalising social relations before attempting to democratise surveillance? These are social, political and economic problems, forged within socio-cultural-economic contexts that generate and shape issues such as conven-tional crime, political violence, domestic and sexual violence and deaths and injury at work. The mode of addressing these problems and the means to redress them lie beyond the capabilities of surveillance as it is presently constituted.

Surveillance and crime: contesting the 'public interest'

The bulk of resources, ideological fervour and technological know-how devoted to the surveillance of crime facilitate a particular notion of 'public interest' that is driven by the accumulation of collective and repetitive representations of 'dangerous' activities and 'dangerous' groups who are usually located at the bottom of social hierarchies. As indicated in this book, states and corporations, and the relations developed historically between them, possess a greater material and ideological command over the shaping of this 'public interest', in which conventional images of crime figure prominently. In parallel, states and corporations are engaged in processes of 'concealing and hence mystifying ... [their] ... own propensity for violence and serious crimes on a much larger scale' than the conventional framework acknowledges (Box, 1983: 14). As we have seen, these twin processes have peculiar impacts for particular social groups. The finger-printing of children in UK schools (up to 2 million by 2008), the experiments underway with RFID tags on school uniforms to track attendance and movement, and the £250 million spent on the now defunct ContactPoint up until 2008 have not only discarded with privacy rights when it comes to children, but have also further stigmatised particularly poor sections of this age group in purveying anti-social identities and reputations (Hayes and Bowlands, 2008). Furthermore, Garrett (2004: 58) has demonstrated that across much of Europe by the late twentieth century two dominant themes stood at the centre of social policy concerning young people – each governed through modern surveillance principles. The first consolidating principle was 'educational', in rendering the young competent for the world of work. The second sought to 'ensure that the criminal proclivities of the children of the unemployed and working poor are detected, regulated and contained'. In the UK, both of these strands have come together under the Crime and Disorder Act (1998) and the Anti-Social Behaviour Act (2003). Together they have heralded the cause of 'alarm, harassment and distress' as a feature peculiar to the young, along with Acceptable Behaviour Contracts, Parenting Contracts and Dispersal Orders to deal with younger civil and criminal offenders (Muncie, 2009: 317–319). Disciplinary surveillance, spatial containment and the criminalisation of youth have, over time, been legitimated as being in the 'public interest', with little or no input from young people themselves in terms of what this 'interest' might mean (Valentine, 2004). Finally, questions of information management in general (Lyon, 2007) and the UK state's inability to manage the data and information accrued in these surveillance processes has been severely criticised in terms of data losses and leakage (Anderson et al., 2009).

However, these systematic and historically conspicuous surveillance developments that construct the 'risky' and the 'anti-social' are not inevitable features of surveillance, determined by either technology or historical 'laws'. The contestations and forms of resistance we explored in Chapter 7 – particularly 'from below' – showed how, in contesting surveillance, the potential exists for new meanings and uses of surveillance technology to be imagined and put into practice. What exactly the 'public interest' is around surveillance at any particular time is never entirely settled, nor is it 'obvious' – it is, however, contested. Thus, surveillance is never a static process and the interests that underpin it are open to challenge, as are the assigning categories, signifiers and artefacts that make up surveillance discourse and practices. In this sense, the possibility has been raised as to incorporating corporate crimes into established community safety and crime prevention agendas (see Croall, 2009). This would mean challenging and changing the terms of prevailing surveillance discourses in relation, for example, to re-assigning the meaning of 'anti-social' currently allotted to groups at the bottom of the social hierarchy (Coleman, 2009b). As argued elsewhere, there is no philosophical reason why 'defining business activities as "anti-social"' cannot be done in order to 'provide a symbolic challenge to the current association of "anti-social behaviour" with relatively powerless groups' (Croall, 2009: 177). Furthermore, as some critical theorists have pointed out, criminalised harms could be extended to include the socially harmful activities of powerful groups against the powerless, and behaviour which violates human rights (Schwendinger and Schwendinger, 1970). For Henry and Milovanovic (1996: 105), this notion of crime as a violation of human rights raises new victim categories such as 'abused women', 'victims of state crimes', or, as we saw in Chapter 6, 'victims of surveillance' (McCahill and Norris, 2003). Gazing upon, and surveilling, the powerful does pose a challenge to some long-standing ideas, interests and institutional arrangements concerning how policing and surveillance have been and continue to be practised (arrangements we explored in Chapters 4, 5 and 6). As we saw particularly in Chapter 6, conventional surveillance practices *do* have anti-social impacts – more broadly defined in terms of disrupting access to social spaces and in fostering discriminatory effects upon the life experiences of vulnerable groups whose 'risky' behaviour is defined ever earlier in life and subject to individualised therapy and criminal justice interventions. Rendering these *anti-social impacts* visible, along with the under-surveilled, yet anti-social, activities practised by powerful agents and agencies, present a two-pronged challenge to the sense – if any – in which surveillance purports to represent the 'public interest'. But it is not only ideas that would need to be challenged here, but their materiality ensconced in the powerful institutional alliances that compose the surveillance state and the legitimate authority to identify, surveil and coerce human subjects.

As this book has maintained a view of surveillance as something which operates within political power plays and cultural norms forged in hierarchical social orders, it has also stressed the ways in which both panoptic and synoptic surveillance target and represent – to borrow Box's words – 'only *a* crime problem and not *the* crime problem' (Box, 1983: 3, emphasis in original). Another key social impact of this partiality of surveillance lies in its synoptical form (when the many see the few) which impacts upon *perceptions* of public sentiment and consciousness (Mathiesen, 1997) or how we come to 'see', understand and respond to 'crime', 'risk' and 'safety' in society. How this understanding is constructed within surveillance discourses and media forums impacts directly on the prevailing 'social mood' concerning responses and attitudes to conventional crime, corporate harm and state violence. Increased surveillance of the latter two areas, coupled with a pro-regulatory and punitive communicative discourse, may indeed shape and reinforce a social mood that perceives harmful activities as 'real crimes'. Challenging the moral, legal and cultural underpinnings of light touch surveillance with a more robust, systematic and legally censuring surveillance agenda may also have a deterrent impact upon questionable and harmful activities of powerful actors (Tombs and Whyte, 2007). Therefore, the knowledge and information we acquire (or fail to acquire) from surveillance sources about these activities will be a crucial determinant in struggles over the 'public interest' concerning what counts as 'tolerable' and 'intolerable' behaviour in the public consciousness as well as who and what should and should not be subject to surveillance.

Summary and conclusion

Paraphrasing Steven Box's words written some 30 years ago, there is more to crime and criminals that either state or corporate surveillance 'knowledge' can reveal, 'but most people cannot see it' (Box, 1983: 15). The partial nature of the 'seeing' process, *and* the differential impacts this has, have formed the basis of this book's analysis. Academics – and books like this one – have a role (whether wittingly or unwittingly) in shaping the social moods and sentiments that comprise the 'public interest', and thus developments in surveillance that are cast in the public's name. For others, 'criminologists should be at the front line as informed citizens, able to identify the dangers of criminalizing dissent, on the one hand, and of letting the powerful off the hook on the other' (Soothill et al., 2002: 170). In short, when the language of official social control talk couches surveillance in terms of 'empowerment', 'safety', 'justice' and the 'public interest', then social scientists and students of surveillance have an opportunity to explore how these normative and value-laden ascriptions work out in practice.

Through exploration using examples, this book has questioned the efficacy of surveillance *not* so much in relation to whether it 'works' in a technical sense, but in relation to the patterning of socio-spatial participation and social justice. Key questions relating to whether it is better, or in some sense 'progressive', to increase monitoring and criminalised sanctions upon 'the powerful' remain issues to debate. It is worth pointing out that adopting a punitive surveillance approach to the powerful may indeed proffer greater rights for workers, citizens and even the incarcerated, but this may also serve to over-simplify complex power relations and even create an impression that power differentials have, in some way, been 'resolved'. A resort to law, policing and surveillance – as we saw in Chapter 6 in relation to responses to violence against women – can mean that 'women risk invoking a [patriarchal] power that will work against them rather than for them' (Smart, 1989: 138). In this sense, we have kept the focus upon the power of surveillance to define social problems as well as disqualify knowledge pertinent to such problems. It is debatable whether 'better' or more accurate surveillance provides the route to 'solving' social problems, let alone managing them equitably.

As surveillance discourses and practices are not immune from structural imbalances and power inequalities inherent in social relations, they do raise questions that require unpacking in terms of *who* is targeted, *why* and in *whose* interests? In doing this, this book has developed a view of the relationship between surveillance, crime and power as one in which contradiction and contestation loom large. Indeed, on the one hand, surveillance holds forth the promise of achieving wider public access to information and civil rights (and thereby achieving a greater 'justice'); on the other hand, it also involves a means to impose coercive control when warranted by particular conditions (and thereby exacerbating existing or creating new 'injustices'). Moreover, the trajectory of surveillance towards the goals of risk prevention, pre-emption and prediction is transforming the landscape of 'justice'. Apart from undermining traditional practices of criminal justice and due process, this, we have shown, is also transforming wider patterns of social 'entitlement' in relation to how participation (particularly for the already marginalised) is practised and managed in social life. Surveillance operates on a theoretical notion of transparency, but this too is asymmetrically constituted. What transpires about 'crime' from the practice of surveillance reflects the priorities, values and categories of surveillance authorities. However, surveillance entails another contradiction in that, under contemporary social conditions, the increasing reliance upon it often denotes an unwillingness to engage in deeper political questions and a failure to debate how 'justice' and 'injustice' are generated within social orders. The same applies to 'risk', the meaning of which cannot be simply read off from a surveillance database as something objectively and accurately reflective of the 'public interest'. Accepting this would mark a retreat into the finality and conclusiveness of surveillance 'knowledge' itself, and into an acceptance on individualising responsibility and 'blame'. In reifying the individual, the visible and the conventional, surveillance displaces deeper political, social and economic questions that contextualise and generate social problems that underlie the labels of 'crime', 'risk' and 'terror'. In this sense, as well as reinforcing social divisions and ideas about risky or troublesome individuals, surveillance may also contribute to simplifying the deeper causes and potential remedies to what are *social* problems. This point has a wider analytical application as well as policy implications. For example, this can be seen 'in relation to crime and "problem families"', where attention has usually been directed 'into identifying and intervening into the lives of "risky" individuals' at the expense of 'addressing the socio-structural factors that shape their "riskiness"' that would include 'poverty, inadequate housing and mental distress' (Garside, 2009: 42). The individualising urge can, if left unchallenged, also displace sociological scrutiny away from those social processes through which surveillance can be, and is, neutralised and undermined by the powerful. As we have stated throughout this book, surveillance emerges out of *and* reflects power relations and it would be too much to ask for surveillance (on its own) to transform the power relations within which it is embedded.

In representing a view of the crime problem, surveillance is never neutral and the knowledge it provides is always partial in addressing the deep-seated problems in any social order. As Loic Wacquant (2009: 283) has argued, 'criminality is, in all societies, too serious a matter to be left to' what he has called 'false experts' and 'true ideologues' – 'even less to the police and politicians eager to exploit the problem without accurately weighing or accurately mastering it'. His call for a rational debate that escapes 'the law and order snare', and in which crime is placed within the social relations 'of which it is the expression' (2009: 282), is also a call to rely less on the kinds of 'knowledge' generated from officiated surveillance that has proscribed *a* crime problem along with the ways in which we 'see' and respond to it in advanced societies.

Glossary

Actuarial – This term originally refers to the activity of a person (an 'actuary') working in the field of insurance to calculate risks and payments for insurance companies by studying the frequency of accidents and other events. In the field of policing and criminal justice, this refers to how similar forms of 'actuarial' thinking are applied to the 'risks' posed by crime and actions that might be taken to 'deter' or 'pre-empt' those 'risks'.

Algorithm – Algorithms use a series of mathematical steps to provide answers to particular kinds of problems or questions. An example of 'algorithmic' surveillance would be when digital CCTV surveillance cameras are linked with sophisticated computer software which compares the faces of people captured by the cameras with those of known offenders on the database.

Anti-Social behaviour orders (ASBOs) – An anti-social behaviour order (ASBO) is a legal order restricting the activities or movements of someone who has repeatedly behaved in a way that upsets or annoys other people.

Automated socio-technical environments (ASTEs) – A term used by Lianos and Douglas (2000) to describe 'technology-based contexts of interaction' designed to regulate human behaviour by integrating it into a 'pre-arranged environment'.

Automated surveillance – Automated surveillance systems rely on machines, rather than people, to collect (or extract) and process personal information.

Big Brother – The term 'Big Brother' was first used in George Orwell's dystopian novel, *Nineteen Eighty-Four* (1949), to describe the figure that appeared on the ever-present telescreens to monitor citizens in his fictitious totalitarian state. In recent years the term has been adopted by the makers of a 'reality' TV show of the same name which uses surveillance cameras to monitor contestants and then displays the images synoptically to the wider nation.

Biometrics – This refers to the methods used to recognise people based upon physical or behavioural traits, such as fingerprints, DNA, iris recognition or behavioural traits such as 'gait' or 'voice' recognition.

187

Bio-power – A term used by Michel Foucault to refer to the practices used by modern states to regulate citizens through the use of a range of techniques directed at the 'body' and the entire 'population'.

Bureaucratisation – A term coined by the German sociologist, Max Weber, to describe rationalised forms of information gathering and the regulations that are in place in large modern organisations to control activity.

Carceral punishment – Carceral punishment refers to the processes of surveillance and classification developed as punishment and control techniques in the nineteenth-century prison. According to Foucault, carceral techniques disseminate throughout society, proliferating disciplinary control in relation to the targeting of a range of human behaviours.

Categorical suspicion – A term used by Norris and Armstrong (1999) to describe suspicion based on personal characteristics (age, ethnicity, dress) or membership of a 'suspect' group.

'Crime' – A term carrying great censuring power that is contested in historical, legal, political and moral terms. In this sense, 'crime' is the result of various constructions (in legal, media and political debate) and its meaning is as much a result of the power to criminalise as the power to eschew criminalisation within particular institutional and historical settings.

Crime mapping and crime analysis (CM/CA) – Crime mapping and crime analysis is used by analysts in law enforcement agencies to gather information on the temporal, spatial and social aspects of crime in an attempt to identify patterns which can then be analysed and used for 'pre-emptive' policing.

Crimes of the powerful – Like the concept of crime, crimes of the powerful do not denote a unitary category. However, in contrast to the routine pursuit of conventional crime ('street' crime), crimes of the powerful refers to those harmful and socially injurious activities (which may or may not be codified in law) committed by relatively powerful groups in the realms of corporate violence, domestic violence and sexual assault, and police 'crimes'. Crimes of the powerful tend to exist on the margins of legal and enforcement priorities and practices.

Cultural toolkits – A set of familiar symbols, skills and rituals that people acquire as they grow up and which shapes their behaviour and worldview.

Data image – An 'electronic' or 'virtual' version of our embodied selves that is created through our use of information technology to conduct transactions with organisations, databases and individuals widely separated in time and space.

Data mining – The use of sophisticated data search capabilities and statistical algorithms to collect information stored in databases in order to find out about people's behaviour, such as shopping habits.

Differential surveillance – Refers to the uneven development and targeting of surveillance (whether panoptic or synoptic) in relation to groups defined in class, 'racial', gender, age or sexual terms.

Disciplinary power – A form of power that aims to make people conform with proscribed rules or regulations.

Electronic monitoring – An electronic device, sometimes described as 'tagging', that can be placed on a convicted offender on community supervision, parole, or mandatory supervision to monitor his/her location and activities.

Entrepreneurial urbanism – The term is used to denote a range of powerful economic, political and social forces whose prescriptions for managing cities in more 'business-like' terms has impacts on the development and targeting of urban surveillance practices (e.g. CCTV, access control, zero-tolerance policing).

Function creep – The process whereby surveillance technologies introduced for one purpose eventually end up being used for other purposes that go beyond the original stated aims.

Great un-watched – Whereas the 'great un-washed' was a derogatory term used to describe 'common people' or the 'working class', the term 'great un-watched' refers to those powerful groups who find that their deviant activities are not subject to any form of surveillance or, when they are monitored, are subject to 'light touch' surveillance (see below).

Lateral surveillance – A term used by Chan (2008) to describe surveillance which takes place not from the 'top-down' or from the 'bottom-up', but in a sideways direction when, for example, one neighbour is encouraged to monitor another neighbour.

Light touch surveillance – Light touch surveillance is characterised as having lesser degrees of enforcement power, resources committed to it and less punitive in its impacts than the routine forms of surveillance aimed at conventional ('street') crime and criminality where more intense and heavy-handed surveillance operates. Most fruitfully, it is applicable to powerful social agencies (states and corporations) where less routine and stigmatising kinds of surveillance discourses and practices apply.

Modernity – 'Modernity' is understood as an historical period lasting from around the mid-eighteenth century through to the latter decades of the twentieth century and was characterised by capitalist industrialisation, urbanisation, the establishment of democratic government and a welfare state. This stands in contrast to 'modernism', which is understood as a philosophy or intellectual outlook that was shaped by the dominant Enlightenment belief in progress and science.

New penology – A term used by Feeley and Simon (1994) to describe the shift away from 'punishment' or 'treatment' programmes directed at individual offenders (Old Penology) towards strategies that aimed instead to identify, classify and manage whole groups and populations 'assorted by levels of dangerousness'.

New surveillance – A term developed by Gary T. Marx (2002) to refer to new monitoring technologies that emerged in the last quarter of the twentieth century that are routine, relatively hidden and ubiquitous. It is thought that such technologies for collecting personal information probe more deeply, widely and 'softly' than older surveillance methods.

Panopticon – Jeremy Bentham's proposal, written in 1787, for an architectural system of social discipline, applicable to prisons, factories, workhouses and asylums, which created a state of conscious and permanent visibility that assured the automatic functioning of self-control and self-discipline.

Policeman-state – A term developed by the historian V.A.C. Gatrell (1990) that refers to the consolidation of classificatory surveillance practices in the mid-nineteenth century in and around the developing state form within which the 'new police' became one, albeit important, dimension.

Primary definers – A term originally developed by Hall et al. (1978). Primary definition indicates a form of cultural and political power within which particular ideologies and preferred meanings are circulated throughout the wider social body so as to set limits upon what is, and what is not, linguistically and practically credible in terms of identifying, understanding and responding to social problems such as crime. The process of primary definition occurs across state and corporate boundaries and reflects and reinforces the interests and values of powerful social actors.

Privacy – A concept that has evolved with modernity and is used as a basis to defend against, and contest, surveillance practice as this may be defined as 'infringements to liberty'. Usually couched in individual terms, the concept is seen as limited in contesting surveillance (Lyon, 2001) and is understood as a *differential* process (see above) replete with *social ordering* properties (see below).

Racialisation of surveillance – The use of surveillance practices not only to target and categorise people on the grounds of 'race', but also the processes by which these individuals and groups are viewed through a racial lens and a culturally invented racial framework.

Resistance – Any active behaviour by individuals or interest groups that opposes the collection and processing of personal data, either through the micro-practices of everyday resistance to defeat a given application, or through political challenges to wider power relations which contest the surveillance regime *per se*.

Responsibilisation strategies – 'Neo-liberal' government policies and strategies designed to devolve the responsibility for crime control on to individuals, organisations and sectors that operate 'beyond-the-state', but which are still connected to the state through a series of complex alignments.

Rhizome – A rhizome is the horizontal stem of a plant that sends out roots and shoots from its nodes.

Risk management – In the context of policing and security, 'risk management' refers to an approach which focuses on governing the future through proactive prevention rather than reactive punishment.

Scopophilia – A term that originates from Latin and refers to a 'love of looking' or to the pleasure that is derived from looking.

Simulation – This refers to the act of imitating the behaviour of some process by means of something suitably analogous. In computer science, simulation refers to the technique of representing the real world by a computer program.

Social control – In its broadest sense, the term 'social control' simply refers to processes designed to produce conforming behaviour. In this book, however, we follow Stan Cohen (1985) and use a much more 'narrow' definition to refer to 'those organised responses to crime and deviance'.

Social ordering – Surveillance works through social ordering via the differential value placed upon its classifications, such as 'young' and 'old', 'foreign' and 'national', 'black' and 'white', 'poor' and 'affluent' and 'feminine' and 'unfeminine'. Someone or some agency makes a decision about what it is necessary to know and for what purpose and in doing so initiates surveillance that reinforces and reflects predominant institutional or social values and power networks.

State assemblage – A state assemblage is a relatively coordinated terrain of power resulting from the institutional alliances and correspondences of interests forged between powerful actors and agencies (for example, those alliances found under conditions of entrepreneurial urbanism between publically constituted authorities and private or corporate bodies) who are involved in the *primary definition* (see above) of 'crime', 'deviance' and 'dissent' as well as the development and deployment of authorised surveillance practices.

Superpanopticon – A term used by Gandy (1993) and Poster (1990) to describe how the emergence of information technology and computer databases has extended and intensified the principles of 'panopticism' in the sense that disciplinary surveillance is no longer confined to the enclosed and controlled settings of buildings.

Surveillance – The collection, processing and analysis of personal information about individuals or populations in order to regulate, control, govern, manage or enable their activities.

Surveillance discourses – Surveillance discourses entail formal and informal rules about what can be said, how it can be said, and who can speak credibly in relation to a surveillance regime. The outcomes arising from such discourses impinge upon the regulation of action and the preferred mode of intervention of a surveillance regime.

Surveillance reach – This term refers to the ability of a surveillance regime to penetrate its targeted domain, activity or group. Surveillance reach is differential (see *differential surveillance*) depending on the terms set by the *surveillance discourse* (see above) that surrounds it and the ability of the surveilled to contest the aims and scope of the monitoring process.

Surveillant assemblage – A term used by Haggerty and Ericson (2000) to refer to a set of loosely linked systems, to be distinguished from the operation of the central state or government, and which 'works by abstracting bodies from places and splitting them into flows to be reassembled as virtual data-doubles' (Lyon, 2003b: 31).

Synopticon – The growth of the mass media has given rise to the 'synopticon', which allows the many to watch and scrutinise the activities of the 'few'. The process of synoptic representation renders *particular* forms of crime as a spectacle for mass consumption.

Totalitarian – A political system in which there is only one political party which controls everything and does not allow any opposition parties.

Zero tolerance policing – Zero tolerance policing is based on a conservative criminology and political philosophy. It came to fruition in the 1990s in the USA and found expression in other national jurisdictions. It imposes surveillance and automatic punishment for infractions of rules with the goal of eliminating 'undesirable conduct'. In particular, zero tolerance policing has punitively applied to poor and vulnerable groups, and features in twenty-first-century 'public–private' urban policing networks.

Bibliography

ACLU (2004) 'The surveillance industrial complex: how the American government is conscripting businesses and individuals in the construction of a surveillance society', American Civil Liberties Union, August.

ACPO ANPR Steering Group (2005) 'ANPR strategy for the police service 2005-8: Denying Criminals the Use of the Road', London: ACPO.

Adey, P. (2004) 'Surveillance at the airport: surveilling mobility/mobilising surveillance', *Environment and Planning A*, Vol. 36, pp. 1365–1380.

Adey, P. (2006) 'Divided we move: the dromologics of airport security and surveillance', in Monahan, T. (ed.), *Surveillance and Security: Technological Politics and Power in Everyday Life*, New York: Routledge.

Aggleton, P.J. and Whitty, G. (1985) 'Rebels without a cause? Socialization and subcultural style among the children of the new middle classes', *Sociology of Education*, Vol. 58, No. 1, pp. 60–72.

Altheide, D. (2009) *Terror Post 9/11 and the Media*, New York: Pete Lang.

Alvesalo, A., Tombs, S., Virta, E. and Whyte, D. (2006) 'Re-imagining crime prevention: controlling corporate crime?', *Crime, Law and Social Change*, Vol. 45, pp. 1–25.

Amnesty International (2005) 'Guantánamo and beyond: the continuing pursuit of unchecked executive power', AMR 51/063/2005, 13 May, available at web.amnesty.org/library/Index/ENGAMR510632005.

Anderson, R., Brown, I., Dowty, T., Heath, W., Inglesant, P. and Sasse, A. (2009) *Database State*, York: Joseph Rowntree Trust.

Andrejevic, M. (2007) *iSpy: Surveillance and Power in the Interactive Era*, Kansas City: University Press of Kansas.

Anon (1994) 'Identity checks in france' immigration laws', November, No. 9, available at www.migrationint.com.au/news/qatar/nov_1994-09mn.asp.

Ass, K.T. (2006) '"The body does not lie": identity, risk and trust in technocultures', *Crime, Media, Culture*, Vol. 2, No. 2, pp. 143–158.

Associated Press (2003) 'Woman claims she was videotaped in Toys R Us restroom', 11 July, available at www.notbored.org/camera-abuses.html.

Bailey, V. (1993) 'The fabrication of deviance: "dangerous classes" and "criminal classes" in Victorian England', in Rule, J. and Macolmson, R. (eds), *Protest and Survival*, London: The Merlin Press.

Baker, E. and Roberts, J.V. (2005) 'Globalization and the new punitiveness', in Pratt, J., Brown, D., Brown, M., Hallsworth, S. and Morrison, W. (eds), *The New Punitiveness: Trends, Theories, Perspectives*, Cullompton: Willan.

Ball, K. (2005) 'Organization, surveillance and the body: towards a politics of resistance', *Organization*, Vol. 12, No. 1, pp. 89–108.

Ball, K. and Webster, F. (2003) 'The intensification of surveillance', in Ball, K. and Webster, F. (eds), *The Intensification of Surveillance: Crime, Terrorism and Warfare in the Information Age*, London: Pluto Press.

Barry, A., Osbourne, T. and Rose, N. (eds) (1996) *Foucault and Political Reason: Liberalism, Neo-liberalism and Rationalities of Government*, London: UCL Press.

Bartky, S.L. (1988) 'Foucault, femininity, and the modernization of patriarchal power', in Diamond, I. and Quinby, L. (eds), *Feminism and Foucault: Reflections of Resistance*, Boston: Northeastern University Press.

Barton, A. (2005) *Fragile Moralities and Dangerous Sexualities: Two Centuries of Semi-Penal Institutionalization for Women*, Aldershot: Ashgate.

Bay City News (2005) 'SF cop who reportedly ogled women is suspended for 9 months', 21 April, available at www.notbored.org/camera-abuses.html.

BBC News (2006a) 'Peeping tom CCTV workers jailed', 13 January, available at www.notbored.org/camera-abuses.html.

BBC News (2006b) 'Trust warning over personal data', 13 July, available at news.bbc.co.uk/1/hi/uk_politics/5172890.stm.

BBC News (2007) 'Assembly CCTV turned on homes', 3 July, available at www.notbored.org/camera-abuses.html.

Beckett, K. and Herbert, S. (2010) *Banished: The New Social Control in Urban America*, Oxford: Oxford University Press.

Bennett, C.J. (2005) 'What happens when you book an airline ticket? The collection and processing of passenger data post-9/11', in Zureik, E. and Salter, M.B. (eds), *Global Surveillance and Policing: Borders, Security, Identity*, Cullompton: Willan.

Bigo, D. (2005) 'Frontier controls in the European Union: who is in control?', in Bigo, D. and Guild, E. (eds), *Controlling Frontiers: Free Movement Into and Within Europe*, Aldershot: Ashgate.

Bindel, J. (2008) 'Two women killed each week', *The Guardian*, 2 July.

Black, K. (2002) 'Regulatory conversations', *Journal of Law and Society*, Vol. 29, No. 1, pp. 163–196.

Blair, T. (2004) 'PM's speech on crime reduction, 30 March 2004', available at www.number-10.gov.uk/output/Page5603.asp.

Blomberg, T.C. and Hay, C. (2007) 'Visions of social control revisited', in Downes, D., Rock, P., Chinkin, C. and Gearty, C. (eds), *Crime, Social Control and Human Rights*, Cullompton: Willan Publishing.

Bogard, W. (2006) 'Welcome to the society of control: the simulation of surveillance revisited', in Haggerty, K.D. and Ericson, R.V. (eds), *The New Politics of Surveillance and Visibility*, Toronto: University of Toronto Press.

Bogard, W. (2007) 'Surveillance, its simulation, and hypercontrol in virtual systems', in Hier, S.P. and Greenberg, J. (eds), *The Surveillance Studies Reader*, Maidenhead: McGraw-Hill/Open University Press.

Bordo, S. (1988) 'Anorexia nervosa: psychopathology and the crystallization of culture', in Diamond, I. and Quinby, L. (eds), *Feminism and Foucault: Reflections of Resistance*, Boston: Northeastern University Press.

Bordo, S. (1993) *Unbearable Weight: Women, Western Culture and the Body*, Berkeley: University of California Press.

Bourdieu, P. (1977) *Outline of a Theory of Practice*, Cambridge: Cambridge University Press.

Box, S. (1983) *Power, Crime and Mystification*, London: Tavistock.

Boyne, R. (2000) 'Post-panopticism', *Economy and Society*, Vol. 29, No. 2, May, pp. 285–307.

Broder, J.F. (1999) *Risk Analysis and the Security Survey* (2nd edn), London: Butterworth-Heinemann.

Brogden, M. (1982) *The Police: Autonomy and Consent*, London: Academic Press.

Brogden, M. (1991) *On the Mersey Beat: Policing Liverpool Between the Wars*, New York: Oxford University Press.

Brooke, H. (2009) 'My five-year fight to reveal the truth about MPs' expenses', *The Guardian*, 15 May.

Brown, A. (2004) 'Anti-social behaviour, crime and social control', *Howard Journal*, Vol. 43, No. 2, pp. 203–211.

Brown, D. (2002) 'The politics of penal excess and the echo of colonial penality', *Punishment and Society*, Vol. 4, No. 4, pp. 403–423.

Brown, D. (2005) 'Continuity, rapture, or just more of the "volatile and contradictory"? Glimpses of New South Wales' penal practice behind and through the discursive', in Pratt, J., Brown, D., Brown, M., Hallsworth, S. and Morrison, W. (eds), *The New Punitiveness: Trends, Theories, Perspectives*, Cullompton: Willan.

Brown, G. (2005) 'Full speech by the Right Honourable Gordon Brown MP to the Confederation of British Industry Interactive Conference 2005', available at www. cbi.org.uk/ndbs/press.nsf/0363c1f07c6ca12a8025671c00381cc7/32fb9342737d4d578 025739f00349766?OpenDocument.

Brown, M. (2005) 'Liberal exclusions and the new punitiveness', in Pratt, J., Brown, D., Brown, M., Hallsworth, S. and Morrison, W. (eds), *The New Punitiveness: Trends, Theories, Perspectives*, Cullompton: Willan.

Brown, S.C. (1998) 'What's the problem, girls? CCTV and the gendering of public safety', in Norris, C., Moran, J. and Armstrong, G. (eds), *Surveillance, Closed Circuit Television and Social Control*, Aldershot: Ashgate.

Bunyan, T. (1977) *The History and Practice of the Political Police in Britain*, London: Quartet Books.

Burton, E. and Carlen, P. (1979) *Official Discourse*, London: Routledge and Kegan Paul.

Butin, D.W. (2001) 'If this is resistance I would hate to see domination: retrieving Michel Foucault's notion of resistance in educational research', *Educational Studies*, Vol. 32, No. 2, pp. 157–176.

Cagatay, T. (2006) 'Surveillance over migrant workers and immigrants from Turkey in Germany: from the disciplinary society to the society of control', unpublished PhD thesis, Department of Sociology, Queen's University, Kingston, ON, Canada.

Campbell, J.C. (2000) 'Promise and perils of surveillance in addressing violence against women', *Violence Against Women*, Vol. 6, No. 7, July, pp. 705–727.

Campbell, N. (2006) 'Everyday insecurities: the microbehavioural politics of intrusive surveillance', in Monahan, T. (ed.), *Surveillance and Security: Technological Politics and Power in Everyday Life*, New York: Routledge.

Campbell, S. (2002) *A Review of Anti-Social Behaviour Orders*. Home Office Research Study 236, London: Home Office.

Carlen, P. (1983) *Women's Imprisonment: A Study in Social Control*, London: Routledge and Kegan Paul.

Carrera, S. (2005) 'What does free movement mean in theory and practice in an enlarged EU?', *European Law Journal*, Vol. 11, No. 6, pp. 699–721.

Carson, W.G. (1981) 'White-collar crime and the institutionalization of ambiguity: the case of the early factory acts', in Fitzgerald, M., McLennan, G. and Pawson, J. (eds), *Crime and Society: Readings in History and Theory*, London: Routledge and Kegan Paul in association with the Open University Press.

Castel, R. (1991) 'From dangerousness to risk', in Burchill, G., Gordon, C. and Miller, P. (eds), *The Foucault Effect: Studies in Governmentality*, London: Harvester Wheatsheaf.

CCTV Image (2005a) 'Cameras can make ASBO's work', *CCTV Image*, May.

CCTV Image (2005b) 'Newark meets rural needs', *CCTV Image*, Summer.

CCTV Image (2006a) 'London's new partnership model', *CCTV Image*, May.

CCTV Image (2006b) 'The view of Lincoln city centre', *CCTV Image*, May.

CCTV Image (2006c) 'Taking the bull by the horns', *CCTV Image*, Spring.

Chan, J. (1999) 'Governing police practice: the limits of the new accountability', *British Journal of Criminology*, Vol. 50, pp. 521–570.

Chan, J. (2003) 'Police and new technologies', in Newburn, T. (ed.), *The Handbook of Policing*, Cullompton: Willan.

Chan, J. (2008) 'The new lateral surveillance and a culture of suspicion', in Deflem, M. (ed.), *Surveillance and Governance: Crime Control and Beyond*, Bingley: Emerald Group Publishing Limited.

Chan, J., Brereton, D., Legosz, M. and Doran, S. (2001) *e-Policing: The Impact of Information Technology on Police Practices*, Brisbane: Criminal Justice Commission.

Chesney-Lind, M. (2006) 'Patriarchy, crime, and justice: feminist criminology in an era of backlash', *Feminist Criminology*, Vol. 1, No.1, pp. 6–26.

Coatman, C. (2009) 'Watching the watchers', *Red Pepper*, No. 166, June/July, pp. 18–19.

Cohen, L. (2005) 'Naval review', *CCTV Image*, Winter.

Cohen, P. (1979) 'Policing the working class city', in Fine, B., Kinsey, R., Lea, J., Picciotto, S. and Young, J. (eds), *Capitalism and the Rule of Law: From Deviancy Theory to Marxism*, London: Hutchinson.

Cohen, S. (1971) *Folk Devils and Moral Panics*, Oxford: Basil Blackwell.

Cohen, S. (1985) *Visions of Social Control*, Cambridge: Polity Press.

Cohen, S. (2001) *States of Denial: Knowing about Atrocities and Suffering*, Cambridge: Polity Press.

Cole, S.A. (2001) *Suspect Identities: A History of Fingerprints and Criminal Identification*, Cambridge, MA: Harvard University Press.

Coleman, R. (2004) *Reclaiming the Streets: Surveillance, Social Control and the City*, Cullompton: Willan.

Coleman, R. (2005) 'Surveillance in the city: primary definition and urban spatial order', *Crime, Media and Culture: An International Journal*, Vol. 1, No. 2, pp. 131–148.

Coleman, R. (2009a) 'Surveillance and social ordering', in Drake, D., Muncie, M. and Westmarland, L. (eds), *Criminal Justice: Local and Global*, Cullompton: Willan in association with the Open University Press.

Coleman, R. (2009b) 'Policing the working class in the city of renewal: the state and social surveillance', in Coleman, R., Sim, J., Tombs, S. and Whyte, D. (eds), *State, Power, Crime*, London: Sage.

Coleman, R. and Sim, J. (1996) 'From the Dockyards to the Disney Store: surveillance, risk and security in Liverpool city centre', paper presented at the *Law and Society Association Conference*, University of Strathclyde, July 1996.

Coleman, R. and Sim, J. (1998) 'From the dockyards to the Disneystore: surveillance, risk and security in Liverpool city centre', *International Review of Law, Computers and Technology*, Vol. 12, No. 1, March, pp. 27–45.

Coleman, R. and Sim, J. (2000) 'You'll never walk alone: CCTV surveillance, order and neo-liberal rule in Liverpool city centre', *British Journal of Sociology*, Vol. 51, No. 4, December, pp. 623–639.

Coleman, R. and Sim, J. (2005) 'Contemporary statecraft and the "punitive obsession": a critique of the new penology', in Pratt, J., Brown, D., Brown, M., Hallsworth, S. and Morrison, W. (eds), *The New Punitiveness: Trends, Theories, Perspectives*, Cullompton: Willan.

Coleman, R., Sim, J., Tombs, S. and Whyte, D. (2009) 'Introduction: state, power, crime', in Coleman, R., Sim, J., Tombs, S. and Whyte, D. (eds), *State, Power, Crime*, London: Sage.

Coleman, R., Sim, J. and Whyte, D. (2002) 'Power, politics and partnerships: the state of crime prevention in Merseyside', in Hughes, G. and Edwards, A. (eds), *Crime Control and Community: The New Politics of Public Safety*, Cullompton: Willan.

Coleman, R., Tombs, S. and Whyte, D. (2005) 'Capital, crime control and statecraft in the entrepreneurial city', *Urban Studies*, Vol. 42, December, pp. 2511–2530.

Conrad, K. (2009) 'Surveillance, gender and the virtual body in the information age', *Surveillance and Society*, Vol. 6, No. 4, pp. 380–387.

Cook, D. (2006) *Criminal and Social Justice*, London: Sage.

Crawford, A. (2003) 'The pattern of policing in the UK: policing beyond the police', in Newburn, T. (ed.), *Handbook of Policing*, Cullompton: Willan.

Crawford, A. (2006) 'Networked governance and the post-regulatory state? Steering, rowing and anchoring the provision of policing and security', *Theoretical Criminology*, Vol. 10, No. 4, pp. 449–479.

Crawford, A., Lister, S., Blackburn, S. and Burnett, J. (2005) *Plural Policing: The Mixed Economy of Visible Patrols in England and Wales*, Bristol: The Policy Press.

Croall, H. (2007) 'Victims of white-collar and corporate crime', in Davies, P., Francis, P. and Greer, C. (eds), *Victims, Crime and Society*, London: Sage.

Croall, H. (2009) 'Community safety and economic crime', *Criminology and Criminal Justice*, Vol. 9, pp. 165–187.

Cunningham, D. and Noakes, J. (2008) '"What if she's from the FBI?" The effects of covert forms of social control on social movements', in Deflem, M. (ed.), *Surveillance and Governance: Crime Control and Beyond*, Bingley: Emerald Group Publishing Limited.

Daily Telegraph (2005) 'Why the rules of the game have changed', 16 September.

Daily Telegraph (2006) `Police want spy planes to patrol troubled estates', October 15.

Damer, S. (1974) 'Wine Alley: the sociology of a dreadful enclosure', *Sociological Review*, Vol. 22, No. 2, pp. 221–248.

Dandeker, C. (1990) *Surveillance, Power and Modernity: Bureaucracy and Discipline from 1700 to the Present Day*, Cambridge: Polity Press.

Davies, S. (1996) 'The case against: CCTV should not be introduced', *International Journal of Risk, Security and Crime Prevention*, Vol. 4, No. 1, pp. 315–331.

Davin, A. (1978) 'Imperialism and motherhood', *History Workshop Journal*, Vol. 5, No. 1, pp. 9–66.

Davis, M. (1990) *City of Quartz*, London: Vintage.

Department of Work and Pensions (DWP) (2009) 'Benefit thieves: it's not if we catch you it's when', available at http://campaigns.dwp.gov.uk/campaigns/benefit-thieves/.

Dews, P. (1987) *Logics of Disintegration: Post-structuralist Thought and the Claims of Critical Theory*, London: Verso.

Dispatches (2007) 'When did you last beat your wife?', *Dispatches*, Channel 4, Broadcast Monday 19 March.

Ditton, J. (1998) 'Seen and now heard: talking to the targets of open street CCTV', *British Journal of Criminology*, Vol. 38, No. 3, pp. 404–428.

Dodsworth, F. (2007) 'Police and prevention of crime: commerce, temptation and the corruption of the body politic from Fielding to Colquhoun', *British Journal of Criminology*, Vol. 47, pp. 439–454.

Doherty, J., Busch-Geertsema, V., Karpuskiene, V., Korhonen, J., O'Sullivan, E., Sahlin, I., Tosi, A., Petrillo, A. and Wygnanska, J. (2008) 'Homelessness and exclusion: regulating public space in European cities', *Surveillance and Society*, Vol. 5 No. 1, pp. 9–29, available at: www.surveillance-and-society.org.

Donajgrodzki, A.P. (1977) '"Social police" and the bureaucratic elite: a vision of order in the age of reform', in Donajgrodzki, A.P. (ed.), *Social Control in Nineteenth-century Britain*, London: Croom Helm.

Doyle, A. (2006) 'An alternative current in surveillance and control: broadcasting of surveillance footage of crimes', in Haggerty, K.D. and Ericson, R.V. (eds), *The New Politics of Surveillance and Visibility*, Toronto: University of Toronto Press.

Dupont, B. (2008) 'Hacking the panopticon: distributed online surveillance and resistance', in Deflem, M. (ed.), *Surveillance and Governance: Crime Control and Beyond*, Bingley: Emerald Group Publishing Limited.

Dwyer, J. (2005) 'Police video caught a couple's intimate moment on a Manhattan rooftop', *The New York Times*, 22 December, available at www.notbored.org/camera-abuses.html.

Emsley, C. (1996) *The English Police: A Political and Social History* (2nd edn), London: Longman.

Ericson, R.V. (1992) 'The police as reproducers of order', in McCormick, K.R.E. and Visano, L.A. (eds), *Understanding Policing*, Toronto: Canadian Scholars Press.

Ericson, R.V. (2007a) 'Rules in policing: five perspectives', *Theoretical Criminology*, Vol. 11, No. 3, pp. 367–401.

Ericson, R.V. (2007b) 'Security, surveillance and counter-law', *Criminal Justice Matters*, No. 68, Summer, pp. 6–7.

Ericson, R.V. and Haggerty, D. (1997) *Policing the Risk Society*, Oxford: Clarendon Press.

Eubanks, V. (2006) 'Technologies of citizenship: surveillance and political learning in the welfare system', in Monahan, T. (ed.), *Surveillance and Security: Technological Politics and Power in Everyday Life*, New York: Routledge.

Evans, R., Lewis, P. and Taylor, M. (2009) 'Is it a rally or is it domestic extremism? How the police rebranded lawful protest', *The Guardian*, 26 October.

Feeley, M. and Simon, J. (1994) 'Actuarial justice: the emerging new criminal law', in Nelken D. (ed.), *The Futures of Criminology*, London: Sage.

Finn, R. (2008) 'Seeing terror: everyday surveillance of South Asian women in New York', *Muslim Geographies*, 4–5 April, University of Liverpool.

Fitzgerald, M., McLennan, G. and Sim, J. (1986) 'Intervention, regulation and surveillance', in The Course Team (ed.), *Law and Disorder: Histories of Crime and Justice*, Milton Keynes: Open University.

Flint, J. and Pawson, H. (2009) 'Social landlords and the regulation of conduct in urban spaces in the United Kingdom', *Criminology and Criminal Justice*, Vol. 9, No. 4, pp. 415–435.

Fooks, G. (2002) 'In the valley of the blind the one-eyed man is king: corporate crime and the myopia of financial regulation', in Tombs, S. and Whyte, D. (eds), *Unmasking the Crimes of the Powerful: Scrutinizing States and Corporations*, New York: Pete Lang.

Foucault, M. (1979) *Discipline and Punish: The Birth of the Prison*, London: Allen Lane.

Foucault, M. (1984) 'The judicial apparatus', in Connolly, W. (ed.), *Legitimacy and the State*, Oxford: Basil Blackwell, pp. 201–221.

Foucault, M. (1994a) 'Truth and judicial forms', in Faubion, D. (ed.), *Michael Foucault Essential Works 1954–1984: Power, Volume 3*, London: Penguin, pp. 1–89.

Foucault, M. (1994b) 'The subject and power', in Faubion, D. (ed.), *Michael Foucault Essential Works 1954–1984: Power, Volume 3*, London: Penguin, pp. 326–348.

Foucault, M. (2004) *Society Must Be Defended*, London: Penguin.

Fussey, P. (2007) 'An interrupted transmission? Processes of CCTV implementation and the impact of human agency', *Surveillance and Society*, Vol. 4, pp. 229–256, available at www.surveillance-and-society.org.

Gadher, D. (2006) 'Cameras set racial poser on car crime', *The Sunday Times*, 14 May, available at www.notbored.org/camera-abuses.html.

Gandy, O.H. Jr. (1993) *The Panopticon Sort: A Political Economy of Personal Information*, Boulder, CO: Westview Press.

Gandy, O.H. (2007) 'Data mining and surveillance in the post-9/11 environment', in Hier, S.P. and Greenberg, J. (eds), *The Surveillance Studies Reader*, Berkshire: Open University Press.

Gargis, J. (2003) 'Strip traffic camera zooms in on bar-goers', 12 September, available at www.notbored.org/camera-abuses.html.

Garland, D. (1996) 'The limits of the sovereign state: strategies of crime control in contemporary society', *The British Journal of Criminology*, Vol. 36, No. 4, Autumn, pp. 445–471.

Garland, D. (2001) *The Culture of Control: Crime and Social Order in Contemporary Society*, Oxford: Oxford University Press.

Garland, D. (2003) 'Penal modernism and postmodernism', in Blomberg, T.G. and Cohen, S. (eds), *Punishment and Social Control*, New York: Aldine De Gruyter, pp. 45–73.

Garrett, P.M. (2004) 'The electronic eye: emerging surveillant practices in social work with children and families', *European Journal of Social Work*, Vol. 7, No. 1, pp. 57–71.

Garside, R. (2009) 'Risky individuals, risky families or risky societies?', *Criminal Justice Matters*, No. 78, December, pp. 42–43.

Garton Ash, T. (1997) *The File: A Personal History*, London: Flamingo.

Gatrell, V.A.C. (1990) 'Crime, authority and the policeman-state', in Thompson, F.M.L. (ed.), *The Cambridge Social History of Britain 1750–1950, Volume 5: Social Agencies and Institutions*, Cambridge: Cambridge University Press.

Giddens, A. (1985) *The Nation State and Violence: Volume 2: A Contemporary Critique of Historical Materialism*, Cambridge: Polity Press.

Gifford, Lord, Brown, W. and Bundey, R. (1989) *Loosen the Shackles: The First Report of the Liverpool 8 Inquiry into Race Relations in Liverpool*, Karia Press.

Gill, M. (2006) 'Police need more CCTV training', *CCTV Image*, December.

Gill, M. and Spriggs, A. (2005) 'Assessing the impact of CCTV', *Home Office Research Study 292*, available at www.homeoffice.gov.uk/rds/pdfs05/hors292.pdf.

Gilliom, J. (2001) *Overseers of the Poor: Surveillance and the Limits of Privacy*, Chicago: University of Chicago Press.

Gilliom, J. (2006) 'Struggling with surveillance: resistance, consciousness, and identity', in Haggerty, K.D. and Ericson, R.V. (eds), *The New Politics of Surveillance and Visibility*, Toronto: University of Toronto Press.

Gilroy, P. (1987) *There Ain't No Black in the Union Jack*, London: Hutchinson.

Giroux, H. (1983) 'Theories of reproduction and resistance in the new sociology of education: a critical analysis', *Harvard Educational Review*, Vol. 53, No. 3, pp. 257–293.

Givens, G.J.R., Beveridge, J.R., Draper, B.A. and Bolme, D. (2003) 'A statistical assessment of subject factors in the PCA recognition of human faces', available at www.cs.colostate.edu/evalfacerec/papers/csusacv03.pdf.

Goffman, E. (1961) *Asylums*, London: Penguin.

Goold, B. (2004) *CCTV and Policing: Public Area Surveillance and Police Practices in Britain*, Oxford: Oxford University Press.

Graham, S. (1998) 'Spaces of surveillant simulation: new technologies, digital representations, and material geographies', *Environment and Planning D: Society and Space*, Vol. 6, pp. 483–504.

Graham, S. (2004) 'Introduction: cities, warfare, and states of emergency', in Graham, S. (ed.), *Cities, War and Terrorism: Towards an Urban Geopolitics*, Oxford: Blackwell.

Graham, S., Brooks, J. and Heery, D. (1996) 'Towns on television: CCTV in British towns and cities', *Local Government Studies*, Vol. 22, No. 3, pp. 3–27.

Graham, S. and Marvin, S. (1996) *Telecommunications and the City: Electronic Spaces, Urban Places*, London: Routledge.

Graham, S. and Wood, D. (2003) 'Digitizing surveillance: categorization, space, inequality', *Critical Social Policy*, Vol. 23, No. 2, pp. 235–256.

Grayling, A.C. (2009) *Liberty in the Age of Terror: A Defence of Civil Liberties and Enlightenment Values*, London: Bloomsbury.

Griffin, J.H. (1960) *Black Like Me*, Boston: Signet.

The Guardian (2002) 'Civil wrongs', 22 June.

The Guardian (2002) 'The EU's surveillance network', 10 September.

The Guardian (2002) 'Draconian laws passed in the UK and the US after September 11 threaten the very democracy they are meant to protect', 11 September.

The Guardian (2002) 'How the world's electronic privacy changed', 12 September.

The Guardian (2002) 'EU agrees to pass on intelligence to FBI', 20 December.

The Guardian (2003) 'ID cards may cut queues but learn lessons of history, warn Europeans', 15 November.

The Guardian (2003) 'FBI uses new powers to bug anti-war groups', 24 November.

The Guardian (2004) 'Met urges public to use new terror hotline', 22 March.

The Guardian (2004) 'Biometrics – great hope for world security or triumph for Big Brother?', 18 June.

The Guardian (2004) 'Police victim's family refuse to meet MET chief', 14 September.

The Guardian (2004) 'EU set to agree sweeping counter terror policies', 25 March.

The Guardian (2005) 'The suicide bomber is the smartest of smart bombs', 14 July.

The Guardian (2005) 'Fearful Europe steps up security', 28 July.

The Guardian (2006) 'Fear of the unknown', 20 January.

The Guardian (2006) 'Bush tells of al-Qaida plot to fly jet into tallest building in Los Angeles', 10 February.

The Guardian (2006) 'Buried inside a Bruce Willis video, the evidence of a plot to kill thousands', 7 November.

The Guardian (2007) 'MPs vote to exempt themselves from anti-secrecy law', 19 May.

The Guardian (2008) 'Lie detector tests to catch benefit cheats', 3 December.

The Guardian (2008) 'Verdicts on the De Menezes inquest', 13 December.

The Guardian (2009) 'A climate of private and state secrecy', 14 February.

The Guardian (2009) 'Right to privacy broken by a quarter of UK's public databases, says report', 23 March.

The Guardian (2009) 'CCTV schemes in city and town centres have little effect on crime, says report', 18 May.

The Guardian (2009) 'Banks face naming and shaming under new code of conduct on tax avoidance', 27 June.

The Guardian (2009) 'Inquiry after police use anti-terror act to search girl, 6', 11 September.

Haggerty, K.D. (2006) 'Tear down the walls: on demolishing the panopticon', in Lyon, D. (ed.), *Theorizing Surveillance: The Panopticon and Beyond*, Cullompton: Willan.

Haggerty, K.D. and Ericson, R.V. (2000) 'The surveillant assemblage', *British Journal of Sociology*, Vol. 51, No. 4, pp. 605–622.

Haggerty, K.D. and Ericson, R.V. (2006) 'The new politics of surveillance and visibility', in Haggerty, K.D. and Ericson, R.V. (eds), *The New Politics of Surveillance and Visibility*, Toronto: University of Toronto Press.

Haggerty, K.D. and Gazso, A. (2005) 'Seeing beyond the ruins: surveillance as a response to terrorist threats', *Canadian Journal of Sociology*, Vol. 30, No. 2, pp. 169–187.

Hall, S. et al. (1978) *Policing the Crisis: Mugging, the State and Law and Order*, Macmillan.

Hall, S. and McLennan, G. (1986) 'Custom and law: law and crime as historical Process', *Law and Disorder: Histories of Crime and Justice, Part 2*, Milton Keynes: Open University Press.

Hall, T. and Hubbard, P. (1996) 'The entrepreneurial city: new urban politics, new urban geographies', *Progress in Human Geography*, Vol. 20, No. 2, pp. 153–174.

Hamilton, S. (2002) 'September 11, the internet, and the affects on information provision in libraries', paper presented at the 68th IFLA Council and General Conference, 18–24 August 2002, available at eric.ed.gov/ERICDocs/data/ericdocs2/content_storage_01/0000000b/80/28/25/a6.pdf.

Harcourt, B.E. (2001) *Illusion of Order: The False Promise of Broken Windows Policing*, Cambridge, MA: Harvard University Press.

Harvey, D. (2005) *A Brief History of Neoliberalism*, Oxford: Oxford University Press.

Hayes, B. (2006) 'Arming big brother: the EU's security research programme', Transnational Institute, TNI Briefing Series, No. 2006/1.

Hayes, B. (2008) 'Surveillance society', *Red Pepper*, No. 157, December/January, pp. 14–18.

Hayes, B. and Bowlands, M. (2008) 'Coming for the kids: big brother and the pied pipers of surveillance', *Statewatch*, available at database.statewatch.org/protected/article.asp?aid=28086.

Hayward, K.J. (2004) *City Limits: Crime, Consumer Culture and the Urban Experience*, London: The Glasshouse Press.

Hayward, K.J. and Yar, M. (2006) 'The "chav" phenomenon: consumption, media and the construction of a new underclass', *Crime, Media Culture: An International Journal*, Vol. 2, No. 1, pp. 9–28.

Heath, C., Luff, P. and Svensson, M.S. (2002) 'Overseeing organizations: configuring action and its environment', *British Journal of Sociology*, Vol. 53, No. 2, pp. 181–201.

Heidensohn, F. (1996) *Women and Crime* (2nd edn), London: Macmillan.

Henry, S. (1987) 'Private justice and the policing of labor', in Shearing, C. and Stenning, P. (eds), *Private Policing*, Beverly Hills, CA: Sage, pp. 45–71.

Henry, S. and Milovanovic, D. (1996) *Constitutive Criminology: Beyond Postmodernism*, London: Sage.

Hier, S.P. (2007) 'Probing the surveillant assemblage: on the dialectics of surveillance practices as processes of social control', in Hier, S.P. and Greenberg, J. (eds), *The Surveillance Studies Reader*, Berkshire: Open University Press.

Higgs, E. (2001) 'The rise of the information state: the development of central state surveillance of the citizen in England, 1500–2000', *Journal of Historical Sociology*, Vol. 14, No. 2, pp. 175–197.

Hillyard, P. (1987) 'The normalization of special powers: from Northern Ireland to Britain', in Scraton, P. (ed.), *Law, Order and the Authoritarian State: Readings in Critical Criminology*, Milton Keynes: Open University Press.

Hillyard, P. (1993) *Suspect Community*, London: Pluto.

Hillyard, P., Pantazis, C., Tombs, S. And Gordon, D. (eds) (2004) *Beyond Criminology: Taking Harm Seriously*, London: Pluto Press.

Hillyard, P. and Tombs, S. (2004) 'Beyond criminology', in Hillyard, P., Pantazis, C., Tombs, S. and Gordon, D. (eds), *Beyond Criminology: Taking Harm Seriously*, London: Pluto Press.

Hollander, J.A. and Einwohner, R.L. (2004) 'Conceptualizing resistance', *Sociological Forum*, Vol. 19, No. 4, pp. 533–554.

Holtorf, K. (1998) *Ur-ine Trouble*, Arizona: Vandalay Press.

Home Office (2003) *Respect and Responsibility: Taking a Stand Against Anti-social Behaviour*, CM5778, London: HMSO.

Howe, A. (1994) *Punish and Critique: Towards a Feminist Analysis of Penality*, London: Routledge.

Hudson, B. (2003) *Justice in the Risk Society*, London: Sage.

Hudson, B. (2009) 'Justice in a time of terror', *British Journal of Criminology*, Vol. 49, pp. 702–717.

Huey, L., Walby, K. and Doyle, A. (2006) 'Cop watching in the Downtown Eastside: exploring the use of (counter) surveillance as a tool of resistance', in Monahan, T. (ed.), *Surveillance and Security: Technological Politics and Power in Everyday Life*, New York: Routledge.

Hughes, G. (2007) *The Politics of Crime and Community*, Basingstoke: Palgrave Macmillan.

Hunter, R. (2004) *Chicago's Surveillance Plan is an Ambitious Experiment*, available at www4.gartner.com/resources/123900/123919/chicagos_survei.pdf.

Hutton, W. (2009) 'The G20 has saved us, but it's failing to rein in those that caused the crisis', *The Observer*, 6 September.

The Independent (2006) 'What freedom of information?', 28 December.

The Independent (2009) 'Muslims hit by trebling in stop and search', 1 May.

INQUEST (2009) 'Briefing on the death of Ian Tomlinson', June, London: Inquest.

Institute of Race Relations (2007) *Community Responses to the War on Terror*, Briefing Paper No. 3, London: IRR.

Introna, L.D. and Wood, D. (2004) 'Picturing algorithmic surveillance: the politics of facial recognition systems', *Surveillance and Society*, Vol. 2, Nos 2–3, pp. 177–198, available at www.surveillance-andsociety.org.

Jefferson, T. and Smith, J. (1985) 'Watching the police', *Critical Social Policy*, Vol. 5, pp. 124–133.

Jessop, B. (1990) *State Theory*, Oxford: Blackwell.

Johnston, L. (1992) *The Rebirth of Private Policing*, London: Routledge.

Johnston, L. (2000) 'Private policing: problems and prospects', in Leishman, F. and Loveday, B. (eds), *Core Issues in Policing*, London: Longman.

Johnston, L. and Shearing, C. (2003) *Governing Security: Explorations in Policing and Justice*. London: Routledge.

Jones, H. (2005) 'Visible rights: watching out for women', *Surveillance and Society*, Vol. 2, No. 4, pp. 589–593.

Jones, T. and Newburn, T. (1998) *Private Security and Public Policing*. Oxford: Clarendon Press.

Jones, T. and Newburn, T. (2002) 'The transformation of policing: understanding current trends in policing systems', *British Journal of Criminology*, Vol. 42, pp. 129–146.

Joseph, A.M. (2001) 'Anthropometry, the police expert, and the Deptford murders: the contested introduction of fingerprinting for the identification of criminals in late Victorian and Edwardian Britain', in Caplan, J. and Torpey, J. (eds), *Documenting Individual Identity: The Development of State Practices in the Modern World*, Princeton, NJ: Princeton University Press.

Jowitt, K. (1992) *New World Disorder*, Berkeley, CA: University of California Press.

Kaluszynski, M. (2001) 'Republican identity: bertillonage as government technique', in Caplan, J. and Torpey, J. (eds), *Documenting Individual Identity: The Development of State Practices in the Modern World*, Princeton, NJ: Princeton University Press.

Kelly, D. (2006) 'We've got your number', *CCTV Image*, Spring.

Kemshall, H. and Maguire, M. (2001) 'Public protection, partnership and risk penality: the multi-agency risk management of sexual and violent offenders', *Punishment and Society*, Vol. 3, 237–264.

Koskela, H. (2000) '"The gaze without eyes": video-surveillance and the changing nature of urban space', *Progress in Human Geography*, Vol. 24, No. 2, pp. 243–265.

Koskela, H. (2006) '"The other side of surveillance": webcams, power and agency', in Lyon, D. (ed.), *Theorizing Surveillance: The Panopticon and Beyond*, Cullompton: Willan.

Kubanek, J. and Miller, F. (1997) 'DNA evidence and a National DNA Databank: not in our name', Vancouver Rape Relief and Women's Shelter, available at www.rapere-liefshelter.bc.ca/issues/dna.html.

Lacey, N. (1994) 'Introduction: making sense of criminal justice', in Lacey, N. (ed.), *A Reader in Criminal Justice*, Oxford: Oxford University Press.

Lee, J.A. (1981) 'Some structural aspects of police deviance in relations with minority groups', in Shearing, C. (ed.), *Organizational Police Deviance*, Toronto: Butterworths.

Levack, K. (2003) 'TIA: terrorism information awareness or totally inappropriate?', *Econtent*, October, available at www.econtentmag.com/Articles/ArticleReader. aspx?ArticleID = 5550.

Lewis, P. (2009a) 'Police: we have network of informers among protesters', *The Guardian*, 25 April.

Lewis, P. (2009b) 'Family claim cover-up over death in police custody', *The Guardian*, 21 August.

Lewis, P. and Evans, R. (2009) 'Activists repeatedly stopped and searched as officers "mark" cars', *The Guardian*, 26 October.

Lianos, M. and Douglas, M. (2000) 'Dangerization and the end of deviance: the institutional environment', in Garland, D. and Sparks, R. (eds), *Criminology and Social Theory*, Oxford: Oxford University Press.

Linebaugh, P. (2006) *The London Hanged: Crime and Civil Society in the Eighteenth Century*, London: Verso.

Loggins, K. (2002) '14 cheerleaders sue over camera in dressing area', *The Tennessean*, 23 March, available at www.notbored.org/camera-abuses.html.

Lomell, H.M. (2004) 'Targeting the unwanted: video surveillance and categorical exclusion in Oslo, Norway?', *Surveillance and Society*, Vol. 2, pp. 347–361, available at www.surveillance-and-society.org/articles2(2)/unwanted.pdf.

Luksch, M. and Patel, M. (2008) 'Faceless: chasing the data shadow', *Variant*, Vol. 31, Spring, pp. 10–12.

Lusher, A. (2006) 'Police want spy planes to patrol troubled estates', *The Daily Telegraph*, 15 October.

Lyon, D. (1991) 'Bentham's Panopticon: from moral architecture to electronic surveillance', *Queens Quarterly*, Vol. 98, No. 3, pp. 596–617.

Lyon, D. (1994) *The Electronic Eye: The Rise of the Surveillance Society*, Cambridge: Polity Press.

Lyon, D. (2001) *Surveillance Society: Monitoring Everyday Life*, Buckingham: Open University press.

Lyon, D. (2002) 'Surveillance studies: understanding visibility, mobility and the phonetic fix', *Surveillance and Society*, Vol. 1, No. 1, pp. 1–7.

Lyon, D. (2003a) 'Surveillance after September 11, 2001', in Ball, K. and Webster, F. (eds), *The Intensification of Surveillance: Crime, Terrorism and Warfare in the Information Age*, London: Pluto Press.

Lyon, D. (2003b) *Surveillance After September 11*, Cambridge: Polity Press.

Lyon, D. (2003c) 'Surveillance as social sorting', in Lyon, D. (ed.), *Surveillance as Social Sorting: Privacy, Risk and Digital Discrimination*, New York: Routledge.

Lyon, D. (2006a) '9/11, synopticism, and scopophilia: watching and being watched', in Haggerty, K.D. and Ericson, R.V. (eds), *The New Politics of Surveillance and Visibility*, Toronto: University of Toronto Press pp. 35–54.

Lyon, D. (2006b) 'The search for surveillance theories', in Lyon, D. (ed.), *Theorizing Surveillance: The Panopticon and Beyond*, Cullompton: Willan.

Lyon, D. (2007) *Surveillance Studies: An Overview*, Cambridge: Polity Press.

MacLeod, G. (2002) 'From urban entrepreneurialism to a "revanchist city": on the spatial injustices of Glasgow's renaissance', *Antipode*, Vol. 34, No. 2, pp. 602–624.

Maidment, B. (2008) 'Caricature and social change 1824–1840: the march of the intellect revisited', in Morgan, V. and Williams, C. (eds), *Shaping Belief: Culture, Politics and Religion in Nineteenth Century Writing*, Liverpool: Liverpool University Press.

Mainwaring-White, S. (1983) *The Policing Revolution: Police Technology, Democracy and Liberty in Britain*, Brighton: Harvester.

Manning, P. (1972) 'Observing the police: deviants, respectables and the law', in Douglas, J. (ed.), *Research on Deviance*, New York: Random House.

Manning, P. (2008) *The Technology of Policing: Crime Mapping, Information Technology and the Rationality of Crime Control*, New York: New York University Press.

Marks, P. (2005) 'Imagining surveillance: utopian visions and surveillance studies', *Surveillance and Society*, Vol. 3, No. 2/3, pp. 222–239.

Martin, A.K., van Brakel, R.E. and Bernhard, D.J. (2009) 'Understanding resistance to digital surveillance: towards a multi-disciplinary, multi-actor framework', *Surveillance and Society*, Vol. 6, No. 3, pp. 213–232.

Marx, G.T. (1981) 'Ironies of social control: authorities as contributors to deviance through escalation, nonenforcement, and covert facilitation', *Social Problems*, Vol. 28, pp. 221–246.

Marx, G.T. (2002) 'What's new about the "new surveillance"? Classifying for change and continuity', *Surveillance and Society*, Vol. No. 1, pp. 9–29.

Marx, G.T. (2003) 'A tack in the shoe: neutralizing and resisting the new surveillance', *Journal of Social Issues*, Vol. 59, No. 2, pp. 369–390.

Marx, G.T. (2005) 'Some conceptual issues in the study of borders and surveillance', in Zureik, E. and Salter, M.B. (eds), *Global Surveillance and Policing: Border, Security, Identity*, Cullompton: Willan Publishing.

Marx, G.T. (2007) 'What's new about new surveillance? Classifying for change and continuity', in Heir, S.P. and Greenberg, J. (eds), *The Surveillance Studies Reader*, Maidenhead: Open University Press.

Marx, G.T. (2009) 'A tack in the shoe and taking off the shoe: neutralization and counter-neutralization dynamics', *Surveillance and Society*, Vol. 6, No. 3, pp. 294–306.

Marx, K. (2009) 'Capital: a critical analysis of capitalist production, Volume 1', in Whyte, D. (ed.), *Crimes of the Powerful: A Reader*, Maidenhead: McGraw-Hill/Open University Press.

Mathiesen, T. (1997) 'The viewer society: Michel Foucault's "Panopticon" revisited', *Theoretical Criminology*, Vol. 1, No. 2, pp. 215–234.

Mathiesen, T. (2000) 'On the globalisation of control: towards an integrated surveillance system in Europe', in Green, P. and Rutherford, A. (eds), *Criminal Policy in Transition*, Oñati International Series in Law and Society, Oxford: Hart Publishing, pp. 167–192.

Mathieson, T. (2004) *Silently Silenced: Essays on the Creation of Acquiescence in Modern Society*, Winchester: Waterside Press.

Mathiesen, T. (2006) '*Lex Vigilatoria*: global control without a state?', in Haggerty, K.D. and Ericson, R.V. (eds), *The New Politics of Surveillance and Visibility*, Toronto: University of Toronto Press.

Mattli, W. and Woods, N. (2008) 'Watching the watchdogs', *The Guardian*, 19 December.

McCahill, M. (1998) 'Beyond Foucault: towards a contemporary theory of surveillance', in Norris, C., Moran, J. and Armstrong, G. (eds), *Surveillance, Closed Circuit Television and Social Control*, Aldershot: Ashgate.

McCahill, M. (2002) *The Surveillance Web: The Rise of Visual Surveillance in an English City*, Cullompton: Willan.

McCahill, M. (2003) 'Media representations of visual surveillance', in Mason, P. (ed.), *Criminal Visions*, Cullompton: Willan.

McCahill, M. (2007) 'Us and them: the social impact of "new surveillance" technologies', *Criminal Justice Matters*, No. 68, Summer, pp.14–15.

McCahill, M. and Norris, C. (2002) *CCTV in London*, Urbaneye Working Paper No. 6, Centre for Technology and Society, Technical University of Berlin, available at www.urbaneye.net/results/results.htm.

McCahill, M. and Norris, C. (2003a) 'Estimating the extent, sophistication and legality of CCTV in London', in Gill, M. (ed.), *CCTV*, Leuester: Perpetuity Press.

McCahill, M. and Norris, C. (2003b) 'Victims of surveillance', in Davis, P., Jupp, V. and Francis, P. (eds), *Victimisation: Theory, Research and Policy*, Basingstoke: Palgrave Macmillan.

McCahill, M. and Norris, C. (2003c) *CCTV Systems in London: Their Structures and Practices*, Working Paper No. 10, available at www.urbaneye.net.

McCahill, M. and Finn, R. (2010) 'The social impact of surveillance in three UK Schools: "Angels", "Devils" and "Teen Mums"', *Surveillance and Society*, Vol. 7, No. 3/4, pp. 273–289.

McCartney, C. (2006) 'The DNA Expansion Programme and criminal investigation', *British Journal of Criminology*, Vol. 46, No. 2, pp. 175–192.

McCormick, K.R.E. and Visano, L.A. (1992) 'Regulating an urban order: policing pathologies in the carceral city', in McCormick, K.R.E. and Visano, L.A. (eds), *Understanding Policing*, Toronto: Canadian Scholars Press.

McCulloch, J. and Pickering, S. (2009) 'Pre-crime and counter-terrorism: imagining future crime in the war on terror', *British Journal of Criminology*, Vol. 49, pp. 629–645.

McGowen, R. (1990) 'Getting to know the criminal class in nineteenth-century London', *Nineteenth Century Contexts*, Vol. 14, No. 1, pp. 33–54.

McGrail, B. (1998) 'Communication technology, local knowledges, and urban networks', paper presented at *Telecommunications and the City*, University of Georgia, Atlanta, GA, March.

McLaughlin, E. (2007) *The New Policing*, London: Sage.

McMullan, J.L. (1998a) 'Social surveillance and the rise of the "police machine"', *Theoretical Criminology*, Vol. 2, No. 2, pp. 93–117.

McMullan, J.L. (1998b) 'The arresting eye: discourse, surveillance and disciplinary administration in early English police thinking', *Social and Legal Studies*, Vol. 7, No. 1, pp. 97–128.

McNay, L. (1994) *Foucault: A Critical Introduction*, Cambridge: Polity Press.

Meehan, A.J. (1998) 'The impact of mobile data terminal (MDT) information technology on communication and recordkeeping in patrol work', *Qualitative Sociology*, Vol. 21, No. 3, pp. 225–254.

Miller, P. and Rose, N. (1990) 'Governing economic life', *Economy and Society*, Vol. 19, No. 1, February, pp. 1–29.

Mitchell, D. (2003) *The Right to the City: Social Justice and the Fight for Public Space*, New York: The Guilford Press.

Mitchell, T. (1988) *Colonising Egypt*, Cairo: American University of Cairo Press.

Monahan, T. (2006a) 'Questioning surveillance and security', in Monahan, T. (ed.), *Surveillance and Security: Technological Politics and Power in Everyday Life*, New York: Routledge, pp. 1–23.

Monahan, T. (ed.) (2006b) *Surveillance and Security: Technological Polities and Power in Everyday Life*, New york: Routledge.

Monahan, T. (2006c) 'Counter-surveillance as political intervention?', *Social Semiotics*, Vol. 16, No. 4, pp. 515–534.

Monahan, T. (2008) 'Editorial: surveillance and inequality', *Surveillance and Society*, Vol. 5, No. 3, pp. 217–226.

Monbiot, G. (2007) 'Because it is illegal, the climate camp is now also a protest for democracy', *The Guardian*, 7 August.

Morgan, R. and Newburn, T. (1997) *The Future of Policing*, Oxford: Clarendon Press.

Mort, F. (1987) *Dangerous Sexualities: Medico-moral Politics in England since 1830*, London: Routledge and Kegan Paul.

Muncie, J. (2001) 'The construction and deconstruction of crime', in Muncie, J. and McLaughlin, E. (eds), *The Problem of Crime*, London: Sage in association with the Open University.

Muncie, J. (2009) *Youth and Crime* (3rd edn), London: Sage.

Mythen, G. and Walklate, S. (2006) 'Communicating the terrorist risk: harnessing a culture of fear', *Crime, Media, Culture*, Vol. 2, No. 2, pp. 123–142.

NACRO (2002) *To CCTV or Not to CCTV? Current Review of Research into the Effectives of CCTV Systems in Reducing Crime*, London: NACRO.

Nayak, A. (2006) 'Displaced masculinities: chavs, youth and class in the post-industrial city', *Sociology*, Vol. 40, No. 5, pp. 813–831.

Neal, A.W. (2006) 'Foucault in Guantánamo: towards an archaeology of the exception', Special Section: *Theorizing the Liberty-Security Relation: Sovereignty, Liberalism and Exceptionalism*, London: Sage.

Nellis, M. (2003) '"They don't even know we're there": the electronic monitoring of offenders in England and Wales', in Ball, K. and Webster, F. (eds), *The Intensification of Surveillance: Crime, Terrorism and Warfare in the Information Age*, London: Pluto Press.

Nellis, M. (2007) 'Tracking offenders by satellite – progress or cost-cutting?', *Criminal Justice Matters*, No. 68, Summer, pp. 110–135.

Neocleous, M. (2000) 'Social police and mechanisms of prevention', *The British Journal of Criminology*, Vol. 40, pp. 710–726.

New Internationalist (2005) 'They are watching you', March.

Newburn, T. and Hayman, S. (2002) *Policing, Surveillance and Social Control: CCTV and Police Monitoring of Suspects*, Cullompton: Willan.

Nieto, M., Johnston-Dodds, K. and Simmons, C. (2002) *Public and Private Applications of Video Surveillance and Biometric Technologies*, Sacramento, CA: Californian Research Bureau, available at www.library.ca.gov/crb/02/06/02-006.pdf.

Nock, S. (1993) *The Costs of Privacy*, New York: Aldine De Gruyter.

Norris, C. (2003) 'From personal to digital: CCTV, the panopticon, and the technological mediation of suspicion and social control', in Lyon, D. (ed.), *Surveillance as Social Sorting: Privacy, Risk and Digital Discrimination*, New York: Routledge, pp. 249–281.

Norris, C. (2007) 'The intensification and bifurcation of surveillance in British criminal justice policy', *European Journal on Criminal Policy and Research*, Vol. 13, Nos 1–2, pp. 139–158.

Norris, C. and Armstrong, G. (1999) *The Maximum Surveillance Society*, Oxford: Berg.

Norris, C. and McCahill, M. (2006) 'CCTV: beyond penal modernism?', *British Journal of Criminology*, Vol. 46, No. 1, pp. 97–118.

Norris, C., McCahill, M. and Wood, D. (2004) 'The growth of CCTV: a global perspective on the international diffusion of video surveillance in publicly accessible space', *Surveillance and Society*, Vol. 2, Nos 2/3, pp. xxx–xxx, available at www.surveillance-andsociety.org.

The Observer (2002) 'Police to spy on all emails: fury over Europe's secret plan to access computer and phone data', 9 June.

The Observer (2006) 'We don't live in a police state yet, but we're heading there', 22 January.

The Observer (2007) 'Civil rights fears over DNA file for everyone', 27 May.

Office for National Statistics (2009) *Public Sector Finances*, August, available at www.statistics.gov.uk/pdfdir/psf0909.pdf.

O'Malley, P. (1992) 'Risk, power and crime prevention', *Economy and Society*, Vol. 21, No. 3, August, pp. 252–275.

O'Malley, P. (2004) 'Penal policies and contemporary politics', in Sumner, C. (ed.), *The Blackwell Companion to Criminology*, Oxford: Blackwell.

Orman, D. (2003) 'Pittsford: girls were videotaped', 4 December, available at www.notbored.org/camera-abuses.html.

Orwell, G. (1949) *Nineteen Eighty-Four*, London: Penguin.

Parliamentary Papers (1829) *A Bill [as amended by the committee] for Improving the Police in and near the Metropolis*, (245) 10 Geo. IV.–Session 15 May, available at parlipapers.chadwyck.co.uk/fulltext/fulltext.do?id = 1829-011372&DurUrl = Yes.

Pasquino, P. (1991) '"Theatrum Politicum": the genealogy of capital – police and the state of prosperity', in Burchell, G., Gordon, C. and Miller, P. (eds), *The Foucault Effect: Studies in Governmentality*, Chicago: University of Chicago Press.

Paterson, C. (2007) '"Street-level surveillance": human agency and the electronic monitoring of offenders', *Surveillance and Society*, Vol. 4, No. 4, pp. 314–328, available at www.surveillance-and-society.org.

Paul, T.V. (2005) 'The national security state and global terrorism: why the state is not prepared for the new kind of war', in Aydinli, E. and Rosenau, J.N. (eds), *Globalization, Security and the Nation State: Paradigms in Transition*, New York: State University of New York Press.

Pearson, G. (1983) *Hooligan: A History of Respectable Fears*, London: Macmillan.

Peck, J. (2001) 'Neoliberalizing states: thin policies/hard outcomes', *Progress in Human Geography*, Vol. 25, No. 3, pp. 445–455

Pelham, D. (2004) 'Owner convicted of taping clients – Danny Eugene Daulton was convicted of eavesdropping with a hidden camera', 17 June, available at www.not-bored.org/camera-abuses.html.

Pfaff, S. (2001) 'The limits of coercive surveillance: social and penal control in the German Democratic Republic', *Punishment and Society*, Vol. 3, No. 3, pp. 381–407.

Phillips, C. and Bowling, B. (2007) 'Ethnicities, racism, crime, and criminal justice', in Maguire, M., Morgan, R. and Reiner, R. (eds), *The Oxford Handbook of Criminology*, Oxford: Oxford University Press.

Poster, M. (1990), *The Mode of Information: Poststructuralism and Social Context*, Cambridge: Polity Press.

Poster, M. (1996) 'Databases as discourse; or electronic interpellations', in Lyon, D. And Zureik, E. (eds), *Surveillance, Computers and Privacy*, Minneapolis: University of Minnesota Press.

Private Eye (2009) 'Browns Britain', No. 1240, July.

Raby, R. (2005) 'What is resistance?', *Journal of Youth Studies*, Vol. 8, No. 2, pp. 151–171.

RCPO (Revenue and Customs Prosecution Office) (2009) *Annual Report and Resource Accounts 2008–09*, London: The Stationery Office.

Reiman, J.H. (2007) *The Rich Get Richer and the Poor Get Prison: Ideology, Class and Criminal Justice* (8th edn), London: Pearson/Allyn & Bacon.

Rigakos, G.S. (1999) 'Risk society and actuarial criminology: prospects for a critical discourse', *Canadian Journal of Criminology*, Vol. 41, No. 2, pp. 137–150.

Riley, C. (2003) 'Overton County schools sued over locker room filming', 1 July, available at www.notbored.org/camera-abuses.html.

Rodger, J.J. (2008) *Criminalising Social Policy: Anti-social Behaviour and Welfare in a De-civilised Society*, Cullompton: Willan.

Rose, N. (1996) 'Governing "advanced" liberal democracies', in Barry, A., Osborne, T. and Rose, N. (eds), *Foucault and Political Reason: Liberalism, Neo-liberalism and Rationalities of Government*, London: UCL Press.

Rose, N. and Miller, P. (1992) 'Political power beyond the state: problematics of government', in *British Journal of Sociology*, Vol. 43, No. 2, June: 173–205.

Rosenberg, T. (1996) *The Haunted Land: Facing Europe's Ghosts after Communism*, New York: Vintage Books.

Rubin, J.W. (1996), 'Defining resistance: contested interpretations of everyday acts', *Studies in Law, Politics and Society*, Vol. 15, pp. 237–260.

Rule, J.B. (1973) *Private Lives and Public Surveillance*, London: Allen Lane.

Rule, J.B. 'Social control and modern social structure', in Hier, S.P. and Greenberg, J. (eds), *The Surveillance Studies Reader*, Berkshire: Open University Press.

Ryan, M. (1996) *Lobbying from Below: Inquest in Defence of Civil Liberties*, London: UCL Press.

Samatas, M. (2008) 'From thought control to traffic control: CCTV politics of expansion and resistance in post-Olympics Greece', in Deflem, M. (ed.), *Surveillance and Governance: Crime Control and Beyond*, Bingley: Emerald Group Publishing Limited.

Sanders, A. and Young, R. (2007) *Criminal Justice* (3rd edn), Oxford: Oxford University Press.

Saner, E. (2009) 'I feel completely violated', *The Guardian*, 25 February.

Schienke, E.W. and Brown, B. (2003) 'Streets into stages: an interview with surveillance camera players', *Surveillance and Society*, Vol. 1, No. 3, pp. 356–374, available at www.surveillance-and-society.org.

Schwendinger, H. and Schwendinger, J. (1970) 'Defenders of order or guardians of human rights', *Issues in Criminology*, Vol. 5, No. 2, pp. 123–157.

Scott, J.C. (1990) *Domination and the Arts of Resistance: Hidden Transcripts*, New Haven, CT: Yale University Press.

Scraton, P., Jemphrey, A. and Coleman, S. (1995) *No Last Rights: The Denial of Justice and the Promotion of Myth in the Aftermath of the Hillsborough Disaster*, Oxford: The Alden Press.

Sharpe, J.A. (1999) *Crime in Early Modern England 1550–1750*, London: Longman.

Shearing, C.D. and Stenning, P.C. (1983) 'Private security: implications for social control', *Social Problems*, Vol. 30, No. 5, pp. 493–506.

Shearing, C.D. and Stenning, P.C. (1987) 'Say "Cheese!": the Disney order that is not so Mickey Mouse', in Shearing, C.D. and Stenning, P.C. (eds), *Private Policing*, Thousand Oaks, CA: Sage.

Shearing, C.D. and Stenning, P.C. (1996) 'From the panopticon to Disney World: the development of discipline', in Muncie, J., McLaughlin, E. and Langan, M. (eds), *Criminological Perspectives: A Reader*, Milton Keynes: Open University.

Shearing, C.D. and Stenning, P.C. (2003) 'From the Panopticon to Disney World: the development of discipline', in McLaughlin, E., Muncie, J. And Hughes, G. (eds), *Criminological Perspectives: Essential Readings*, London: Sage.

Shearing, C.D. and Wood, J. (2003) 'Nodal governance, democracy, and the new "denizens"', *Journal of Law and Society*, Vol. 30, pp. 400–419.

Sheptycki, J. (2003) *Review of the Influence of Strategic Intelligence on Organised Crime Policy and Practice*, Final Report, London: Home Office.

Shesgreen, S. (2002) *Images of the Outcast: The Urban Poor and the Cries of London*, New Brunswick, NJ: Rutgers University Press.

Shilling, C. (2003) *The Body and Social Theory*, London: Sage.

Showalter, E. (1987) *The Female Malady: Women, Madness and English Culture 1830–1980*, London: Virago.

Sibley, D. (1995) *Geographies of Exclusion*, London: Routledge.

Sim, J. (1990) *Medical Power in Prisons: The Prison Medial Service in England 1774–1989*, Milton Keynes: Open University Press.

Sim, J. (2000) 'The victimized state', *Criminal Justice Matters*, Vol. 42, No. 1, pp. 26–27.

Sim, J. (2009) *Punishment and Prisons: Power and the Carceral State*, London: Sage.

Sim, J. and Tombs, S. (2008) 'State talk, state silence: work and "violence" in the UK', in Panitch, L. and Leys, C. (eds), *Violence Today: Actually Existing Barbarism*, London: Merlin Press.

Simon, J. and Feeley, M.M. (2003) 'The form and limits of the new penology', in Blomberg, T.G. and Cohen, S. (eds), *Punishment and Social Control*, New York: Aldine De Gruyter.

Simon, R.I. (1997) 'Video voyeurs and the covert videotaping of unsuspecting victims: psychological and legal consequence', *Journal of Forensic Science*, Vol. 42, No. 5, pp. 884–889.

Simpson, L.C. (1995) *Technology, Time and the Conversations of Modernity*, London: Routledge.

Smart, B. (1985) *Michel Foucault*, London: Tavistock.

Smart, C. (1989) *Feminism and the Power of the Law*, London: Routledge.

Smith, G.J.D. (2004) 'Behind the screens: examining constructions of deviance and informal practices among CCTV control room operators in the UK', *Surveillance and Society*, Vol. 2, Nos 2/3, pp. 377–396, available at www.surveillance-and-society.org/articles2(2)/screens.pdf.

Smith, N. (1996) The *New Urban Frontier: Gentrification and the Revanchist City*, London: Routledge.

Snider, L. (2009) 'Accommodating power: the "common sense" of regulators', *Social and Legal Studies*, Vol. 18, No. 2, pp. 179–197.

Solheim, S. (2005) 'Airport arms with ipaqs', available at www.eweek.com/article2/0,1759,1780278,00.asp.

Soothill, K., Peelo, M. and Taylor, C. (2002) *Making Sense of Criminology*, Oxford: Polity Press.

Sorensen, A. (2003) 'Building world city Tokyo: globalization and conflict over urban space', *The Annals of Regional Science*, Vol. 37, pp. 519–531.

Southern Metropolis Daily (2008) 'Eye in the sky', 10 May, available at www.notbored.org/camera-abuses.html.

Spalek, B. and Lambert, B. (2007) 'Muslim communities under surveillance', *Criminal Justice Matters*, summer.

Squires, P. (1990) *Anti-social Policy: Welfare, Ideology and the Disciplinary State*, London: Harvester Wheatsheaf.

Stallybrass, P. and White, A. (1993) 'Bourgeois hysteria and the carnivalesque', in During, S. (ed.), *The Cultural Studies Reader*, London: Routledge.

Stanley, J. and Steinhardt, B. (2002) 'Drawing a blank: the failure of facial recognition technology in Tampa, Florida', an ACLU Special Report, 3 January 2002, available at www.epic.org/privacy/surveillance/spotlight/1105/aclu0302.pdf#search = %22 Drawing%20a%20blank%3A%20the%20failure%20of%20facial%20recognition%20 %22.

Steinwedel, C. (2001) 'Making social groups, one person at a time: the identification of individuals by estate, religious confession, and ethnicity in late imperial Russia', in

Caplan, J. and Torpey, J. (eds), *Documenting Individual Identity: The Development of State Practices in the Modern World*, Princeton, NJ: Princeton University Press.

Stenson, K. (2005) 'Sovereignty, biopolitics and the local government of crime in Britain', *Theoretical Criminology*, Vol. 9, pp. 265–287.

Stenson, K. and Edwards, A. (2001) 'Rethinking crime control in advanced liberal government: the "Third Way" and return to the local', in Stenson, K. and Sullivan, R.R. (eds), *Crime, Risk and Justice: The Politics of Crime Control in Liberal Democracies*, Cullompton: Willan.

Stephan, A. (2004) 'America', *New Statesman*, 12 January, available at www.newstatesman.com/nssubsfilter.php3?newTemplate = NSArticle_NS&newDisplayURN = 200401120004.

Storch, R.D. (1981) 'The plague of blue locusts: police reform and popular resistance in Northern England 1840–57', in Fitzgerald, M., McLennan, G. and Pawson, J. (eds), *Crime and Society: Readings in History and Theory*, London: Routledge and Kegan Paul in association with the Open University Press.

Surveillance and Society Network (2006) *A Report on the Surveillance Society*, available at http://news.bbc.co.uk/1/shared/bsp/hi/pdfs/02_11_06_surveillance.pdf.

Sutherland, E.H. (1983) *White Collar Crime: The Uncut Version*, New Haven, CT: Yale University Press.

Sykes, G.M. (1958) *The Society of Captives: A Study of a Maximum Security Prison*, Princeton, NJ: Princeton University Press.

Taylor, I. (1999) *Crime in Context: A Critical Criminology of Market Societies*, Oxford: Polity Press.

Taylor, I., Evans, K. and Fraser, P. (1996) *A Tale of Two Cities: Global Change, Local Feeling and Everyday Life in the North of England*, London: Routledge.

Taylor, M. (2009) 'Secret police intelligence was given to E.ON before planned demo', *The Guardian*, 20 April.

Thomson, P. (1836/1973) 'The evils of protection: labour the Factories Regulation Bill', in Hollis, P. (ed.), *Class and Conflict in Nineteenth-Century England 1815–1850*, London: Routledge and Kegan Paul.

Thrift, N. (2000) 'Entanglements of power: shadows?', in Sharp, J.P., Routledge, P., Philo, C. and Paddison, R. (eds), *Entanglements of Power: Geographies of Domination and Resistance*, London: Routledge.

The Times (2009) 'Rogue bankers "more a threat that terrorists"', 23 February.

Times of India (2002) 'Cameras to be installed at city airport', 20 July, available at http://timesofindia.indiatimes.com/articleshow/16593947.cms.

Tombs, S. (2002) 'Understanding regulation', *Social and Legal Studies*, Vol. 11, No. 1, pp. 113–133.

Tombs, S. (2007) 'Violence, safety crimes and criminology', *British Journal of Criminology*, Vol. 47, No. 1, pp. 531–550.

Tombs, S. and Whyte, D. (2002) 'Scrutinizing the powerful: crime, contemporary political economy and critical social research', in Tombs, S. and Whyte, D. (eds), *Unmasking the Crimes of the Powerful: Scrutinizing States and Corporations*, New York: Pete Lang.

Tombs, S. and Whyte, D. (2006) 'Corporate crime', in McLaughlin, E. and Muncie, J. (eds), *The Sage Dictionary of Criminology*, London: Sage.

Tombs, S. and Whyte, D. (2007) *Safety Crimes*, Cullompton: Willan.

Tombs, S. and Whyte, D. (2010a) 'A deadly consensus: worker safety and regulatory degradation under New Labour', *British Journal of Criminology*, Vol. 50, No. 1, pp. 46–65.

Tombs, S. and Whyte, D. (2010b) 'Brown-nosing the rich', *Criminal Justice Matters*, Vol. 79, No. 1, pp. 32–33.

Töpfer, E., Hempel, L. and Cameron, H. (2003) *Watching the Bear: Networks and Islands of Visual Surveillance in Berlin*, Urbaneye Working Paper No. 8, Centre for Technology and Society, Technical University of Berlin, available at www.urbaneye.net/results/results.htm.

Torpey, J. (2005) 'Imperial embrace? Identification and constraints on mobility in a hegemonic empire', in Zureik, E. and Salter, M.B. (eds), *Global Surveillance and Policing: Borders, Security, Identity*, Cullompton: Willan.

Travis, A. (2007) 'Ground floor perfumery, stationary … and cells', *The Guardian*, 15 March.

Travis, A. (2009) 'Police told to ignore human rights ruling over DNA database', *The Guardian*, 7 August.

Urbaneye (2004) *On the Threshold to Urban Panopticon? Analysing the Employment of CCTV in European Cities and Assessing its Social and Political Impacts*, Final Report to the European Union, Technical University of Berlin.

Valentine, G. (2004) *Public Space and the Culture of Childhood*, Aldershot: Ashgate.

van Dijk, T.A. (1998) 'Opinions and ideologies in the press', in Bell, A. and Garrett, P. (eds), *Approaches to Media Discourse*, Oxford: Blackwell.

van der Ploeg, I. (2003) 'Biometrics and the body as information: narrative issues of the socio-technical coding of the body', in Lyon, D. (ed.), *Surveillance as Social Sorting: Privacy, Risk and Digital Discrimination*, London: Routledge.

Wacquant, L. (1999) 'How penal common sense comes to Europeans: notes on the transatlantic diffusion of the neoliberal doxa', *European Societies*, Vol. 1, No. 3, pp. 319–352.

Wacquant, L. (2005) 'The great penal leap backward: incarceration in America from Nixon to Clinton', in Pratt, J., Brown, D., Brown, M., Hallsworth, S. and Morrison, W. (eds), *The New Punitiveness: Trends, Theories, Perspectives*, Cullompton: Willan, pp. 3–26.

Wacquant, L. (2009) *Punishing the Poor: The Neoliberal Government of Social Insecurity*, Durham, NC, and London: Duke University Press.

Wakefield, A. (2003) *Selling Security: The Private Policing of Public Space*, Cullompton: Willan.

Wakefield, A. (2005) 'The public surveillance functions of private security', *Surveillance and Society*, Vol. 2, pp. 529–545, available at www.surveillance-and-society.org.

Walklate, S. (2008) 'What is to be done about violence against women? Gender, violence, cosmopolitanism and the law', *British Journal of Criminology*, Vol. 48, pp. 39–54.

Wallace, H. (2009) 'Keeping the right people on the DNA database?', *Criminal Justice Matters*, No. 78, December, pp. 2–3.

Wazir, B. (2002) 'Lost Angeles', *The Observer Magazine*, 7 July, pp. 26–31.

Webster, W.R. (1998) 'Surveying the scene: geographic and spatial aspects of the closed-circuit television surveillance revolution in the UK', paper presented at the XII meeting of the Permanent Study Group on Informatization in Public Administration, European Group of Public Administration Annual Conference, Paris, France, 14–17 September.

Webster, W.R. (2004) 'The evolving diffusion, regulation and governance of closed-circuit television in the UK', paper presented at the CCTV and Social Control: The Politics and Practice of Video Surveillance, University of Sheffield, 7–8 January.

Weeks, J. (1989) *Sex, Politics and Society: The Regulation of Sexuality Since 1800*, London: Longman.

Weiss, L. (1997) 'Globalisation and the myth of the powerless state', *New Left Review*, No. 225, September/October, pp. 3–27.

Wells, H. and Wills, D. (2009) 'Individualism and identity: resistance to speed cameras in the UK', *Surveillance and Society*, Vol. 6, No. 3, pp. 259–274.

Welsh, K. (2008) 'Current policy on domestic violence: a move in the right direction or a step too far?', *Crime Prevention and Community Safety*, Vol. 10, No. 4, pp. 226–248.

Whitaker, R. (2006) 'A Faustian bargain? America and the dream of total information awareness', Haggerty, K.D. and Ericson, R.V. (eds), *The New Politics of Visibility and Surveillance*, Toronto: University of Toronto Press.

White, S.G. (2008) 'Academia, surveillance, and the FBI: a short history', in Deflem, M. (ed.), *Surveillance and Governance: Crime Control and Beyond*, Bingley: Emerald Group Publishing Limited.

Whyte, D. (2006) 'Regulating safety, regulating profit: cost-cutting, injury and death in the British North Sea after Piper Alpha', in Tucker, E. (ed.), *Working Disasters: The Politics of Recognition and Response*, New York: Baywood Publishing Company.

Whyte, D. (2007) 'Gordon Brown's charter for corporate criminals', *Criminal Justice Matters*, No. 70, pp. 31–32.

Whyte, D. (2009) 'The problem of criminalization', in Whyte, D. (ed.), *Crimes of the Powerful: A Reader*, Maidenhead: McGraw-Hill/Open University Press.

Wiecek, C. and Rudinow-Saetnan, A. (2002) *Restrictive? Permissive? The Contradictory Framing of Video Surveillance in Norway and Denmark*, Urbaneye, Working Paper No. 4., Centre for Technology and Society, Technical University of Berlin, available at www.urbaneye.net/results/results.htm.

Wiener, M.J. (1990) *Reconstructing the Criminal: Crime, Law and Policy in England 1830–1914*, Cambridge: Cambridge University Press.

Wilson, B. (2007) *The Making of Victorian Values: Decency and Decent in Britain, 1789–1837*, New York: The Penguin Press.

Wilson, J.Q. and Kelling, G.L. (1982) 'Broken windows', *The Atlantic Online*, March, available at www.theatlantic.com/doc/print/198203/broken-windows.

Wilson, S. (2006) 'Law, morality and regulation: Victorian experiences of financial crime', *The British Journal of Criminology*, Vol. 46, No. 6, November, pp. 1073–1090.

Wolf, N. (1993) *Fire with Fire*, London: Chatto & Windus.

Worrall, A. (1990) *Offending Women: Female Law Breakers and the Criminal Justice System*, London: Routledge.

Yar, M. (2003) 'Panoptic power and the pathologisation of vision: critical reflections on the Foucauldian Thesis', *Surveillance and Society*, Vol. 1, No. 3, pp. 254–271.

Young, J. (2007) *The Vertigo of Late Modernity*, London: Sage.

Youth Justice Board (2006) 'Who is ISSP for?', available at www.youthjusticeboard.gov.uk/YouthJusticeBoard/Sentencing/IntensiveSupervisionAndSurveillanceProgramme/WhoIsISSPFor.htm.

Zedner, L. (2006) 'Policing before and after the police', *British Journal of Criminology*, Vol. 46, pp. 78–96.

Zureik, E. (2001) 'Constructing Palestine through surveillance practices', *British Journal of Middle Eastern Studies*, Vol. 28, No. 2, pp. 205–227.

Zureik, E. and Salter, M.B. (2005) 'Introduction', in Zureik, E. and Salter, M.B. (eds), *Global Surveillance and Policing: Borders, Security, Identity*, Cullompton: Willan.

Index

1984 (Orwell) 148, 166, 187

Aas, Katja Franko 98
actuarial justice 69–70, 187
  see also new penology (Feeley and Simon)
air travel 98, 109
al-Qaeda 104
algorithm 187
Andrejevic, Mark 107, 164, 178
Anti-Social Behaviour Act of 2003 (UK) 182
anti-social behaviour orders (ASBOs) 79, 82,
  115–116, 138, 156, 187
Anti-Terrorism, Crime and Security Act of
  2001 (UK) 97
Aounit, Mouloud 109
Armstrong, Gary 71, 105, 113–114, 118, 188
Ash, Timothy Garton 156
Association of Chief Police Officers
  (ACPO, UK) 72, 74
Aum Shinrikyo (Japan) 94
automated socio-technical environments
  (ASTEs) 23, 119, 187
automated surveillance 187
Automatic Number Plate Recognition (ANPR)
  72, 78

Baker, Estella 96
Barot, Dhiren 103
Bartky, Sandra 30
Barton, Alana 57
Bennett, Colin 98
Bentham, Jeremy 48, 51, 101, 104, 190
Big Brother 187
Bigo, Didier 117
bio-power (Foucault) 18
biometrics 20–21, 29, 97–98, 118–119, 187
Bishopsgate bombing (1993) 94, 96
Blair, Tony 93
Blomberg, Thomas G. 19
Bogard, William 22–23, 26
Bordo, Susan 30
Bourdieu, Pierre 128

Bow Street Police 48
Bowling, Benjamin 118
Box, Steven 183, 184
Brogden, Michael 60
broken windows theory 85–86
Brown, Alison P. 81
Brown, Bill 155
Brown, David 86
Brown, Gordon 162
Brown, Mark 94
Brown, Sheila 120
Bulger, Jamie 129
bureaucratisation (Weber) 188

Campbell, Siobhan 115
Cannistraro, Vincent 103
capitalist modernity 40
CAPPS (Computer-Assisted Passenger
  Prescreening System) 95, 98
carceral punishment (Foucault) 16–17,
  29, 188
Carson, W.G. 55
Castel, Robert 21
categorical suspicion (Norris
  and Armstrong) 188
Cava, Sam 100
CCTV surveillance systems
  as actuarial technology 70
  in custody suites 137
  effectiveness 170–171
  funding 173
  in housing estates 81–82, 116
  in mass private property 79–80,
    83–84, 114
  media usage 127
  open-street systems 70–72, 77, 113–114
  power 101–102, 137–138
  privacy and 164
  resistance and 146, 149–151
  terrorism and 94, 98–99
  usual suspects and 83–84, 87, 113–114,
    118, 128–129

CCTV surveillance systems *cont.*
  women and 120–122
  in the workplace 80, 151–152
  see also Automatic Number Plate
    Recognition (ANPR)
Chadwick, Edwin 50, 87
Chan, Janet 76, 77–78, 119
chavs 49, 127–128
children 54–55, 114, 177, 182
civic duty 107
Clarke, Peter 95
co-option 78–83
Coatman, Clare 165
Cohen, Phil 62
Cohen, Stan 18–19, 41, 65, 175
Cole, Simon 117
Coleman, Roy 3, 26, 27, 32, 33, 34, 35,
  60, 69, 85, 105, 128, 171, 183
colonialism 104–105, 117
Colquhoun, Patrick 48, 49–50, 51
community policing 80–81, 95, 107–108
Community Safety Officers (CSOs) 81
Computer-Aided Dispatch (CAD) 78
Computer-Assisted Passenger Prescreening
  System (CAPPS) 95, 98
computers 20
ContactPoint 177, 182
Contagious Diseases Acts (UK) 56–57
Cook, Dee 5
Copwatch 154
corporate crime 10, 63, 130–135, 158–160
counter surveillance 152–153, 154–155, 165
Counter-Terrorism Act of 2008 (UK) 165
Crawford, Adam 79, 115
crime
  definitions 8, 188
  surveillance and 2–3, 5–6, 15–16
Crime and Disorder Act of 1998 (UK) 182
crime mapping and crime analysis (CM/CA)
  76, 188
crimes of the powerful 188
  see also light touch surveillance
Crimestoppers 127
Crimewatch (BBC show) 2, *126*
criminal classes 43–44, 59, 64,
  125, 175–177
  see also usual suspects
Criminal Justice and Public Order Act of
  1994 (UK) 72–73, 118
criminals, perception and depiction of 42–44,
  48, 125–129
cultural toolkits 188
Cunningham, David 156
Customer Relationship Management
  (CRM) 102

Damer, Sean 116
Dandeker, Christopher 41
dangerous classes 59
data-doubles 20–21
data image 20, 188
data mining 20, 102, 189
Data Protection Act of 1998 (UK) 164
databases 20, 177–178
  see also specific databases
dataveillance (Whitaker) 70, 113
Davis, Mike 85
democratisation of surveillance 25–26, 124
Department of Work and Pensions (DWP) 4
  see also social security benefit fraud
differential surveillance 28–31, 189
disappearance of the body (Lyon) 20
disciplinary power 16–17, 189
disciplinary societies 17
DNA databases 113, 114–115
  see also National DNA Database (UK)
DNA Expansion Programme 73
domestic extremism 74
domestic violence 122–124
Douglas, Mary 23, 112, 119
  see also automated socio-technical
    environments (ASTEs)
Doyle, Aaron 125, 154

Echelon 100
Einwohner, Rachel L. 145
electronic monitoring (EM) 115, 189
endowment mortgages 159–160
entrepreneurial urbanism 189
Ericson, Richard V. 24, 32, 78, 79, 93, 151
  see also surveillant assemblage
    (Haggerty and Ericson)
Eubanks, Virginia 178
Eurodac 98, 100–101
European Security Research Programme
  (ESRP) 100, 105
Europol 97, 99
Explosive Substances Act of 1883 (UK) 93

face-to-face surveillance 12, 19, 23
Facial Images National Database (FIND) 72
Factory Act of 1833 (UK) 54–55
factory laws 54–55
Feeley, Malcolm *see* new penology
  (Feeley and Simon)
female self-surveillance 29–30
Fielding, John 48, 50, 75
The File: A Personal History (Ash) 156
file-based surveillance 12, 19
Financial Services Authority (FSA)
  159–160, 180

finger-printing 98, 100–101, 117, 182
Finn, Rachel 119, 128
Fitwatch 152–153
Flint, John 81
Forward Intelligence Teams (FITs, UK)
   74, 152–153
Foucault, Michel
  on carceral punishment 16–17, 29, 144, 188
  Cohen and 18–19
  on disciplinary technologies of the self 30
  on panoptic surveillance 17–18, 27, 51,
    58, 101–102, 103
  on surveillance developments 32, 46
Framework Decision on combating
   terrorism (EU) 106
Freedom of Information (Amendment)
   Bill of 2007 (UK) 164
function creep 189

Gandy, Oscar H. 102
Garland, David 33, 65, 94–95, 175
Garrett, Paul Michael 182
Gaszo, Amber 26, 94, 103
Gatrell, Victor 41, 62–63
  see also policeman-state (Gatrell)
Giddens, Anthony 16
Gilliom, John 144–145, 149, 179
Giroux, Henry 153
Givens, Geof 119
global migrants 117
global surveillance networks 70
globalisation 96–104
Goffman, Erving 149
Goold, Benjamin 71, 77, 118
Graham, Stephen 105–106
great unwashed 52–53, 124, 189
great unwatched 156–161, 189
Griffin, J.H. 119

Haggerty, Kevin
  on CAD systems 78
  on expansion of surveillance 32
  on panoptic surveillance 102
  on public police 79
  on resistance 151
  on synoptic surveillance 26
  on terrorists 103
  on USA Patriot Act 94
  see also surveillant assemblage
    (Haggerty and Ericson)
Harcourt, Bernard E. 86
Hay, Carter 19
Hayes, Ben 98, 105
Hayman, Stephanie 137
Hayward, Keith 127–128, 150

Hazards.org 152
Health and Safety Executive (HSE) 132,
   133, 158–159, 162
Henry, Stuart 183
Higgs, Edward 104–105
Hillyard, Paddy 93, 94, 108
Hollander, Jocelyn A. 145
Holliday, George 152
home curfew systems 115
Howard, John 50–51
Howe, Adrian 30
Hudson, Barbara 174–175
Huey, Laura 154

Industrial Schools 54
INQUEST 136
Institute for Applied Autonomy (IAA)
   149–150, 151
Intensive Supervision and Surveillance
   Programme (ISSP) 115, 176
interface surveillance 13
internet 97, 104, 150–151
Introna, Lucas 98, 107
Irish Republican Army (IRA) 94, 96

Jemaah Islamiyah (JI, Indonesia) 103
Johnston, Les 68n1, 69–70, 75, 80–81
Joseph, Anne M. 150
Jowitt, Kenneth 149
juvenile delinquency 53–54, 182

King, Rodney 152, 154–155
Koskela, Hillie 121, 155
Kubanek, Julia 114–115

Lacey, Nicola 34
lateral surveillance 189
Lianos, Michalis 23, 112, 119
   see also automated socio-technical
    environments (ASTEs)
light touch surveillance 113,
   129–130, 140–141
  defined 189
  over policing 135–140, 165–166, 167
  over the powerful 46, 55, 130–135,
    156–161, 167, 179–180
Linebaugh, Peter 49
Liverpool City Police 60–61
Livingstone, Ken 99
Lock Hospitals 56–57
London bombings (2005) 99, 118
Louima, Abner 155
Luksch, Manu 164–165
Lyon, David
  on data users 181

Lyon, David *cont.*
on the disappearance of the body
and data-doubles 20, 21
on the panopticon 101, 102
on the power of surveillance 12, 34
on racial profiling 109
on scopophilia 27
on social sorting 15
on surveillance 145
on surveillance societies 16
on terrorism 96
on theoretical perspectives 16

Manning, Peter 75, 76
Marine Police 49–50
Marx, Gary T. 22–24, 146, 149, 151, 154
see also new surveillance (Gary T. Marx)
mass private property 70
Mathiesen, Thomas 26–28, 101, 106
Mattli, Walter 160
McCahill, Michael 32, 72, 82, 95,
120, 128, 129
McCartney, Carole 73
McCulloch, Jude 93–94, 108
McDonald, Ken 180
McGowen, Randall 44
media
portrayal of benefit fraudsters 5–6
and September 11 attacks 96
TV shows 2, 29, 44, 125–129, *126*
Meehan, Albert J. 78
Menezes, Jean Charles de 138–139
Metropolitan Police 60
Metropolitan Police Act of 1839 (UK) 63
Miller, Fiona 114–115
Milovanovic, Dragan 183
Mitchell, Timothy 104
mobile data terminals (MDTs) 78
mobile populations 117
modernity 189–90
Mohammed, Khalid Sheikh 103
Monahan, Torin 31–32, 116, 149–150,
152, 153, 154–155
Monbiot, George 164
moral panics 43, 61, 125, 129
Mort, Frank 56
Myners, Paul 162

National DNA Database (UK) 72–73,
114, 171, 176
National Extremism Tactical Coordination
Unit (NETCU, UK) 74
National Public Order Intelligence Unit
(NPOIU, UK) 74
National Security Entry-Exit Registration
System (NSEERS, USA) 98

Nayak, Anoop 128
new lateral surveillance (Chan) 70
new penology (Feeley and Simon) 21, 24,
69, 175, 190
new police 44, 52, 58–62
see also policeman-state (Gatrell)
new punitiveness 87, 96
new surveillance (Gary T. Marx)
and construction of crime problem 172
defined 190
powerful groups and 112–113
public and private police and 68–69
risk mentality and 70, 75
and surveillance societies 22–24
and synoptic surveillance 26
usual suspects and 108–110, 112–119
new terrorism 92–101
Newburn, Tim 137
Nineteen Eighty-Four (Orwell) 148, 166, 187
Noakes, John 156
nomads 117
normalizing society (Foucault) 18
see also surveillance societies
Norris, Clive
on categorical suspicion 188
on CCTV surveillance systems 71, 82, 98,
113–114, 118, 129
on databases 72, 73
on global security companies 105
on new surveillance technologies 32, 95
on persistent offenders 115
on surveillance and women 120
on terrorism 94

Obama administration 102
Obscene Publications Act (1857) 47
old penology 69
Oliver, Anne Marie 103
O'Malley, Pat 175
ONSET 177
Orwell, George 148, 166, 187

panoptic sorting (Gandy) 102
panoptic surveillance
dispersal of surveillance and 18–19
in prisons 17
synoptic surveillance and 25, 27–28,
96, 124–127
technology and 20–21
see also superpanopticon (Poster)
Panopticon (Bentham) 51, 101, 190
Patel, Mukul 164–165
Patriot Act of 2001 (USA) 94, 95, 97
pauperism 53
Pawson, Hal 81
penal modernism (Garland) 65

Penal Servitude Act of 1864 (UK) 63
Persistent and Prolific Offender (PPO) 176
Persistent Offender Strategy 115
Pfaff, Steven 148–149
Phillips, Coretta 118
Pickering, Sharon 93–94, 108
plural policing 87–88
    see also public-private surveillance
        networks
police 45, 48–50
    see also light touch surveillance; new
        police; policeman-state (Gatrell);
        public-private surveillance networks
Police Information Technology Organisation
    (PITO) 100
Police National Computer (PNC) 72, 73
police property 83–87
policeman-state (Gatrell) 52, 58, 62–64, 190
    see also new police
Policewatch (TV format idea) 126
political dissent 63, 73–74, 104–105
politics of prevention see new penology
    (Feeley and Simon)
Poor Law Amendment Act of 1834 (UK) 53
Poster, Mark 20
pre-emptive surveillance 22–23, 75,
    93–94, 95
    see also risk management
Prevention of Crimes Act of 1871 (UK) 63
Prevention of Terrorism (Temporary
    Provisions) Act of 1989 (PTA, UK) 93
primary definers 190
prisons/imprisonment 16–17, 30, 50–51, 57
privacy 7, 25, 31, 164, 190
Privium 109
Proclamation Society 46
profiling 23
    see also racial profiling
Protection from Harassment Act of 1997
    (UK) 164
Prüm Treaty 101, 177
public interest 153, 159–160, 161, 181–184
public order 62–63
public-private surveillance networks 69,
    70–71, 73–74, 78–89
public safety 105, 161
punishment 16, 69–70, 86–87
    see also carceral punishment (Foucault)

Raby, Rebecca 147
racial profiling 108–110
racialisation of surveillance 116–119, 190
Radio Frequency Identification (RFID)
    tags 182
Reformatory Schools 54
Reiman, Jeffrey H. 179

resistance
    defined 145–147, 191
    new police and 61–62, 64
    power and 156–166
    to speed cameras 153–154
    to state surveillance regimes 148–149, 166
    strategies and moves 149–153, 154–155,
        165, 166–167
responsibilisation strategies 80–81, 191
Revenue and Customs Prosecutions Office
    (RCPO) 4, 10
rhizome 191
Ridge, Tom 103
ring of steel (London) 96
risk management 69–70, 75, 161–166, 191
    see also new penology (Feeley and Simon)
Roberts, Julian V. 96
Rodger, John 81, 115–116, 128
Rosenberg, Tina 151
Rule, James B. 14–15
Rural Constabulary Act of 1839 (UK) 60

Sanders, Andrew 165–166
Schengen Information System (SIS)
    99–100, 106
scopophilia (love of looking) 27, 191
Scorecard.org 153
Scott, James C. 146
Secure Flight 98
self-surveillance 29–30, 163
September 11 attacks 92–93, 94–95, 96
Shearing, Clifford D. 21–22, 69–70, 78, 81
Sheptycki, James 76–77
Sim, Joe 33, 175
Simon, Jonathan 122
    see also new penology (Feeley and Simon)
simulation 191
SIRENE (Supplementary Information Request
    at the National Entry) 99
Snider, Laureen 180
Social Construction of Technology
    (SCOT) 75
social control 18–19, 191
social enemies 42
social ordering 191
social security benefit fraud 3–6
social sorting (Lyon) 15
Society for the Improvement of Prison
    Discipline and the Reformation of
    Juvenile Offenders 53–54
Society for the Reform of Manners 46
Society for the Suppression of
    Mendicity 46
Society for the Suppression of Vice
    (SSV) 46–47
sousurveillance 136, 165

speed cameras 153–154
state assemblage 191g
Stenning, Philip C. 21–22, 78
Stenson, Kevin 88
stop and search 117–118
Storch, Robert 60, 61, 62
suffragettes 150
superpanopticon (Poster) 20, 191–192
surveillance
    crime and 2–3, 5–6, 15–16, 171–174
    definitions 2, 192
    effectiveness 170–171, 184
    power of 12–13, 15–16, 28, 171–172
    spatial borders and 14
    types of 12–13
Surveillance Camera Players (SCPs) 155
surveillance discourses 192
surveillance reach 29, 192
surveillance societies 7–8, 14–15, 16,
    22, 40–65
    see also new surveillance (Gary T. Marx)
surveillant assemblage (Haggerty and Ericson)
    24–25, 68, 70–72, 192
sus laws (stop and search) 117–118
Sutherland, Edwin H. 133
Sykes, Gresham M. 149
synoptic surveillance 25, 26–28, 96, 124–129,
    133, 192

tax evasion 3–6
technology 19–21
terrorism 92–110
Terrorism Act of 2000 (UK) 106
Thomas, Richard 7
Tomlison, Ian 136
Topal, Cagatay 117
Total Information Awareness (TIA) 100, 102
totalitarianism 192
TV shows 2, 29, 44, 125–129, *126*

United States Visitor and Immigrant Status
    Indicator Technology (US-VISIT) 98
unmanned aerial vehicles (UAVs) 106
US-VISIT (United States Visitor and Immigrant
    Status Indicator Technology) 98
USA Patriot Act of 2001 (USA) 94, 95, 97, 138
usual suspects
    CCTV surveillance systems and 83–84, 87,
        113–114, 118, 128–129
    new surveillance and 108–110,
        112–119, 176–177
    as victims of surveillance 172
    see also criminal classes

Vagabond Act of 1572 (UK) 45–46
Vagrancy Act of 1824 (UK) 63
victims of surveillance 172
viewer society (Mathiesen) 26–28
visibility 3–6, 15, 24, 85, 103, 132–133

Wacquant, Loic 186
Wakefield, Alison 83–84
Walby, Kevin 154
war on terror 94–96, 104–110, 119
Weber, Max 188
Wells, Helen 154
Wills, David 154
Wilson, Sarah 56
women 29–31, 54–55, 56–58, 119–124
Wood, David 98, 107
Woods, Ngaire 160
workhouses 53
workplace 54–55, 132, 133–134, 158–159

Yar, Majid 127–128
Young, Richard 165–166
youth *see* juvenile delinquency

zero tolerance policing 192